EDUCATION, CULTURE AND POLITICS IN MODERN FRANCE

BY

W. D. HALLS

PERGAMON PRESS

OXFORD · NEW YORK · TORONTO
SYDNEY · PARIS · FRANKFURT

U.K.	Pergamon Press Ltd., Headington Hill Hall, Oxford, England
U.S.A	Pergamon Press Inc., Maxwell House, Fairview Park, Elmsford, New York 10523, U.S.A.
CANADA	Pergamon of Canada Ltd., P.O. Box 9600, Don Mills M3C 2T9, Ontario, Canada
AUSTRALIA	Pergamon Press (Aust.) Pty. Ltd., 19a Boundary Street, Rushcutters Bay, N.S.W. 2011, Australia
FRANCE	Pergamon Press SARL, 24 rue des Ecoles, 75240 Paris, Cedex 05, France
WEST GERMANY	Pergamon Press, GmbH, 6242 Kronberg/Taunus, Pferdstrasse 1, Frankfurt-am-Main, West Germany

First edition 1976

Library of Congress Cataloging in Publication Data

Halls, W. D.

Education, culture and politics in modern France.

(Society, schools, and progress series) (Pergamon international library of science, technology, engineering, and social studies)

Bibliography: p.

1. Education—France—History. 2. Education and state—France. I. Title.

LA691.8.H34   1976   370'.944   75–44309

ISBN 0–08–018962–8

ISBN 0–08–018961–X pbk.

Printed in Great Britain by A. Wheaton & Co., Exeter

PERGAMON INTERNATIONAL LIBRARY
of Science, Technology, Engineering and Social Studies

*The 1000-volume original paperback library in aid of education,
industrial training and the enjoyment of leisure*

Publisher: Robert Maxwell, M.C.

EDUCATION, CULTURE AND POLITICS IN

MODERN FRANCE

THE PERGAMON TEXTBOOK
INSPECTION COPY SERVICE

An inspection copy of any book published in the Pergamon International Library
will gladly be sent to academic staff without obligation for their consideration for
course adoption or recommendation. Copies may be retained for a period of 60 days
from receipt and returned if not suitable. When a particular title is adopted or
recommended for adoption for class use and the recommendation results in a sale
of 12 or more copies, the inspection copy may be retained with our compliments.
If after examination the lecturer decides that the book is not suitable for adoption
but would like to retain it for his personal library, then a discount of 10% is
allowed on the invoiced price. The Publishers will be pleased to receive suggestions
for revised editions and new titles to be published in this important International
Library.

SOCIETY, SCHOOLS, AND PROGRESS SERIES

General editor: Professor Edmund J. King

OTHER TITLES IN THE SERIES

Contents

Preface

This study deals with the interplay of educational theory and practice in France with culture and politics. Its main focus is on the process of educational change during the first fifteen years of the Fifth Republic. It is therefore a contemporary history of education and suffers accordingly from all the disadvantages of writing about the present day: to name but two, the lack of perspective and the inaccessibility of important primary sources of a political kind. On the other hand, it seeks to catch the cut and thrust of the present-day debate about schools and universities in France, and to distinguish some of the underlying factors that account for the passion of the argument.

The main thesis of the book is that a new view of culture — here defined as all the artefacts of men, whether these be material objects or their thoughts, ideas, beliefs and opinions — has enlarged the narrower, more literary concept that has swayed French education for 170 years. This metamorphosis has not occurred without resistance on the part of those most closely concerned. But the impact of science, technology and an economic view of the world on education has been inexorable, so that a fresh synthesis of what is meant by "culture générale" now seems to be emerging.

On the other hand, the political forces that have clashed upon the educational question, although they may have donned a new garb, seem basically to be in the historical succession that may be traced back to La Chalotais, Rousseau and the Philosophes, if not earlier. The labels may change, as may the emphases in the discussion, but the dialectic of the warring factions of the Left and Right continues as before.

Education in modern society is about power. "To ask who is to be educated is to ask who is to rule." Culture and politics, which shape educational systems, must ultimately determine the answer to that question. In France the battle has been long and the issue is still in the balance.

Why the conflict has been so fierce, so unrelenting, is itself an interesting incidental question. It may be because the French care

vii

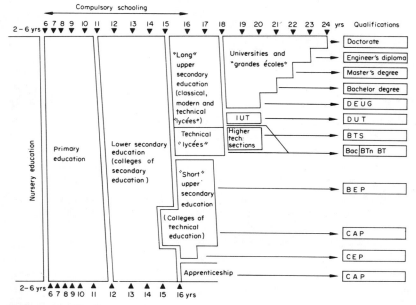

Notes on qualifications:
DEUG = Diplôme d'Etudes universitaires générales; DUT = Diplôme universitaire de technologie; BTS = Brevet de Technicien supérieur (Higher technician's diploma); Bac = Baccalauréat; BTn = Brevet de Technicien (Lower technician's diploma); BT = Baccalauréat de Technicien (specialised Technician's baccalaureate); BEP = Brevet d'Etudes professionnelles (Diploma of Vocational Studies); CAP = Certificat d'Aptitude Professionelle (Certificate of Vocational Aptitude); CEP = Certificat d'Etudes Professionnelles (Certificate of Vocational Studies).

Fig. 1 The general structure of education in France

passionately about the things of the mind. Thus education becomes a matter of high seriousness, rather than a peripheral interest of politicians. What distinguishes the educational debate across the Channel is the quality of the argument, as contrasted with the indifference, the superficiality or the polemics with which the subject is treated in England.

Since I published a first attempt to examine French education some ten years ago,[1] only one major book in English has appeared on the subject.[2]

[1] *Society, Schools and Progress in France,* Oxford, Pergamon Press, 1965.
[2] W. R. Fraser, *Reform and Restraints in Modern French Education,* London, RKP, 1971.

Although the number of books written by Frenchmen about their educational system is still a trickle as compared with the torrent of works on English education that have poured forth in recent years, the evolution of French education has been so swift, the documentation available has now become so abundant, that this present work must necessarily also act as a textbook, providing essential information for further study. This constraint has to some extent determined the plan of the book. A discussion of the historical and cultural background is followed by a section devoted to administration and planning. The third part is given over mainly to an analysis of the school system, with some indication· of the social factors involved, particularly in relation to pupils and teachers. The last section is devoted to what might loosely be termed the politics of education, with an analysis of higher education, since it is mainly round the universities and similar institutions that political discussion has revolved. The book ends with a brief evaluation of the issues that have emerged, and an appraisal of the future evolution of French education.

This is not a view of a foreign educational system seen from the study. It is the outcome of visits to schools and universities, and countless discussions with pupils, parents, teachers, inspectors and administrators. If there is any good in the book, it is because of them; the errors and misapprehensions are all my own. My French friends will lament the seeming severity of my judgements; my English colleagues will say that I have been too encomiastic. Whether stringent or eulogistic, I must, however, declare my own great predilection − to put it no higher − for France and French culture, which I have studied for half a lifetime.

My thanks go not only to the many anonymous friends already mentioned, but in particular to the following: M. Jean Auba, Director of the Centre International d'Etudes Pédagogiques at Sèvres for his personal kindness and the unfailing hospitality of the unique institution that he directs; to the Director and his associates at the Institut National de la Recherche et de la Documentation Pédagogiques, whose information service was a never-failing resource; to those who kindly allowed me to use the following libraries: the Bibliothèque Nationale, the library of the Musée Pédagogique; in Oxford, the libraries of the Maison Française and of St. Antony's College; and lastly, to Pamela, my wife, who also bore the heat and burden of the day.

Oxford   W.D.H.
December 1975

PART I

HISTORICAL AND CULTURAL

CHAPTER 1
Historical Background

Jean-Jacques Rousseau has often been dubbed "the Copernicus of education". By coincidence the publication in 1762 of his *Emile*, from which may be deduced those principles of egalitarianism and secularism over which many battles have been fought in France, was matched by another notable landmark. In the same year the Jesuits, whose *Ratio Studiorum* had formed the basis for the education of future élites, were expelled from France. A certain polarity exists about these two events. On the one hand secularism which, in the mind of Napoleon, led to State supremacy and nationalism in education; on the other, the primacy of the Church in the education of the young, which was accompanied by an anti-national Ultramontanism. Rousseau's more strictly educational ideas have taken a long time to permeate the French schools, although today his views on the stages of child development are at least partially reflected in the French concept of "phases" ("cycles") in education. By contrast, the formalism of the Jesuit college, with its accent on the humanities, has taken a long time to die out of French secondary schools. There is no doubt, however, that the ideas of the Swiss Rousseau and the Spanish soldier-priest, Ignatius de Loyola, have considerably influenced the course of education in France.[1]

The other Philosophes were less concerned with the process of education and more with its social role. They viewed education as an instrument for reducing the inequalities among men. Condorcet believed that greater equality in education would consummate "greater equality in industry and so in wealth".[2] The Revolutionary Constitution of 1791 stipulated that

[1] Two indispensable recent histories of French education since the Revolution are: F. Ponteil, *Histoire de l'enseignement en France. Les grandes étapes, 1789–1944*, Paris, 1966; and A. Prost, *L'Enseignement en France, 1800–1967*, Paris, 1968.
[2] Condorcet, *Sketch for a Historical Picture of the Progress of the Human Mind*, London, 1955, pp. 183–184.

3

there should be set up "a public system of education, common to all citizens, free for those parts of education indispensable to all men".[3] Yet, having in effect specified universal and free primary education, they expelled religious such as the Christian Brothers whose vision had likewise been to establish a school in every parish of France. It is true that Condorcet assumed this ambition, but the plan he outlined to the Legislative Assembly remained a dead letter.

Equality was not the only Revolutionary goal in education. The men of 1789 saw education as a means of promoting national sentiment. Thus in primary schools the teaching of French was to be highlighted. They also saw new types of élites arising to run the Republic. The foundation of the Ecole Polytechnique in 1794 and of the "écoles centrales" the following year, in which the stress was upon modern subjects, represented practical steps towards achieving this aim. As First Consul Bonaparte later reinforced both the inculcation of national feeling and the training of new cadres to replace the old aristocracy, but was scarcely interested in the diminution of inequality to be brought about by the education of the masses.

A measure of prime importance was taken in 1802 by Bonaparte when he created the "lycée", a new type of academic secondary school to replace the "collèges royaux" of the Ancien Régime and the Jesuit institutions. The "lycée" remained at the pinnacle of the French school system for 150 years, without evolving radically from the Napoleonic conception of its function in society. Around it the Emperor created the Imperial University in 1808. Even today the term "Université" retains as one of its meanings the distinctive sense then given it, to designate the totality of State educational institutions. To administer this new entity Fontanes was appointed as Grand Master, an office from which developed the Ministry of Education. The teaching body to operate the new schools was conceived of almost as a religious order, hierarchical and owing a personal allegiance to the Emperor. Those appointed to it would be "the guarantee against pernicious and subversive theories of social order . . .

---

[3] "Il sera créé et organisé une *Instruction publique,* commune à tous les citoyens, gratuite à l'égard des parties d'enseignement indispensables pour tous les hommes, et dont les établissements seront distribués graduellement, dans un rapport combiné avec la division du royaume." (Title I of the Constitution accepted by the king on September 14, 1791.)

defenders of morality and the principles of the State".[4] Creator of political divisions, military districts and even episcopal dioceses, Napoleon divided France educationally into "académies", each under a Rector who reported to the central administration in Paris. Fontanes, as well as being Grand Master, was also Rector of the academy of Paris. To ensure that the orders emanating from the central administration were obeyed, a general inspectorate was set up to visit each academy regularly. Corresponding to the national hierarchy, a similar chain of command was established in each lycée. The schools were run like military institutions: the pupils were dressed in uniforms and their day was regulated by the beat of the drum. The mission of the school was to mould future officers for the Imperial armies and administrators for the territories they conquered, as well as for France itself. The curriculum followed was both literary and scientific, although Napoleon himself gave primacy to the former. A passing-out examination, the baccalaureate, was instituted in 1808. Considered the first degree of higher education, it gave automatic access to the newly constituted university faculties. In obedience and loyalty to the Emperor and in respect for the Catholic religion the future élites of the nation would be trained for their task.

Napoleon was well content to hand back to ecclesiastics the lesser task of educating the masses. The Concordat of 1801 had restored to religious the right to teach and already as Consul Napoleon had given back to the communes the responsibility for primary schools. These became once more parochial institutions, many again in the charge of the Christian Brothers, who had returned to France in 1804. By 1833 Guizot could insist that every commune should maintain its own primary school, either independently or in conjunction with the Church. Each "département" (the political unit into which France had been divided by Napoleon) should set up a teacher training college and all teachers in State schools should possess a teaching certificate. For both future teachers and primary pupils moral and religious instruction was to be the staple of the curriculum. The rudiments of education were to be given not to ensure greater equality but to acquaint future citizens with their duties. Thus far had the Revolutionary dream declined.

To Guizot must also be attributed the doubtful honour of having formalized primary and secondary education into two separate educational

[4] Napoleon's *First Instructions* to Fontanes.

channels rather than into two consecutive levels, a state of affairs that lasted until 1959.

In 1850 the Falloux Law reasserted the legal right of anyone to open a school, thus formally breaking the monopoly in secondary education created by Napoleon, although in practice the monopoly had already been greatly infringed. This revival of the "liberté d'enseignement" ("freedom in education") benefited principally the Church, which at the same time gained considerable freedom from State control in matters such as the inspection of schools and teaching qualifications, whilst securing representation on the central bodies concerned with the organization of the educational system. The Falloux Law represents the high-water mark in the ebb and flow of ecclesiastical influence in education. The violence of 1848 had frightened the bourgeoisie into giving more power to the Church, which was considered to be an element of stability in society.

The Second Empire is noteworthy for the measures of Victor Duruy, a Minister who was both "democratic and innovating". He was a protagonist of free primary education — by 1866, 41 per cent of primary pupils were being educated free.[5] He took practical steps to ensure greater opportunity for girls, particularly in secondary education. The secondary curriculum gave greater emphasis to science and vocational subjects than before. Despite greater centralization and the reinforcement of State education, the reign of Napoleon III also saw a large expansion of private education, both secular and denominational. Whether this greater enthusiasm for schooling was shared by the pupils is difficult to say. For them, conditions were harsh. A boarder in a lycée rose at 5.30 a.m. in winter and went to bed at 8.30 p.m. He worked an 11½-hour day, of which only 4 hours were spent in actual classroom learning, the rest being devoted to supervised private study.[6] This Spartan-like régime was to subsist during the Third Republic.

That régime had its uncertain birth in defeat by Prussia, a defeat which, it was alleged, owed something to the Prussian schoolmaster, a cry which was to be re-echoed in 1940. It was nevertheless the new Republic which was to be the first to implement an overall, coherent policy in education. In 1870 Jules Ferry, the architect of the new system, proclaimed his belief: ". . . . Among all the questions and necessities of the times, among

[5] Prost, *op. cit.*, p. 94.
[6] *Ibid.*, p. 50.

all the problems, I shall choose one to which I shall devote all my intelligence, my spirit, my heart, my physical and moral powers: it is the problem of the education of the people." Like Danton in his insistence on the primacy of education, like Condorcet in his belief that education could reduce inequalities in the human condition, Ferry realized eventually the old dream of the Revolutionaries, an education that should be compulsory for all, secular in character, and free. Thus in 1881 fees were abolished in State schools; in 1882 schooling was made compulsory for all children between the ages of 7 and 13; in the same year religion was forbidden to be taught in State schools and the curriculum was secularized. The Catholics found their educational privileges curtailed. In 1879 already, the right they had enjoyed to grant degrees in their own institutions of higher education was rescinded and the State monopoly restored. The theoretical basis for the Catholic right to educate had been pithily summed up by Pio Nono: ".... In spite of the discomfiture that may be felt by our opponents, I am obliged to repeat that it was to the apostles and their successors, and not to others, that Jesus Christ commanded, 'Euntes docete'." Nevertheless, religious belonging to orders not officially authorized to teach, such as the Jesuits, were no longer allowed to teach in either State or Catholic schools. The right of inspection of schools by religious authorities, a right which they had enjoyed since the Falloux Law, was withdrawn. By 1886 no ecclesiastic whatsoever was allowed to teach in State schools.

The educational debate thus became one about the nature of French society. In 1870, to hark back to the war, the Catholics had attributed the Prussian victory to irreligion and moral decadence. On the other hand, "Ferry and the Republicans, the Masonic lodges, the Ligue de l'Enseignement [a liberal and secularist movement founded by Jean Macé in 1863], and societies of Freethinkers answered that illiteracy, ignorance of the modern world, of science and technology, had earned France defeat at the hands of enlightened, Protestant Prussia".[7] The Positivist attitude of Ferry aroused fierce hostility. He was accused of creating the "Godless school". His retort was that religion acted as a divisive factor in an educational system which should "mix up, on the school benches, the children who will later find themselves serving under the flag of our country". For a morality based on religion he wished to substitute a secular one, "... the

[7] P. Gagnon, *France Since 1789,* New York, 1964, p. 233.

old morality of the philosophers: it is the morality of Socrates, it is the morality of Aristotle, it is the morality of Cicero, a morality that Christianity has refined, perfected and revealed — with that I agree. But it is a morality as eternal as the human soul itself." This is the tone of reason, but there is no doubt that others such as Macé saw the school as the instrument of a more militant secularism to promote a different notion of the State. The State would adopt a posture of "neutrality", founded on democracy, flatly opposed to the hierarchical form of society, based since the Restoration on the alliance of "throne and altar" so beloved by writers such as Bonald and de Maistre and which the militant secularists alleged to be the ideal of Catholicism.

To teach the children of the people who were drawn into the primary school Ferry realized that teacher training institutions must be expanded. The number of "écoles normales" was increased, particularly those for girls, and schools to educate the future staffs of these institutions were opened at Fontenay-aux-Roses and St. Cloud. The "instituteur", the primary teacher, educated in what has been described as a "secular seminary", was to become the lay missionary of the new Republican ideals, a counterweight to the influence exerted by the priest in every village of France.

In strictly educational terms the effect of the Ferry laws was salutary. By the turn of the century no child, however remote his home, had to walk more than 2 kilometres to the nearest primary school. But education had become more than ever the symbol of conflict, a struggle that ranged Republicans, freemasons, radicals and secularists on the left, and Royalists, whether their allegiance was to the houses of Bourbon, Orleans or Bonaparte, and Catholics on the right. It was a cleavage in French society that was to last till 1940 and beyond.

In secondary education a grand reform of syllabuses was carried out in the closing decades of the century. Latin and French teaching was refurbished and curricula in modern languages, history and science were strengthened. The Instructions of 1890 speak of the acquisition of culture no longer in terms of the mere accumulation of knowledge, but as "learning to learn". Indeed there is a very modern, platitudinous ring about them: education must be "general in its principles, but not encyclopedic in its content". Knowledge is not so important as the acquisition of a taste for study, of habits of work, and of the ability to understand.

In higher education also Ferry initiated a series of reforms that took until the end of the century to complete. In the university faculties work was being carried on in tumbledown buildings lacking in equipment. Speaking in the Chamber of Deputies, Ferry had occasion to allude to "the damp and unhealthy cellar in which Claude Bernard had carried out his work".[8] Not only were the faculties refurbished, but the number of chairs was increased. By 1896 fifteen universities, one for each academy, were constituted by linking faculties together. This was not the solution that reformers such as Liard wanted, but it was nevertheless a structure that subsisted until 1968.

For a brief interval in the 1890s the Ralliement, the rallying of Catholics to the Republican régime, was encouraged by Leo XIII. Passions were, however, revived by the Dreyfus Affair. The prohibition preventing any member of a religious order from teaching even in a Catholic school, passed in 1904, and the abrogation a year later of the Concordat, with the separation of Church and State, exacerbated the educational rift. Combes began to close schools run by unauthorized religious orders. Even those institutions run by authorized orders were to be closed within ten years. The result was that many Catholic schools ostensibly became non-religious private institutions whose teachers doffed the cassock for the frock-coat. Religious belief had become a private matter, in which the authorities of the State were not involved. But before Catholic education had completely vanished from the scene the First World War had consummated the "union sacrée" of all Frenchmen as they closed ranks against the enemy of 1870. Yet, as one historian has remarked, "the France which enters upon the war in 1914 is still a France in which the "schools question [i.e. the question of religion and education] decides the dividing line between right and left".[9]

As if to redress the inherent beastliness of war, the end of conflict always sees an upsurge of idealism. In France this was expressed in 1918 in the field of education. From the trenches came a call from a group of young idealists styling themselves the Compagnons de l'Université Nouvelle, urging a common primary school for all children, free secondary education and selection on merit. The cry was for a single school − the "école unique" − to break down the hermetic divisions that separated the

[8] Quoted in J. Minot, *L'Entreprise Education Nationale*, Paris, 1970, p. 46.
[9] Prost, *op. cit.*, p. 210.

children of agricultural and industrial workers and of petty bourgeois, all of whom remained trapped in the primary school system, from the scions of the richer bourgeoisie and upper classes, who frequented the "lycée" with its own primary preparatory classes. Such a system, it was argued, was the breeding ground of class distinctions, a hindrance to social mobility and an obstacle to real political and civic equality. In short, a truly meritocratic educational system must be installed in a democracy, so that all had an equal chance to improve their lot. Hence the three planks on which the Compagnons stood: "école unique", "gratuité", "sélection".[10]

From the outset their programme encountered either opposition or indifference. Although they were careful to point out that they did not seek a State monopoly in education and that the Catholic colleges would remain intact, many Catholics were themselves violently opposed or at best reserved to the new proposals. Among the political parties the Radicals led by Herriot, himself a former schoolmaster, were vaguely sympathetic; under Léon Blum the Socialists gave general support. However, the elections of 1919 brought in a government of the Right which was to last four years.

The administration known as the Bloc National included monarchists, Catholics and all shades of right-wing opinion. The Catholics were less preoccupied with the école unique than with obtaining State subsidies for their schools. Despite strenuous efforts in the Chamber of Deputies this they failed to do: "The vote showed that 'laïcité' remained one test of republicanism that most deputies did not care to fail."[11] In 1923 the campaign for the école unique was renewed through agencies such as the Ligue des Droits de l'Homme. The Radical and Socialist opposition were stimulated to concerted action on education by the actions of Bérard, the then Minister of Education. Bérard declared himself against "subordinating to material progress and economic necessity the conditions of intellectual culture" and accordingly made Latin compulsory again for all secondary pupils.

A weak alliance between Radicals and Socialists, the Cartel des Gauches, succeeded the Bloc National as the government and in 1924

[10] For an account of French educational controversy between the Wars cf. J. Talbott, *The Politics of Educational Reform in France, 1918–1940,* Princeton, N.J., 1969.
[11] Talbott, *op. cit.,* pp. 71–72.

promptly reinstated the "modern" option in the lycée so that classics became merely one alternative among a number. There were fears that root and branch reform in education might occur. The Catholics were wary of a State monopoly in education being established, an idea long canvassed by the Freemasons. Other opposition groups mounted attacks on the concept of the école unique on the grounds that it would lead to the "primarization" of the school system and that selection for the lycée on merit alone would lead to social unrest and in any case would encroach upon the rights of parents. Turning the argument round, they also averred that a single school for all would merely cause the bourgeoisie to remove their children from State to confessional schools, thus strengthening the latter. The one practical step towards equality that was taken was the introduction of a common curriculum for the two types of primary classes that existed: those which received the majority of pupils and those which were fee-paying and acted as a "feeder" system for the lycée. Before other issues came to a head, however, in 1926 the Cartel des Gauches was overthrown and a government of national union, under Poincaré, assumed power.

Herriot became Minister of Education in Poincaré's administration and took the first steps towards the abolition of fees in the lycée. By a gradual phasing-out this was finally achieved by 1933, although for a short period under the Vichy régime the clock was put back and the top classes once again became fee-paying. The practical effects of this measure were not very striking and the principal beneficiaries were in fact the lower middle class rather than the workers. During the early 1930s education took a back seat as a political issue. However, with the advent of the Popular Front in 1936 the programme of economic and social reforms included raising the school-leaving age to 14.

Blum, however, eventually appointed as Minister of Education Jean Zay, the youngest Minister ever to hold any office in government.[12] He was to continue as Minister even after the Popular Front had dissolved, right up to late 1939, when he joined the Army. Zay, one of the Radical "young Turks", was a lawyer by profession, but in 1936 gave notice that he intended to reform the education system. He presented a plan to the Cabinet in March 1937, declaring that "the time appears to have come to

[12] For Jean Zay cf. M. Ruby, *La Vie et l'oeuvre de Jean Zay* (Thèse de doctorat de troisième cycle, Faculté des lettres et sciences humaines, Paris, 1967), Paris, 1969.

give primary, secondary and higher education the general statute that has been awaited for many years and for which a number of measures and experiments have paved the way".[13] The principal innovation that he effected — and one which later became the lynch-pin of the de Gaulle reforms of 1959 — was the introduction of an "orientation" period (which he limited to one year) at the outset of secondary education. After this initial year pupils would be "oriented" into one of three branches, classical, modern or technical. The first two branches would cover a full secondary course of seven years; the technical branch would stop after four years. More children would enter the "lycée". Zay expressed his aim as one of social justice, so that "each may go in his chosen direction as far and as high as his abilities permit him".[14] Reaction to this plan was at first muted, although later right-wing Catholics attacked it as being an example of State direction and thus an attack upon parental liberty. Administrators such as Gustave Monod, the director of secondary education, gave Zay their support, although traditionalists such as members of the Société des Agrégés were openly hostile. However, in the teeth of enormous difficulties the "orientation" experiment got under way in September 1937, only to be all but abandoned two years later in the twilight of war.

Thus the high hopes and endeavour that had inspired the Compagnons twenty years before had largely remained unrealized. Educational reform foundered between the wars because the intellectual tradition in France was so deeply inrooted; because Catholics feared, and secularists fiercely advocated, a State monopoly in education; because the efforts of the reformers were concentrated too much on equalizing opportunity for the gifted but deprived few rather than on ensuring secondary education of an appropriate kind for all children; because the bookish, literary content of secondary education was not seen as being no longer appropriate to a new age; because vested interests, whether political, religious or professional, were too powerful. It took the shock of defeat to act as the catalyser for new beginnings.

The new era, however, had to await 1944 and the Liberation. After the débâcle of 1940 Pétain launched a call for the intellectual and moral regeneration of the nation — an echo of Renan[15] — in which the schools

---

[13] From the "exposé des motifs" of the bill presented by Zay to the Chamber of Deputies, March 5, 1937.

[14] Quoted in Talbott, *op. cit.*, p. 215.

[15] E. Renan, *La Réforme intellectuelle et morale de la France,* Paris, 1871.

would play a fundamental role. There foregathered at Vichy a motley crew composed of members of the Action Française, ex-Cagoulards, Army officers (who, following Pétain and his great exemplar Lyautey, believed that both the Army and the schools were the educational forces of the nation), sprinkled with a few genuine idealists and a few self-seeking collaborators. These launched the so-called "Révolution Nationale".[16] In education, however, the measures that were taken might best be termed reactionary rather than revolutionary. The teacher training schools were abolished, because they had been the forcing ground for the staunchest upholders of secularism and the Third Republic and their influence upon the young was reckoned to have been pernicious. Teachers' unions were disbanded and the teacher representatives on the various advisory and consultative bodies connected with education were either eliminated or reduced in numbers. The militantly secularist Ligue de l'Enseignement was dissolved. Members of religious orders were allowed to teach in State schools. Religious education was reintroduced for a time into these schools as well. The crucifix was reinstated on the classroom walls. The picture of Marshal Pétain, "Head of the French State", had to be displayed — although some recalcitrant teachers stuck it on the inside of a cupboard door kept firmly shut! The Republican motto was effaced from the school walls. Jews and Freemasons were excluded from teaching; eventually Jewish pupils were not allowed to attend school. It is true that Jérôme Carcopino, the noted classical scholar who occupied for a while the post of Vichy Minister of Education, tried covertly to undo or mitigate the worst effects of the measures taken by his predecessors, particularly Jacques Chevalier. But Carcopino's tenure was short-lived and the last Minister of Education of the tottering régime was Abel Bonnard, writer, reactionary and homosexual.

However, not all that the Vichy régime accomplished in education turned out in the end to be evil. The revival in interest in physical education and sport — although perhaps for the wrong motives — was salutary. The abolition of the écoles normales presaged the end of a teacher training system which began at the age of 15 and resembled a junior seminary. Henceforth all entrants should take the baccalaureate

[16] A summary account of the educational measures taken by the Vichy régime in the period of the "Révolution Nationale" is given in R. Paxton, *Vichy France. Old Guard and New Order, 1940–1944,* London, 1972, pp. 153–165.

examination, thus putting an end to the vicious circle of the so-called "esprit primaire", within which the future primary teacher was intellectually imprisoned. The subsidies to private education paved the way for the religious settlement in education successfully accomplished by Debré in 1959. Moves were also made to rationalise the different types of primary and secondary schools. Not all these measures survived the Liberation, but some were revived later. In any case the gains of Vichy were negligible in comparison with the policy of repression that turned itself against the work of Ferry and his companions then and since. "L'Etat Français", with its narrowly interpreted motto of "work, family and motherland", was no substitute for the Republic and its more universal ideals.

Even before the recovery of the metropolitan territory the provisional government of de Gaulle had begun to plan the reform of the educational system. The Commissioner of National Education, René Capitant, set up a body in North Africa in 1944 which took up the task of planning changes virtually where Jean Zay had left off. The Algiers Plan proposed secondary education, free and compulsory, for all children up to the age of 15.[17] The first two years of secondary education would become an "orientation" phase which would determine the future course the pupil would follow, classical, modern or technical. The baccalaureate would confer unrestricted access to higher education, which in the first two years would be unspecialized. The post-baccalaureate classes preparing for competitive entrance to the "grandes écoles" would be abolished.

This plan was, however, rapidly superseded by the Langevin–Wallon Plan, published in 1947.[18] Set up in Paris after the Liberation, a commission presided initially over by Professor Langevin and then, after his death, by Professor Wallon, drew up a very ambitious project founded upon the twin principles of "démocratisation" and "orientation" which has become the reference framework for all later proposals for reform. The aims of education were defined as to promote the maximum development of the individual child regardless of his social origins, to prepare him for

[17] For the various reform proposals cf. L. Decaunes (ed.), *Réformes et projets de réforme de l'enseignement français de la Révolution à nos jours,* Paris, 1962.
[18] The Plan is reprinted in: *Le Plan Langevin–Wallon de réforme de l'enseignement. Compte rendu du colloque organisé par le groupe français d'éducation nouvelle et la Société française de Pédagogie,* Paris, 1964.

the world of work and to fit him to take his place in society. Preparation for employment was important, and equal dignity should be attached to both manual and intellectual work. Compulsory education from 6 to 18, divided into three phases, was envisaged. The first phase, for children aged between 6 and 11, would comprise a uniform programme, although teaching methods would be adapted to the level of ability. From 11 to 15 all pupils would pass through a phase of "orientation", consisting of a common core and, · after two years, a choice of options, but with maximum transfer possibilities from one to another. This would finally lead to a phase of "determination", for pupils from 15 to 18, divided into three tracks. The first track would be a "practical" one, for children whose manual rather than intellectual skills were predominant, and would constitute a kind of apprenticeship course. The second track would be designed for those children who were "executants" rather than inclined to theoretical studies, and would prepare for commercial, industrial, agricultural and artistic occupations. The last track would be academic, leading to the baccalaureate: here a common core of French, history and modern languages would be supplemented by literary, scientific and technical subjects, depending upon the pupil's aptitudes. The leit-motif of the secondary stage is one of "orientation", in which the pupil would be guided along the educational path which best befitted him. The stage would be characterized by the use of active methods, the promotion of co-operative as well as individual endeavour and a form of assessment in which a distinction would be drawn between the evaluation of knowledge and the evaluation of future ability. In higher education there would be a preparatory phase lasting a year, followed by specialization. Such specialization could have three main orientations: to professional training, to scientific research or to the diffusion of culture. Teachers would no longer be divided according to whether they were to teach in primary or in secondary education, but rather according to whether they taught a number of subjects or were specialists in one only. They would all undergo a four-year course, the first two years of which would be spent in a teacher training institution and the last two in the university proper, preparing for a degree.

The Plan was imbued with the same spirit of idealism that had, at the end of the First World War, animated the Compagnons de l'Université Nouvelle. Langevin and Wallon sought to remedy "the divorce between school education and life", which leaves out of account scientific development. The authors invoked the principle of "justice" for all children, regardless of social origins. Children must be oriented towards their appropriate form of employment without mutual prejudice arising because some become intellectual and others manual workers. "General culture represents what draws men closer together and unites them, whilst an occupation too often represents what separates them." Yet the analysis of "general culture" made in the Langevin–Wallon Plan reveals an open flank of ambiguity:

> Education must therefore offer to all equal possibilities of development, must open to all an access to culture, must be democratised less by a selection which segregates the most gifted from the mass than by a continued raising of the cultural level of the nation as a whole.

In other words, although schooling must take into account individual talents, a loftier aim must be to make accessible to the many the high culture that until then had been open only to the few. In a situation where the Pétain régime had reintroduced fees into the top classes of the lycée and had therefore attempted to limit access to the high culture to the rich, such a preoccupation is understandable. There is insufficient attention paid to the problem of redefining secondary education for the majority, for whom the heady wine of intellectualism may prove unsuitable and even distasteful. A similar manifestation of the *Zeitgeist* is to be found in the legitimate preoccupation, after a divisive war, with civic education. "The civic training of youth", the Report declares, is one of the most fundamental duties of a democratic state and it is incumbent upon the school system to fulfil this role. In a nation which had in part ascribed the defeat of 1940 to the shortcomings of the educational system and had under Vichy witnessed the growth of youth movements basically hostile to the democratic ideal, civic education was reckoned to be important.

The pressure of other priorities of reconstruction – housing, transport, food, industrial renovation – rather swept the Langevin–Wallon Plan under the table, at least for the time being. Nonetheless, other projects which more or less adopted its principles were continually being brought before the National Assembly, notably those of Depreux (1948), Delbos (1949) and Marie (1953). All foundered upon the treacherous rock of Parliamentary politics, which under the Fourth Republic were marked by frequent ministerial crises.

Meanwhile within the educational system itself modest reforms that did not require legislation arose from the initiative of teachers and administrators. One of the most notable successes was the creation of the "classes nouvelles" in 1945. (These classes were later renamed "classes pilotes.") They were set up by Gustave Monod, Director of Secondary Education within the Ministry of Education, in six "lycées pilotes". Their purpose was to continue the practice of the "orientation classes" created before the war by Jean Zay, and at the same time to achieve greater flexibility in the organization and methods of teaching. The classes were characterized by regular meetings of the teachers, where the progress of each pupil was carefully recorded. Parents, school psychologists and guidance counsellors were drawn into these regular consultations. To counter the passivity of the pupil, so-called "active" methods were adopted in which the stress was on self-discipline and co-operative work. "L'étude du milieu", the study of the local environment, was one of the ways in which the child's interest was stimulated. In half-classes what was known as "directed work" was undertaken. This involved the development of the child's capacity to work independently. He was taught how to apply what he had learnt in formal lessons. Techniques such as how to use a dictionary, how to use a library, how to draw up the plan for a French composition — in short, learning how to work — were fostered. The practice of handicrafts, the use of work sheets in French grammar and mathematics, and the working on projects in a team were all encouraged. Today such a description of what went on seems rather ordinary, but in the context of the then formalism of the French classroom it was revolutionary. The "classes nouvelles" experiment, which in its hey-day affected only about 8000 pupils, had an influence quite disproportionate to its size.

On the legislative front other reform projects were presented to the National Assembly, but foundered on the reef of political dissension. The Berthoin project of 1955 was perhaps the most realistic of all the schemes mooted since the Liberation, based as it was on the Langevin—Wallon Plan. It would have extended compulsory schooling, then ending at 14, to 16 and have preserved the concept of a phase of observation and guidance to determine in secondary education the best course for each pupil to follow. It propounded the notions of either "long" (extended) general or vocational secondary education or of a "short" or terminal phase. When this project was not adopted a similar scheme was proposed a year later by

Billères, but which had the additional novelty of stressing scientific and technical education.

Not only party politics prevented the realization of reforms. The expansion of education — any education — became a pressing necessity as the post-war "baby boom" reached the primary schools. Whereas in 1942 only 573,000 children had been born, by 1950 the figure had risen to 858,000. At the same time the pool of teachers available, born in the hollow years of declining population before the war, was clearly insufficient.

The real opportunity to break away from the past did not come until 1958. During the brief interregnum when de Gaulle governed by decree Berthoin, by this time Minister of Education, seized the opportunity to promulgate an ordinance which may be considered as the first of a long series of measures undertaken during the Fifth Republic aimed at reforming the education system from top to bottom. Yet the reforms promulgated in 1959 were comparatively modest. The school-leaving age was formally raised to 16, but this was not to come into effect until 1967 and thus was merely a declaration of intent. The real nub of the reform was the stipulation, twenty-one years after it had first been tried out experimentally by Jean Zay, of a two-year phase of observation for all children between 11 and 13, regardless whether they remained in the primary school or moved on to a school of higher status at that age.[19] At the end of the two-year period they were to be allocated to follow a short terminal course, or to another short course vocationally oriented, or to a "long" general or vocational course. To facilitate transfer between schools where it was necessary "bridging" or reception classes were instituted in the lycées. The snags in this arrangement soon became apparent. At the end of the observation phase it was patently difficult to move a pupil from one type of school to another. In any case entry into the observation phase itself was to be limited. Some who lacked the ability to "understand concepts" were eliminated from the beginning and placed in classes which were largely of the same kind as they would have had before. Those that were allowed into the observation phase were sorted at the end of the first term into those deemed suitable to study Latin and those who were not. With the prestige that still attached to the classics this classification

[19] For a complete review of the "phase of observation and orientation" cf. Gisela Knaup, *Die französische Beobachtungs- und Orientierungβtufe,* Hanover, 1974.

assumed undue importance. Nevertheless, from these new dispositions two positive gains emerged. The first was that the former entrance examination to the "lycée", the equivalent of the English 11+, was abolished and a much larger proportion of pupils than ever before had the chance of following a truly secondary course. The second was the systematic arrangements that were made to follow the educational career of children closely for at least the first two years of secondary education; thus the definitive judgement about their educational future, arrived at by a "class council" ("conseil de classe") which included all the teachers that taught them, was deferred until the age of 13.

If one seeks to understand why the reforms so long advocated in theory failed to be realized earlier the reasons are complex. Other priorities had to be met before that of education. The perpetual instability of successive governments of the Fourth Republic impeded progress. And there were perhaps deeper reasons: the proud intellectual tradition of the lycée, grounded in an élitist concept of education, made the politicians, most of whom had been nurtured within that tradition themselves, reluctant to take measures which would harm what was, with the "grandes écoles", the acme of French educational institutions. This consideration blocks partially even today that free educational development whose roots have been traced back to 1918, which was given further impetus by Jean Zay in 1938, reaffirmed in principle in the charter of reform outlined by the Council of the Resistance clandestinely during the Occupation, and given an up-to-date formulation by Langevin and Wallon in 1947. The constant theme, the major one if France was to "join its century", was that of equalization of opportunity, which would lead, it was firmly believed, to a true democratization of society.

CHAPTER 2

Education, National Sentiment and Culture

Modern educational systems have developed as instruments for the transmission, diffusion and enlargement of a nation's cultural patrimony, which is partly that of all mankind, partly peculiar to one linguistic area and to one special political entity. Since the mid-eighteenth century rulers and others among the older nations of Europe have attempted to use education and, through schools and universities, culture to achieve national purposes. In Prussia the "Landschulreglement" of 1763 was in part a political move by Frederick the Great to ensure the growth of national unity. In France La Chalotais' *Essai d'éducation nationale* urged the suppression of the Jesuits because they were educating a youth whose loyalty was not to France but to Rome. Indeed, in France the education system, and thereby the culture that it imparts, has been an instrument for ensuring the perpetuation of the State, which has always been regarded as a legitimate aim of government. Whereas in some countries such as Britain this inculcation of what might be termed patriotism has been carried out almost unconsciously, France, partly because of historical circumstances such as the threat of invasion, has used its schools more openly to engender national sentiment. As has already been noted, the Revolutionaries saw the school as a means of realizing ideals of liberty and equality. For the Napoleonic régime education was a school of duty to train Frenchmen to take over leadership in the State and to rule the Empire. Fourcroy's *Rapport* of 1806 speaks of establishing a teaching body which will be "eminently French, namely that all will have one single aim, that of forming characters virtuous from religious principle, useful to the State by their abilities and knowledge, attached to the government and devoted to its august leader in love and duty".

The Napoleonic legend sustained the schools even after the Restoration. An ordinance of 1821 set out a charter for education which was to consist of "religion, the monarchy and legitimacy". Later, Guizot was alive to the role of the school in promoting social stability and national loyalty. His circular letter to all primary teachers, dated July 16, 1833, placed education as being "for the benefit of the State itself": the schools were to aid in the task of suppressing riot and revolution, which had so alarmed the bourgeoisie in 1830. For Guizot religion was to be a controlling force against revolt. Not that Louis Philippe cared overmuch for religiously controlled schools. He said, "The children are taught too much the verse of the Magnificat, 'deposuit potentes de sede' ".

It was Michelet's *Le Peuple* (1846) which gave to education and ·patriotism their populist expression. For Michelet the father is the first educator of the child. When he begins to grow up the father takes him to a big public procession in Paris and points out to him the crowds of people, the Army and the Tricolour flag, saying solemnly, "There, my boy, look; there is France, there is our country".[1] This is the vision for which the child must be ready to die. Likewise the priority for formal schooling is also fixed: "One's country first, as dogma and as principle. Then one's country as a legend: our two redemptions, by the Holy Maid of Orleans, by the Revolution. . . ."[2] It is these ideals that for generations coloured the kind of history taught in French schools.

Duruy's patriotic emphasis was slightly different. For him it was the civilizing mission of France in the world that was paramount. In a memorandum to Napoleon III he stated baldly that since France was the moral centre of the world she must make provision for those who are destined for the liberal professions, for the higher offices in the State, for literature and science, philosophy and history, and thus justify an aristocracy of the intellect. For Ferry the military failure of 1870 was attributable to the lack of education, as we have already seen, and his legislative work to strengthen and reform the schools is undoubtedly linked to his desire to see the infant Republic flourish and France revive. All that ran counter to these ambitions, in particular the Catholic claim to regulate education, must be overcome. Secularism and patriotism went hand in hand. Speaking in the Senate on December 23, 1880 he declared, "It is important for the Republic, for civil society, and for all those who hold dear the tradition of 1789, that the direction of schools and their inspection should not be in the hands of ministers of religion. . . ." In

[1] Michelet, *Le Peuple,* Paris, 1846, pp. 317 ff.
[2] *Ibid.*, p. 343.

1905, at its annual congress, the Ligue de l'Enseignement stipulated that pupils should be trained in "citizenship, fidelity to the principles of democracy and to the Republic which is the highest form of it and, first and foremost because it comes before all other considerations, patriotism. . . ." When a more conciliatory note was struck in the relationships between secularists and Catholics the unifying force between them, as the one educational point on which both sides could agree, was the necessity for patriotism. In 1914, so well had the fathers of the Third Republic done their work, that it was the primary teachers who were among the most courageous in action, when called up as reserve NCOs' and officers. In 1940 Pétain condemned the insufficient inculcation of patriotic sentiment in schools between the Wars. Capitant's Commission for Educational Reform, meeting in Algiers in 1944 at the instigation of de Gaulle, was also categorical about the alleged shortcomings in this respect of the education that had been proffered to the national elites:

> The defeat and the tyranny would not have been what they have been but for the faintheartedness, the default or the treason of the controlling groups in the navy and the army, in politics and finance, in industry and commerce. Those who could claim to have come from the summit of our educational system are those whose conduct has been the most scandalous.[3]

De Gaulle was fully conscious of the important role that the school might play as a unifying force in national life. On the occasion of the revolt of the OAS in Algeria teachers of civics were instructed to set their pupils an essay on a text of Victor Hugo consisting of a proclamation addressed to the army in 1851:

> There are two things that are sacred: the flag, which represents military honour, and the law, which represents national honour. Soldiers, the greatest of all attacks is the flag raised against the law.[4]

The school is the instrument of the State to promote national feeling, the sacrifice of self to one's country; to induce a sense of civic responsibility, of respect for the law; to be a bulwark against all that divides the people; to foster loyalty to the régime, whether this be revolutionary, imperial, monarchical or democratic. Until 1968, and perhaps beyond, this was one of the most important facets of education, where patriotism and culture flowed together. Durkheim has hypothesized that the phases of

[3] Quoted by C. H. Dobinson in *World Year Book of Education*, 1952, p. 336.
[4] Circular of April 25, 1961, given in *Bulletin Officiel de l'Education Nationale* (BOEN), No. 15 of April 27, 1961.

educational evolution correspond to the "states of society".[5] Ever since the Revolution French society has been polarized into two groups, the one seeking to preserve what might be termed traditional values, the other for ever striving after radical solutions. Culturally Vial[6] has likewise identified two similar opposing tendencies, the one idealist, imbued with "l'esprit des anciens collèges", the other utilitarian, imbued with "l'esprit des écoles centrales". The meeting ground for both sets of dichotomies has been patriotism.

The guiding light of French education has been intellectualism, the "doctrine that knowledge is wholly or mainly derived from the action of the intellect, i.e. from pure reason". The belief that this is so has informed, consciously or unconsciously, the relationship perceived by the French between their culture and their educational system. This predominantly mental mode of educating the young may be deduced from the widespread use until comparatively recently of the term "instruction" rather than "éducation". It has been assumed that schooling, given in the form of instruction, will automatically stimulate the broader process of education. Faith in this pathetic fallacy has been held by many; Victor Hugo, for example, is often quoted: "A child that one instructs is a man that one wins." A change in this view was slow in coming. In 1932 Edouard Herriot, himself a former schoolmaster, allowed his Minister of Education, Anatole de Monzie, to change the title of the portfolio that he then held from that of Minister of Public Instruction to that of Minister of National Education. Even today, however, inspectors of the central administration are designated as "Inspectors-General of Public Instruction". As late as 1959 official texts emanating from the Ministry spoke of "instruction" rather than "education". A circular of December 1969 instituting forms of extracurricular activities stressed what had been up to then inadequately acknowledged, that "education can no longer be limited to instruction through the acquisition of knowledge". A slightly earlier circular (September 2, 1969) on the renewal of elementary education defined the task as that of "the overall work of education of the child". Nevertheless the view that the work of schools is purely intellectual dies hard.

In particular, the task of primary education has been considered to be

---

[5] E. Durkheim, *L'Evolution pédagogique en France,* Vol. II, *De la Renaissance à nos jours,* Paris, 1938.
[6] F. Vial, *Trois siècles de l'enseignement secondaire,* Paris 1936.

one of "instruction", conceived differently from that of the "lycée". Here it is important to draw a distinction between two attitudes of mind. The primary teacher, the "instituteur", has traditionally been held to be imbued with "l'esprit primaire", which has been both a term of abuse and of admiration. Until fairly recently the whole schooling of the future primary teacher, even his training, had come under the régime of primary education. To its admirers "l'esprit primaire", which he embodied, represented the will to provide all Frenchmen, regardless of social class or belief, with a form of education that would develop all capacities to the full. To those who execrated the "primary mentality" it connoted the way in which those only half-educated have constituted themselves as judges of people, affairs and events, when they themselves lack the cultural background essential to make a balanced appraisal. Hence what is being condemned in "l'esprit primaire" is a pseudo-intellectualism.

However, true intellectualism, as practised in the schools, was until recently more related to instruction than to education. Today, however, the task of educating as well as instructing has been forced upon the schools. The enlarged clientele of universal mass secondary education required to be culturally adjusted to a different set of values – some would say, middle-class values. This cultural adjustment had hitherto been encompassed by the bourgeoisie, for their own children, in the home. It now became incumbent upon the teachers.

J. R. Pitts has identified the characteristic of French culture as the cult of "intellectual prowess". In education this has been expressed as the pursuit of excellence of the mind, which has been a constant ideal. The medieval schoolmen insisted that logic was the foundation of education and the indispensable tool for sharpening the intellect. Rabelais believed that happiness lay in the fount of knowledge, of which all men must drink "because it has the power of filling the spirit with all truth". The Jesuits were partly the victims of the postulate that knowledge automatically brings goodness in its train, when, using a subtle blend of Antiquity and Christianity, they sought to promote what they conceived to be the right religious and moral ideas. Yet the domain of character formation *per se* has never really been an active field of concern for French educationists. Rather has the inculcation of desirable moral and personal traits been held to lie within the purview of the family or the Church. Despite an intellectual tradition that in its literary overtones has close affinities with the beliefs of von Humboldt or Matthew Arnold, the French have clung to the sophism that "to know the right is to do the right". Future élites have been schooled in the moral examplars of ancient and French classical authors, and been obliged to study philosophy in the final year of secondary education. Thus far, and no farther, has the school ventured to go in teaching ethical viewpoints. The secular nature of the State educational system made it virtually impossible to propound absolute moral standards sanctioned by a metaphysical view of human existence.

The efforts of reformers have nevertheless been persistently directed towards creating a secondary school less intellectually oriented. These efforts have been frustrated because of the strongly conservative nature of French educational tradition. Even in the primary school the approach has been intellectually rigorous. Wylie, observing the village schoolmarm and her methods, describes the class as follows: "She first introduces a principle or rule. Then a concrete illustration or problem is presented and studied or solved in the light of the principle."[7] By the time the bright pupil has got to the lycée, whose task has in the past been to form a leadership élite, he has accepted that the training imparted ("la formation") should be intellectual and little else.

The nature of that intellectual training has, moreover, been essentially literary. The prominent place accorded to the humanities at first made it difficult for the French to accept science at all into the educational pattern. When Duruy first introduced a special science option into the "lycée" it was scornfully dismissed as "classes for grocers". Science was held to be too closely connected with the business of earning a living. Durkheim[8] sees the slowly increasing esteem of science as waxing in inverse proportion to the decline in religious belief. Religion was related to Man, to men and the human condition; science, in contrast, dealt with things, inert, inanimate matter. Until comparatively recently the highfliers of the lycée were not allowed to concentrate unduly upon science: the most prestigious section of the baccalaureate was that in which the study of mathematics and science was combined with Latin.

Indeed the place of Latin in the curriculum is worthy of special note. Although the study of Greek almost died out in French schools during the Second World War Latin has continued to struggle on. Perhaps even more

[7] L. Wylie, *Village in the Vaucluse,* New York, 1957.
[8] Durkheim, *op. cit.,* Vol. II, p. 139.

than the Italians the French have in the past believed in the civilizing mission of Latin, holding that their own language and its classical literature are its direct successor. They have accepted the "roots of civilization" argument, the view that Rome has a message for every generation. Latin has been held to be the bearer of a complete system of values; this concept of "timeless values" and "eternal verities" embodied in Antiquity is, of course, today under constant attack. Latin is no longer the "mother tongue" of the Church, a Church which was held to sustain Western civilization and of which France was "the eldest daughter". A humanist education was long considered to be a vital part of the training of a leadership élite, because the study of Latin texts was held to impart a knowledge of the highest moral values essential for those who would eventually wield high responsibility in the State. For its devotees the strictly linguistic training that Latin gave was self-evident. Speaking at Albi in 1970, the late President Pompidou, himself a former teacher of the classics, expressed himself in laudatory terms regarding the value of Latin. Jean-Pierre Hébert has summarized the arguments for the classics in a nutshell:

> ... we must learn those methods of work which impart a taste for free thought, sound judgement and criticism. And nothing is better fitted to that purpose than the exercise of translating the ancient languages. Because it teaches nothing. Because it *trains*. [9]

Nevertheless, the place of the classics in French education has been progressively downgraded. The "common school" of lower secondary education, which once possessed a prestigious section in which Latin was started after one term in the school, now begins Latin (and Greek, which is also an option) only in the third year ("quatrième"), where it is chosen less and less by the gifted pupils. The motives of Edgar Faure, who postponed the beginning of Latin when he was Minister of Education in 1968, may be partly ascribed to a desire to placate the Fédération de l'Education Nationale whose largest constituent union, the Syndicat National des Instituteurs, was campaigning for a "common core" of all subjects for all children in the first two years of secondary education. This step was impossible to take if Latin were retained for the 11-year-olds. Faure's successor, Olivier Guichard, upheld this decision for a different

[9] Quoted in W. R. Fraser, *Education and Society in Modern France,* London, 1963, p. 45.

reason: he wished to see a reform of French language teaching, which should henceforth acquire a status unconnected with Latin and would concentrate more upon the communication skills. This relegation of the "noble disciplines" *par excellence* to a subordinate place in the curriculum represents a victory for the instrumentalists and utilitarians in education. They have paid little heed to their opponents, who declare that "democratization", which should signify the universalization of standards accepted as the hallmarks of the "high culture" and thus of civilization itself, has been cheapened under the influence of a populist ideology of "relevance".

Another far-reaching consequence of the intellectualist approach to education has been the independence of thought and strong individualism that it has fostered among the brightest pupils. David Thomson has argued that "the powerful traditions of classical humanism" have conspired "to exalt the individual in French thought, habits and social organization".[10] There can be little doubt that such traditions were inculcated in the "lycée" where they were transmitted by such schoolmaster philosophers as "Alain" (Emile Chartier), who encouraged their charges to question all values. The typical exercises of the "lycée" have been the detailed study of literary texts – the "explication de texte" – and the solution of complicated mathematical problems, both processes of analysis and logic which are highly individualistic. Until very recently no attempt had been made in French schools to stimulate co-operative effort. Today, however, such excessive individuality is deplored by some in authority: hence the insistence upon collaboration, the practice of group work in the classroom and the encouragement of "le team-spirit" by sport and outdoor activities. But the spirit of emulation, itself an inheritance of the tradition of the Jesuit college, dies hard and has wide ramifications. It has undoubtedly nurtured intellectual brilliance, but it may also partially explain the typically French disdain of authority. The private individual feels himself in no way inferior to the public official and this manifests itself in a certain unyieldingness in social behaviour. A case in point is the quarrel between confessionalism and secularism, which has been exacerbated because of this incapacity for intellectual compromise. Logically, each side feels its position unassailable. Competitiveness is joined to intellectual obstinacy. There is difficulty at arriving at a consensus, which may account for the

[10] D. Thomson, *Democracy in France since 1870,* 4th ed., London, 1964, p. 122.

fact that political passions in France, once aroused, have often been more singularly embittered than elsewhere. The "modal personality" of the French intellectual is that of the "lone wolf" rather than that of the urbane personality willing to compromise with those equally cultured. If national traits can be said to endure, at least for generations, then André Siegfried[11] has seen the cult of the individual as one abiding characteristic of Frenchmen.

The belief in the powers of the intellect has also not infrequently stifled the efforts of French educationists to add an aesthetic dimension to the education of gifted pupils. Not until the mid-1960s was an "artistic" option added to the baccalaureate examination.

This intellectualist view of the nature of education has expressed itself in the peculiarly French concept of "culture générale" which has held sway since the Renaissance. This concept is now at last undergoing a change of focus and enlargement. Nevertheless, because of its continuing influence upon formal education the traditional view of what has been considered cultural — formative of the mind — must be mentioned. The classics, their languages, literature and philosophy, constituted the nub of what should be taught. In the seventeenth century, at the instigation of Fermat, Pascal and Descartes, mathematics were added. These have formed the core of knowledge through which "culture générale" has been inculcated, although other disciplines such as history have also played their part. The stress is always upon the links between the various aspects of knowledge. Indeed the Cartesian method, with which French culture is indissolubly associated, holds that, because of their interrelationship, all sciences must be studied together. The ability to know must be cultivated not in order to accumulate knowledge but in order to acquire understanding. Paul Valéry affirms that what must be developed is "the ability to situate oneself" in relation to a whole all parts of which one cannot possibly master. The mind must therefore be *trained* to exhibit qualities of critical thinking, analysis, logic, abstraction, generalization and effective judgement, whilst at the same time preserving an openness to new ideas. The body of knowledge the mind has to assimilate must be essentially non-vocational and non-utilitarian in any immediate sense. In any case, process is more important than content: the trained mind, it is argued, can

[11] A. Siegfried, *Tableau des partis politiques en France*, Chap. 1: "Le caractère français", Paris, 1930.

turn itself to anything. Reasoning and reason are sovereign.

Now, however, the concept of "culture générale" is undergoing a transformation. The ambition had formerly been to give the student a mastery over his total environment. Now there is a more restricted aim which chimes better with the more specialized nature of modern society:

> ... the older high bourgeois culture, which assumed that an autonomous intelligence could apprehend and act upon the world as a totality, has disappeared. ... The new conception of higher culture is in practice a specialized one that reflects, consolidates and legitimates the intellectual division of labour.[12]

The "new men" in France rule as technocrats or bureaucrats and are best characterized as cultural relativists. That "unity of school and life" which Langevin postulated is now seen as a link between education and *contemporary* culture rather than with the eternal values that the classics allegedly epitomized. "Real life culture" is now to be preferred to "la culture universitaire", that devotion to the ideal, to the world of abstraction, the withdrawal from "the harsh imperatives of life as it is", which Vincent has claimed to be the life style of the traditionalist lycée teacher.[13] Administrators, technologists and the owners of the means of production now rate as paramount educational objectives those relating to material prosperity rather than those concerning the disinterested pursuit of knowledge or the fostering of metaphysical values.

These changes have been documented by a French sociologist, Mme Viviane Isambert-Jamati, in a longitudinal study of the lycée from 1860 to 1965.[14] Taking the speeches made at school prizegivings (which were very often written by teachers within the school) as well as educational literature, she has attempted to discern what were the objectives of the lycée during this period. Five aims are distinguished:

(a)   To allow the pupil "to participate in the supreme values" – presumably the true, the good, the beautiful. Whether these values postulate a supreme being is irrelevant in this context.

(b)   To allow the pupil to accede to "a socially superior class of people", which may be interpreted as an élite based either on wealth or intellect and to which the happy few may accede by virtue of their noble birth.

[12] N. Birnbaum, quoted in Talbott, *op. cit.*, p. 259.
[13] G. Vincent, *Les Professeurs du second degré*, Paris, 1967.
[14] Viviane Isambert-Jamati, *Crise de la société, crise de l'enseignement*, Paris, 1970.

(c) To allow him to acquire an individual refinement sought for its own sake. This aim is clearly linked to the gratuitousness of culture.

(d) To enable him to carry out a certain number of intellectual operations. This would seem to be a form of mental gymnastics the purpose of which is not entirely clear.

(e) To enable him to acquire the means of transforming the world outside the school. Such a goal can only be strongly associated with an instrumentalist, almost utilitarian view of society.

Mme Isambert-Jamati traces the different emphases given to these aims throughout the hundred years with which she deals (she omits the Vichy interlude) and arrives at some interesting conclusions. Whereas the first aim, participation in the supreme values, is placed at the top of the hierarchy in 1860, by 1932 it had sunk to bottom place and has remained there. In contrast, the aim of enabling the pupil to acquire the means of transforming the world outside the school, which may be classed as instrumentalist or even utilitarian and which started at the bottom of the ladder in 1860, fluctuated violently throughout the period but ended up in 1964 as the foremost aim of secondary education. It may be inferred that the view of education as individual and collective investment for the production of wealth and as an agent for the reshaping of society is the predominant ethic in modern French society.

According to the study, there has been a "loss of the eternal". The subject-matter of education has assumed greater importance; the so-called "eternal values", the "symbolic aspects of culture" which still predominated at the end of the nineteenth century, have considerably diminished in importance. From 1918 to the Second World War the atmosphere in the lycée was one of intellectual discipleship between teacher and pupils. Intellectual flexibility was highly esteemed and thus the study of languages and mathematics as "intellectual gymnastics" was of greater importance than the content of the actual curriculum. Since 1944 it would seem that the moral themes of obedience and discipline, the development of intellectual initiative, even the inculcation of democratic ideals, have all receded into the background. Mme Isambert-Jamati concludes that whereas previously classical humanism, which had been the dominant feature of French secondary education, had signified the quest for *eternal* man, the assimilation of modern values had led merely to the discovery of *permanent* man — the one an ideal type, the other merely an historical one.

One of the consequences of this modification of culture is the revulsion of the academic teachers from the concept of education as "investment", as having economic profitability. They have tended to insist, as will be seen, upon the gratuitousness of culture and have concentrated upon subject-matter for its own sake rather than its utility. Finding themselves, as they believe, in a society which has disinherited them and robbed them of status, they have sought revenge by emphasizing the disinterested pursuit of knowledge. They have been reinforced in their beliefs by the cavalier fashion in which politicians have plunged into educational reform without consulting them. To a certain extent their attitude is one that students share. In 1968 even non-political students — of which there were and are many — felt that their own individual development counted little; society's leaders were training them to serve as "production fodder", to become businessmen, industrialists or bureaucrats to satisfy the needs of the consumer society. (The students' attitude was, of course, ambivalent: at the same time they were complaining that at the end of their studies there were no jobs for them to go to.) More particularly, young people in France have shunned scientific and technological courses and have studied the humanities and the social sciences, whereas exactly the opposite tendency was desired by the Government. But this is not a phenomenon confined to France.

To this extent, therefore, it may be argued that academic secondary education in France is floundering, since neither pupils nor teachers accept the profit motive as the basis for culture. The bourgeoisie, whose offspring still comprise a disproportionate number of those who find themselves in an élitist form of schooling, have shown themselves to be more willing to come to terms with the politicians and technocrats, for whom a prime educational criterion has been economic "rentabilité". Remembering their own more disinterested schooling, these parents do have occasional misgivings, but they are nevertheless genuinely surprised at the rejection of contemporary material values by their children and the teachers. French education, however, does not face a unique dilemma. The attitude of pupils is as ambiguous as that of the students. On the one hand they reproach the old dispensation with lacking contact with the real world; in 1968 the high walls surrounding the barrack-like lycée buildings were the symbol, as they expressed it, of a "cultural ghetto". On the other hand, they rejected the world outside.

There can be little doubt that a shift is taking place in the French idea of culture. It represents an attempt to reconcile the reality of modern industrial civilization with European intellectual and cultural traditions of a bygone age. France, it is alleged, is now governed by a technocracy, despite the fact that its leading political figures have been trained in the humanities rather than the sciences. Conscious of the country's industrial potential, they have accepted a machine-dominated civilization. The grand updating of the French economy, a scientific modernization that seems almost unbelievable to those who knew the country before 1939, has added a technological dimension to culture and education. Jean Capelle,[15] one of the few scientists who for a while achieved eminence in the educational administration of the Fifth Republic, has condemned those French intellectuals who cling desperately to an exclusively humanist view of culture and derided the "Mediterranean mentality" that tends to despise technology. He argues cogently that technology must be part of a *liberal* education if the adjective implies, as it should, the freeing of the human mind. Gadgets, machines and technical know-how not only free men from ignorance of how the world of today functions, but also from the drudgery of routine tasks. The intelligent organization of work, which seeks to replace the carrying out of heavy manual tasks by the use of push-button technology, will indeed allow men to concentrate on more essential intellectual problems. But Man has first to learn how to live with the machines that his genius has invented. Thus culture, and hence education, must embrace technology, because Man has to learn how to control his own inventions, to become their master and not their slave. Therefore ingrained attitudes must be eradicated: those of the bourgeoisie who regard technical education still as manual and therefore degrading; those of their student offspring who view industrial technology as the symbol of their future enslavement to work. Hence compulsory technical education in the lower secondary school, the institution of technical lycées and colleges, the creation of university institutes of technology, to mention only three expedients of the Gaullist régime in its attempt to integrate technology into a new concept of "culture générale". The idea

---

[15] J. Capelle, *Tomorrow's Education: the French Experience* (tr. W. D. Halls), London, 1967.

meets with resistance, but is perfectly consistent with the view that a liberal education is a transitional process from knowing to being able, from the rational to the operational.

Other straws in the wind indicate a revision of the traditional view of "culture générale". "Nihil doceatur nisi ad usum praesentem", wrote Comenius. This is a pedagogical precept held in honour not only in socialist countries; in France also culture has become more utilitarian. Even that most sacrosanct subject of the curriculum, French, is no longer exempt. The language must be taught, it is argued, more than the literature, because of its basic communication value. There was indeed something grotesque in the study of medieval French texts by the 14-year-old. Now the teaching of the mother tongue implies more the mastery of language than the learning of literary history, or the study of literature.

PART II

ADMINISTRATION, FINANCE AND PLANNING

CHAPTER 3

The Government and Administration of Education

Promulgated on October 4, 1958, the Constitution of the Fifth Republic declared that France is an indivisible, secular, democratic and social republic (Art.2).[1] For education the secular nature of the State is important. It means that whilst a private system of education, which may be run by religious institutions, is permitted, State schools must be neutral, neither teaching any religious doctrine nor (with certain exceptions) permitting religious teaching in their buildings. From the administrative viewpoint France is divided up into a number of areas known as "academies", each headed by a Rector. So highly is this office esteemed that the Constitution stipulates that Rectors are appointed directly by the President (Art.13). During the life of the Fifth Republic, because of the efforts to decentralize educational administration, the Rector has acquired greater power than before, so much so that, contrary to previous practice, whereby he was appointed until retirement at the age of 70, the President retains the right to dismiss a Rector at any time.

The Constitution distinguishes between two types of laws: those which determine "fundamental principles" and those which lay down "rules" (Art.34). The laws of the Fifth Republic that relate to education have fallen into the first category, laying down a "framework" or deciding generally upon the "orientation" of education, specifying objectives which may be general, such as equality of opportunity, or detailed, such as the raising of the leaving age. The actual process by which such laws may be applied has been left in the hands of the Minister. This he does by means of decrees. In general decrees are used for promulgating regulations of a broad kind or for announcing high-ranking appointments. They are signed by the President, counter-signed by the Prime Minister and also signed by

[1] For the text of the Constitution cf. Dorothy Pickles, *The Government and Politics of France,* Vol. I, London, 1972, Appendix II, pp. 300 et seq.

the Minister of Education.[2] In addition to the use of "décrets" certain dispositions relating to education have been made by ordinance, a process peculiar to the Fifth Republic. Further and more detailed regulations are made by means of "arrêtés", circulars, instructions and "notes de service" published in the *Bulletin Officiel de l'Education Nationale,* all of which are implemented by an hierarchical system of administration. The fact that the sole duty of Parliament as stipulated in the Constitution is to determine "the basic principles of education" has had the effect of reinforcing the bureaucracy. Indeed the very complexity of education would preclude elected representatives from scrutinizing minutely the stream of regulations that are published.

In certain respects the powers of the Ministry of Education have nevertheless diminished under the Fifth Republic. Interests such as architecture and the national archives have reverted to other ministries. Educational planning is partly carried out on an inter-ministerial basis, particularly in so far as it concerns the supply of trained manpower. The new laws on technical education passed in 1971 were implemented by a special secretariat reporting directly to the Prime Minister. The recent appointments of secretaries of State for nursery and higher education respectively — the latter being completely autonomous — may be viewed also as a diminution of the powers of the Ministry of Education.

The centralized character of French administration predates the Revolution and was apparent even in the absolute monarchy of Louis XIV. The modern argument for its retention is based on the principle that in a democracy the locus of power must be the central government, because this alone is the true expression of the will of the electorate. The Minister of Education is ultimately accountable to the National Assembly. In England the local education authority (as indeed the school board in the U.S.A.) comprises in the main locally elected councillors, whose mandate to control education may be based on as little as the 30 — 40 per cent who turn out to vote at local elections. Anglo-Saxons may argue that the concentration of power centrally can lead to arbitrary decisions. It might be argued that the concept of a "partnership" between the central and local authorities is a check on arbitrariness in England, but there is also a lack of sharp definition in distinguishing between the powers and

---

[2] F. Ridley and J. Blondel, *Public Administration in France,* 2nd ed., London, 1969, pp. 22–24.

responsibilities of each partner. This does not exist in France. By law the Minister cannot delegate many of his powers — a legacy of the Napoleonic tradition which makes, incidentally, the application of modern management techniques more difficult. Where the Minister does delegate, subordinates act in his name; only chosen assistants have the "powers of signature" and they may act only in accordance with the degree of responsibility that he has allotted them. The Minister himself is subject to a code of administrative law and may be called upon to justify the legality of his acts before the Conseil d'Etat. However, the Fifth Republic has recognized the cumbersome, unwieldy nature of the system of centralized power. When Guichard was Minister decentralization was tried out by creating a number of "pilot rectorates" which had the responsibility for administering directly all levels of education within their academies without reference back to Paris, although, of course, the ultimate control, that of the purse, remained firmly in the hands of the central government.

Nevertheless, French educational administration remains bureaucratic. Max Weber, for whom a bureaucracy represented an ideal form of organization, listed its attributes succinctly in terms that could well apply in this case also: a well-defined hierarchy of authority; division of labour based on functional specialism; a system of rules covering the rights and duties of those holding offices; a system of procedures for dealing with work situations; impersonality in interpersonal relationships; selection for employment and promotion based on professional competence. To a varying degree, these characteristics of bureaucracy can well be applied to French educational administration.

Thus, with the focus of activity in Paris, the Ministry of Education runs directly 800,000 teachers and ancillary staff. Decisions taken centrally affect them all. The *Bulletin Officiel de l'Education Nationale,* which appears regularly and emits a constant flow of instructions, is compulsory reading for all teachers and impinges directly upon their professional life. Yet this constraint upon professional activity may well be more apparent than real: a recent development has been the adoption by teachers of the maxim that "what is not expressly forbidden is allowed". Moreover, there are patently great difficulties in enforcing some of the numerous rules. The primary teacher running a school of some twenty pupils, living in a remote village of the Massif Central, is hardly likely to worry overmuch that an official will suddenly descend upon him to check that he is conforming to requirements (unlike the situation in England, where local advisors and inspectors are well within hailing distance all the time). The larger an organization the greater the possibilities of evasion. Moreover, reasonable conformity with the rules is all that is usually required.

The reverse of the medal may, of course, also apply: the source of power may be felt to be too distant, so that feelings of alienation may arise. Curricula, methods, textbooks: everything is prescribed. Teachers lack the authority to experiment: all research into teaching must be officially sanctioned. In England, on the contrary, it has been said that no innovations which spring from abroad will be really new: one can always find some teacher somewhere who is already carrying out innovations on the same lines.

If physical distance has its good and bad points, the "distance" of power may at times be salutary. The French have a great desire for personal independence. Yet this desire is ambivalent, because at the same time they reason that there is a need for authority and order. Thus they "resolve their dilemma by shunting off most of the problems of human relations off on to an impersonalized and centralized bureaucracy".[3] Indeed, bureaucracy, government by officials, is often in the French context government by official regulations. This is not a distinction without a difference. Issues can in this way readily become depersonalized. The superior who rebukes the subordinate may point to the regulation that enjoins him to do so, and remark that they are both the prisoner of the regulations. Such as approach to administration rules out flexibility but has the advantage that if one goes "by the book" personal acrimony may be obviated. Indeed the hankering for bureaucracy represents a desire for maximum protection: the rule of the game is "impersonal, immoveable".[4]

Such impersonality may even spill over into a bureaucracy of the classroom. It is reflected in the gulf between teacher and taught, according to Crozier, in the over-abstract content of learning, in the lack of a meeting-point between education and the practicalities of life or the personal preoccupations of the pupil. In general, he says: "Authority is converted . . . into impersonal rules. The whole structure is so devised that

[3] J. Ambler, *The Government and Politics of France,* Boston, 1971, p. 58.
[4] M. Crozier, *The Bureaucratic Phenomenon,* Chicago, 1963, p. 249.

whatever authority cannot be eliminated is allocated, so that it is at a safe distance from those affected.[5]

One important aspect of bureaucracy is its potentiality for being more equitable. Government from the centre may achieve a fairer distribution of educational opportunities. In the Ministry is maintained a "school map" on which is plotted every educational institution. When deficiencies arise in schooling because of population mobility, when the rural/urban pattern changes, or regional tendencies become apparent, it is possible to adjust educational provision more easily than when replanning is left to local initiative. Within the educational academy are a number of educational "districts", each comprising a number of "sectors" of some 10,000 inhabitants. As compared with the difficulties created by the disparate size of local educational authorities in England, the divisions of the "school map" make redistribution of facilities easier.

Although the French teacher, on the whole, views bureaucracy with a jaundiced eye, there are some advantages for him. Appointments are made centrally and changes of appointment are effected by means of "commissions paritaires", committees on which teachers' unions and the authorities are equally represented and which consider applications for transfer from one area to another. The local system of appointment, as practised in Britain and the United States, is considered by the French to lend itself to corrupt practices — which indeed it occasionally has done. Furthermore, bureaucracy at least gives the teacher a well-defined career structure, although it is one based upon intellectual capacity rather than sheer teaching ability. Yet the teacher sees his administrative superiors earning a higher salary for doing what he considers to be the less important job. He resents his own lack of autonomous powers of decision, which are the prerogative enjoyed by professionals in other occupations such as medicine and law. He feels that bureaucracy almost by definition is excessive, and too much bureaucracy is intolerable. Hence there is often a tendency on his part to strike over comparatively minor matters.

Critics of the central administration, particularly teachers, have claimed that the restructuration on a "vertical" basis (see below) of the Ministry, which was carried out in the early 1960s, was a deliberate move to weaken opposition. Whereas the old organization, it is alleged, was functional and articulated according to the nature of the tasks that had to be performed,

[5] *Ibid.*, p. 222.

the new one was an attempt to raise up a monolithic structure capable of withstanding an educational body opposed to it and corporately well organized. It must, however, be said that the new organization of the Ministry, which is now expressed in terms of "objectives" and "ways and means", has also been seen by others as merely an attempt to introduce modern management techniques as found in industry and commerce. However, critics argue that not only has the Ministry been structured "against" them, but so have other bodies, such as the Higher Council for National Education ("Conseil Supérieur de l'Education Nationale") which has an important consultative role to play and on which teacher participation has been considerably reduced.

Within the Ministry itself, during the Gaullist period, the various cadres have been "deprofessionalized", in the sense that those without practical experience of education but are purely professional administrators have been brought in increasing numbers. In 1963 it was urged that what the Ministry needed was not only *new* blood, but different blood. After the dismissal of M. Capelle, one of the key administrators, who had been both a university professor and a Rector of an academy, a new post, that of secretary-general, was created and this and other key positions were filled by what have been termed "technocrats". However, in comparison with other Ministries, very few graduates of that breeding ground of the technocracy, the Ecole Nationale d'Administration, have as yet penetrated into the fastnesses of the Rue de Grenelle or the brand new buildings in which the Ministry is now housed at La Défense. Although it employs one-half of *all* French civil servants, the Ministry of Education employs only 57 graduates of ENA, as compared with 393 in the Ministry of Finance and 181 in the Ministry of the Interior, two smaller ministries.[6] Indeed, there may well be a swing in the opposite direction. The Institut National d'Administration Scolaire et Universitaire is busy training up recruits for administration drawn from the ranks of teachers and inspectors. Already in 1968 Edgar Faure had abolished the post of secretary general within the Ministry, using the apt but probably apocryphal phrase, "M. le Secrétaire Général, vous êtes irremplaçable – et on ne vous remplacera pas" ("Secretary General, you are irreplaceable – and you will *not* be replaced"). One suspects that it was the distaste that de Gaulle felt for the resistance to his régime on the part of the teachers

[6] P. Avril, *Politics in France*, Harmondsworth, Middlesex, 1969, p. 206.

that prompted him to introduce a new kind of civil servant into the Ministry.

In any case, it was from 1968 onwards that American-style management techniques firmly took hold. It was conceived that three director delegates would look after the objectives of educational policy, acting as a kind of "think-tank" and giving general guidelines for action to seven directors whose tasks were linked to more immediate concerns and to finding the ways and means of implementing policy. According to one authority,[7] Guichard, when Minister, had wished the directorates relating to objectives to be held by politicians, but had been overruled in this by his colleagues. Such an expedient might well have pleased the teachers more — or displeased them less — than the appointment of "non-professionals". At a lower level, up to yet the appointment of administrators as headmasters of schools has been successfully resisted.

One weakness of the bureaucratic approach is that every facet of education is "officialized". Meetings of school administrative bodies, of teachers and parents, must be held at stipulated times. Duties are minutely prescribed. Even the scale of sanctions that may be taken against teachers and of punishments to be meted out to pupils must be closely followed. Such a system may be traced back to the Napoleonic codifications and even to Roman law. The watchword is order.

To do it justice, the central government is sensitive to the charges levelled against bureaucracy and have tried to leaven authority by introducing a process of "participation". "Participatory administration", which is perhaps seen at its best in Swedish education, implies essentially consensus-formation. It entails well-defined groups of interest groups who must be free to speak their minds freely, uninhibited by any hierarchy; more "face-to-face" contact; and better procedural arrangements. It was not until after the events of May 1968 that "participation", which will be discussed more fully later, became firmly established. Nevertheless, there are voices raised to uphold that the principle is of limited application in education. Mme Fortunel, an inspector-general, is firm on this point:

> There are decisions which are the preserve of the teacher, others of the school principal, others reserved to the Rector, others to the Minister. This must be clear in everyone's mind — and far from being in conflict with participation, this clear distinction is one of the conditions of participation. It is a principle of realism.[8]

[7] J. Hayward, *The One and Indivisible French Republic*, London, 1973, p. 203.
[8] Statement reported in: *Education et Gestion*, Paris, numéro spécial, 1972, p. 44.

Bureaucratic, technocratic and participatory: at present all three elements are represented in the administration of French education. From them may well arise a new synthesis which may well supplant the old "absolutism" of former days.

THE CENTRAL ADMINISTRATION

At the time of writing the structure of the Ministry of Education is undergoing some modifications. As at June 1974, however, it would appear to be organized as in Fig. 2.[9]

The Minister stands at the centre of an organization which, apart from special services, revolves substantially round the two concepts of the determination of objectives and the determination of ways and means to realize these goals.

If the National Assembly votes the "framework laws" ("lois-cadres") for education, it is the Minister who has vast powers in prescribing how these should be implemented in detail. All the powers that in England the Secretary of State for Education does *not* exercise may be exercised by his French counterpart, even down to the prescribing of syllabuses and curricula. (In practice, however, such minutiae of education are usually elaborated by inspectors and teachers working in ministerial committees.) The Minister has also wide financial powers: he can expend the credits voted him in the National Assembly. But he is controlled in this function by a high official of the Ministry of Finance, and actual payments are made by that body. This dual financial system is typical of all French public law, and is a model which is followed in secondary schools and institutions of higher education.

---

[9] A reorganization of the Ministry just announced (July 1975) in outline seems to imply a drastic reorganization of the central body, as regards the directorates. In future there will be one Directorate General for Programming and Coordination, assisted by separate directorates for general education, for technical education, and for administration. The Directorate General will control seven separate directorates for the following: elementary schools; colleges; lycées; lycée teaching personnel; general administration; administrative teaching personnel; equipment and building; and financial affairs. It would appear that the Directorate General now embodies both "objectives" and "ways and means". For "objectives" he is assisted by the three separate directorates; for "ways and means" he has at his disposal the seven directorates mentioned above. But the position has not yet been clarified.

The Ministry of Education*

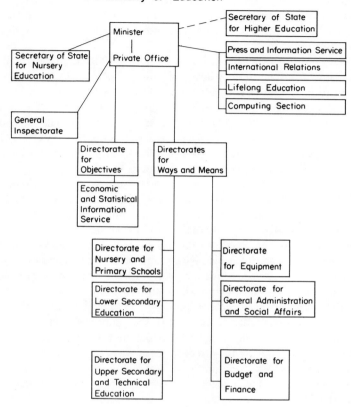

Fig. 2

The present Minister has preferred to call himself Minister of Education rather than Minister of *National* Education. The exact significance, if any, to be attached to this change of nomenclature is discussed elsewhere. Furthermore, at present a Secretary of State for Higher Education, completely independent of the Minister, has been appointed. Another Secretary of State for Nursery Education and Social Action, but responsible to the Minister, has also been appointed.

The Minister appoints his own Private Office ("cabinet"). This often includes politicians. The Private Office is automatically dismissed when a new minister is appointed. The fact that the Fifth Republic has had no less than eleven Ministers of Education already renders very important the position of the top civil servants, who consequently wield much power and assure continuity.

Certain positions are attached directly to the Minister, among them that of the general inspectorate whose role will be dealt with later. Another such position is that of the adviser for lifelong education, a post which emphasizes the importance that the French attach to "L'éducation permanente". The adviser's role is to ensure that "initial" education, whether at school or post-secondary level, is envisaged always in terms of life-long education. The possibilities here are clearly immense: if the adult will return to education in later life it should theoretically be possible to lighten the burden of initial schooling so that not so much learning needs to ·be crammed into the ages of 6 and 21. Services also attached to the Minister directly relate to the press and information, international relations and one that provides computer information.

The directorate for objectives comprises three departments: for higher education and research; for elementary and secondary education; and for guidance and continued education. The task of the directorate is "to conceive operations and commission studies from the directorates of planning and ways and means; to proceed to the evaluation of the means necessary to carry out the operations; to seek approval for their inclusion in the programme . . . and to publish the general instructions necessary for them to be carried out by the directorates of ways and means".

There are now six directorates of ways and means: for nursery and primary schools; for lower secondary education; for upper secondary and technical education; for equipment; for general administration and social affairs; and for the budget and general finance. The directorates are responsible for the deployment of resources in order to attain the goals that have been prescribed. Those responsible meet regularly with the director of the departments relating to objectives.

The outside observer cannot but be impressed by the Cartesian logic of this hierarchical system, which seems to place much responsibility on the directorate concerned with objectives, which must nevertheless engage in a continuing dialogue with the directorates for ways and means to ensure the feasibility of any proposals that emerge. The danger is that such a concentration of power might favour change for its own sake and that the lesser directorates of ways and means might be reduced to mere executants rather than innovatory forces in their own right. Such a sharp division between the "thinkers" and the "doers" is certainly one that does not commend itself to ministries of education elsewhere.

The service providing computerized information reporting directly to the Minister may well be a key one in achieving decentralization. It is intended to facilitate "automatized management procedures" connected with the "school map", the provision of the requisite number of school places at the beginning of each academic year, guidance, medical examinations, the control and upkeep of buildings, the award of scholarships, fees, and matters connected with staffing. These facilities will enable many matters to be settled at academy level, without reference to Paris. Similarly, by delegation of the ministerial "signature" it is hoped to allow subordinate officials, right down to school principals, to assume greater responsibility. As Guichard put it when he was Minister, "A hyper-centralized system which has weakened initiative and discouraged the taking of responsibility cannot be decentralized without some upsets".[10]

The French concept of the central administration, if decentralization is effective, will no longer apply with such force. However, ultimately each echelon will continue to control, when necessary, all subordinate echelons and Minot's judgement may well continue to hold: "Thus all is decided from Paris, for all people, for everything, by virtue of the conception that lays down that unity in administration throughout the national territory guarantees the equality of all in the face of the system."[11] Indeed, the modern and democratic version of absolutism in government may well be that all power proceeds from the centre, from the elected to the electors — although cynics have observed that the presidential regime of the Fifth Republic is in danger of becoming the July Monarchy.

Nevertheless, in the more limited field of educational administration there is no doubt that the great achievement of the last decade has been the partial success of a reform based on a double distinction, that between conception and management ("objectives" and "ways and means") and that between modernization and deconcentration.

Although the Minister alone has powers of decision, there are various consultative bodies to which matters may, and in certain cases must, be

[10] Reported in: *Le Monde,* March 13, 1970.
[11] Minot, *op. cit.,* p. 24.

referred. The most important of these is the Conseil Supérieur de l'Education Nationale (Higher Council for National Education). The origins of the Council can be traced back to the legal privileges enjoyed by the medieval university,[12] although it was created by Napoleon as a tribunal to deal with disciplinary matters relating to teachers in the Imperial University and to advise generally. These juridical and consultative functions are retained today.

The composition of the Council has varied considerably throughout its history. Under the Third Republic its membership was limited solely to educational interests. This continued until 1964, when de Gaulle decided that it should be enlarged to include other interested bodies, although it is alleged also that he found the teachers who constituted the majority of its members too difficult to handle. Today the Council comprises seventy-five members. Twenty-five of these come from the central administration of the Ministry, and ten of these must have been teachers at some stage of their career. The same number form a second group, composed of representatives of other ministries and of other organizations with an economic or social interest in education; thirteen of their number at least must represent parents' associations, student bodies and associations of employers and trade unions. The remaining third of the members comprise teaching members elected by other subordinate advisory Councils. Some teachers want a return to the former régime, where teachers had a majority, or even to a Council with a purely "educational" membership.

The Minister has used the Council less frequently than in the past as a consultative body. Certain matters, however, must be referred to it, although the Minister is still free to accept or reject the advice that is proffered. In its juridical capacity — a survival of those rights of extra-territorial jurisdiction once enjoyed by the Sorbonne — the Council acts as a court of appeal from subordinate Councils, which also possess disciplinary powers over teaching staff.

These other Councils have competence within a particular field: in higher education and research, in school education, and in matters relating to youth and sport.

One last important element in the central administration remains to be mentioned: the general inspectorate. General inspectors are of two categories: those concerned with the inspection of the financial and

---

[12] *Ibid.*, p. 75 et seq.

economic aspects of all the services controlled by the central Ministry, and those concerned directly with the schools, particularly secondary schools. The first category, the "administrative" inspector, has no counterpart in England. The second category corresponds approximately to that of Her Majesty's Inspectorate, inasmuch as the inspectors act as the "eyes and ears" of the Minister as to what goes on in the schools – although it must be said that they do not enjoy quite the same freedom of action as their English counterparts. On the other hand, they number only about 160 in all, and are therefore far more of an élitist body. Just as on this side of the Channel, their role has changed considerably over the years. As one of their number remarked, "For too long has the inspection been conceived of as a terrorist raid."[13] Today they must act as advisers not only to the Minister, but also to the teachers they inspect; they must be the stimulators and transmitters of new ideas. However, in France they have still a strict obligation to evaluate teachers in their particular subject discipline. Upon the "mark" that the inspector has by law to award depend the possibilities of promotion of the teacher. He may well arrive unexpectedly in the classroom and find the luckless teacher unprepared. At the end of the day he will retire to the headmaster's study and receive (one by one), in what is familiarly known as the "confessional", the teachers he has inspected. To ensure that he is not for ever saddled with the same group of schools (nor they with him!) he is usually assigned to inspect a different academy every three years. Today he is often assisted in his task by regional pedagogical inspectors ("inspecteurs pédagogiques régionaux").

If bureaucracy and "participation" characterize the central administration, at least in higher education a third principle, that of autonomy, has also been introduced. The working out of this principle will be discussed later.

---

[13] Wadier, *La Réforme de l'enseignement n'aura pas lieu,* Paris, 1970, p. 101.

CHAPTER 4

Local Administration, Schools and School Administration

The Napoleonic division of France into educational areas known as "academies" still survives, and today there are twenty-five of these. Each one covers several of the political administrative units known as "départements". Each academy is headed by a Rector, who is the representative of the central Ministry in Paris. The Rector is not responsible to the various "préfets" who are the political representatives of the départements in his academy. His main task is to act as the channel through which all instructions from the central government must pass and to see that they are implemented. He is Chancellor of the local universities, although he no longer intervenes actively in university affairs and has only a "delaying power" of decision in regard to them. He has the oversight of all primary and secondary schools in his area, is responsible for allocating staff to them and generally controls all personnel. When scholarship awards are proposed by the authorities of the département he must approve them. He supervises all government-subsidized private education. As the process of "deconcentration" or decentralization from Paris continues efforts are being made, at this intermediate level also, to introduce a system of management by objectives.

In each of the départements that comprise the academy is placed an "academy inspector" ("inspecteur d'académie") who is responsible to the Rector. Because the préfet of a département has certain responsibilities regarding education at this level, the academy inspector has to some extent to liaise with him. He has nevertheless wide powers in regard to primary education, in which he is aided by departmental inspectors. He has also the right of inspection of all secondary schools and is chairman of the "administrative council" (see Fig. 3) that exists in each of these schools. He has also certain responsibilities for inservice training for senior appointments in schools.

The National Administration

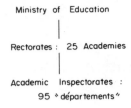

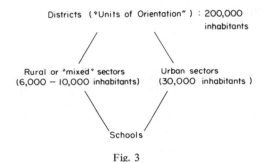

Fig. 3

Other specialized inspectors, such as those that assist the general inspectorate, the chief inspectors for technical education, for youth and sports and for vocational guidance within each academy report to the Rector. Moreover, a number of local advisory councils, parallel to those that exist at national level, function also within the academy.[1]

THE SCHOOLS

Since 1816 the basic unit for primary schooling has been the commune, which is the smallest French political administrative unit. Today there are some 38,000 such communes, which may range from mere hamlets to large towns. Each commune, no matter how small, has a mayor and a municipal council, who have an active part in running the primary schools. (The running costs of the schools form part of the commune's budget, and the mayor initiates all expenditure.) In 1972–1973 there were 51,937

[1] I am greatly indebted to the Institut National d'Administration Scolaire, Paris, for much of the information used in this chapter.

primary schools. The smallest communes have now been grouped together so that in theory no school containing less than five age groups exists: in the space of five years the number of schools has been reduced by 8000. This was a necessary step because 35,000 of the 38,000 communes had an average population of only 450 inhabitants.

This grouping of school facilities has been carried even farther in secondary education. Reference has already been made to the "school map" ("carte scolaire"). This is divided, at the lowest level, into "sectors", each containing one college of secondary education for 10,000 inhabitants. A number of sectors are grouped together in a "district", which contains one or more lycées and colleges of technical education, offering as many options as possible in upper secondary education. Today secondary schooling must be provided for almost four million pupils. These are housed, for lower secondary education, either in colleges of secondary education or in colleges of general education (which are rapidly being converted into colleges of secondary education); for upper secondary education, lycées and colleges of technical education are provided. The total number of secondary schools is 6510, distributed as shown in Table 1.

Table 1. 1972–1973

Lower secondary education	
Colleges of general education	1744
Colleges of secondary education	2426
Upper secondary education	
Colleges of technical education	1198
Lycées	1142
Total	6510

The colleges of secondary education, the lower secondary comprehensive schools, have almost trebled in number in the space of five years, and the colleges of general education, which are being phased out, have correspondingly been halved in number during that time. The number of upper secondary institutions of either type has remained almost the same. About 85 per cent of all colleges of secondary education contain between 300 and 1000 pupils, and the most usual size is between 500 and 600 pupils. Only 15 per cent of the colleges of technical education exceed 600 pupils. Since 1968 this deliberate effort to create smallish schools represents an attempt to promote greater contact between pupils and teachers. However, the lycées remain substantially larger, although three-quarters of them contain less than 1500 pupils and twenty-three of them contain over double that number.

SCHOOL ADMINISTRATION

To describe the functions of the administration in each of the various school types would be too onerous a task. Thus the organization of the lycée will be taken as perhaps the most important example.

The head of the school administration is the "proviseur". He is assisted in his task by a deputy, the "censeur", and an "intendant" (or bursar). These three meet in daily consultation. The proviseur is officially responsible for carrying out the instructions handed down by higher authority and the decisions arrived at by the school "administrative council" (see below). Like many headmasters elsewhere, he spends most of his time in his office and rarely penetrates into the classroom, even to see beginners teach. Since 1968 he no longer enjoys permanent tenure, and his status officially is that of a teacher charged with administrative functions. He has no say in the appointment of staff to the school. He usually sets aside religiously one hour a week to receive parents, but complains frequently that this opportunity is hardly used except at the beginning of the school year. Much of his administrative work has to be done before the beginning of the school year. Indeed, preparations for the "rentrée" of September are begun as early as the previous December, when he has to forecast the number of new pupils to be admitted, the number of teachers required and how they are to be allocated, as well as fill in numerous questionnaires. The norms for all such forecasts and for the allocation of staff are, of course, all laid down centrally, including the number of hours each teacher may be employed in teaching, the number of teaching hours per subject and per class. He is responsible also for all boarding arrangements.

(It is not generally known to what extent there has always been a boarding tradition in French state schools. During the nineteenth century, when there was only one lycée in each département, the sole possibility for many children living in rural areas was to become boarders. This tradition has continued. In 1971—1972 there were some three and a half million pupils in secondary schools of all kinds, of which some 10 per cent were full boarders. This, incidentally, represented a decrease of 5 per cent over the previous five years. Although there has been a decline in boarding in lower secondary education, in upper secondary education the proportion of boarders has remained unchanged: 25 per cent of pupils in the colleges of technical education and 20 per cent in lycées; in the special post-baccalaureate classes in the lycées, comprising pupils preparing for entrance to the grandes écoles, the proportion of boarders is as high as 26 per cent. As is to be expected, the industrial and urbanized areas, such as Lille, Lyon, Paris, Rouen and Strasbourg, have fewer boarders than do schools in the agricultural regions of Western and Central France.)

The sheer complexity of the matters with which the proviseur has to deal has made him more an administrator than a teacher. Today a special three-month training period for headmasters has been instituted and in some quarters there has been talk of replacing the proviseur by a trained manager, perhaps a graduate of the Ecole Nationale d'Administration, with no teaching experience whatsoever. This increasing responsibility has unfortunately been matched by a loss of power, particularly since the introduction of the principle of "participation" into the schools.

The "censeur" acts as the deputy of the headmaster in all matters except those concerning the school budget, where he has no legal power. He looks after all administrative details concerning the pupils; he is responsible for the detailed elaboration of the timetable; he oversees the day-to-day running of the school, including the provision of substitute teachers in case of illness, and discipline and the enforcement of school rules ("le régime intérieur"), and must check for damage the school premises and equipment. The librarian and the school resources officer ("le documentaliste") are also responsible to the "censeur".

The "intendant" (or school bursar) is responsible for the logistics of the school, seeing that money spent is within the budget, that teaching materials are available, that pupils and staff are fed and the buildings are maintained.

Assisting the "censeur" are a number of "education counsellors" ("conseillers d'éducation", formerly known as "surveillants"), headed by a principal "education counsellor" (the former "surveillant-général", familiarly known as the "Surgé"), who can only be compared to a senior NCO. These "counsellors" — one for every 100 pupils — are neither teachers nor administrators. Their job is to organize and supervise the pupils, to take registration, to ensure discipline in private study and in the "interclasse" – the intervals between lessons – by patrolling the corridors, and to stimulate extra-curricular activities of all kinds. This last role is a recent innovation, although increasingly younger teachers are also taking to organizing out-of-school activities.

In boarding schools students are employed as "maîtres d'internat" (in slang, "pions" – "pawns"). They do duty for 30 hours a week. In exchange for board, lodging and a modest salary they look after the general welfare and supervise the pupils, even taking a turn of night duty in the dormitories. (One account of these dormitories, by a former headmaster, speaks of long bare rooms, often housing fifty beds, with no bedside lamps, no individual washbasins and not even enough showers to allow pupils to shower more than once a week. At night the pupils and the "pion" on duty are locked in by the school night watchman, their only means of escape from the dormitory being by breaking a glass case in which is kept a key for use in an emergency!) On the whole the supervisory staff entertain a friendly relationship with their charges and they are probably less resented than the old-style English prefects. Indeed the same headmaster whose depressing account of boarding accommodation has just been quoted writes:

> Much is spoken about self-discipline. If this means, as certain people seem to believe, a similar system to that in English schools where certain pupils, like the "Kapos" in a concentration camp, are promoted to be school or class prefects and invested with power over their fellows (whether they are appointed by the school authorities or elected, whether their function is an institutionalized one or not, this comes to the same thing), the cure seems to be much worse than the evil.[2]

This is an interesting view of a survival of Victorian England in English schools, and one which is shared elsewhere on the Continent.

The fact that responsibility for discipline is partly taken out of the hands of the class teacher alleviates problems to some extent, although there is no doubt that problems of order in French schools are as acute as elsewhere. After 1968 one lycée teacher wrote bitterly:

> Let us say that on the whole the situation is as follows: the administration of the "lycée", no more than the teachers – this is a fact – can no longer impose anything on pupils. All the former disciplinary sanctions have been, by

[2] R. Brechon, *La Fin des lycées,* Paris, 1970, p. 121.

common agreement, abolished since the beginning of the last school year. So there are no longer any punishments or reprimands . . . no more suspensions or expulsions. The "lycée" belongs to the pupils.[3]

The Network of School Administration

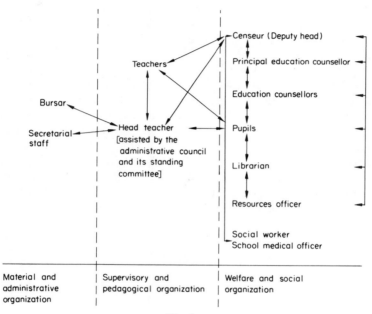

| Material and administrative organization | Supervisory and pedagogical organization | Welfare and social organization |

Fig. 4

Up to now, the description given of the administration of a French school has been one of a bureaucracy in miniature. As the synoptic Fig. 4 shows, however, there is provision for participation in the government of the school by others also. Indeed, "participation" has been the order of the day since 1968, and to a lesser extent, throughout the currency of the de Gaulle reforms. Thus every school must have an "administrative council" ("conseil d'administration"). In primary and nursery schools this must comprise representatives of the parents, the teachers and the local

[3] P. Buriez, "Je ne peux plus être professeur", *Le Nouvel Observateur,* Feb. 17, 1969.

council. The aim (as stated in a Circular of June 27, 1969) is to suggest improvements and to resolve the educational problems that arise from the reforms. In secondary schools administrative councils must also include pupils. The purpose behind pupil participation is stated as to give an opportunity to exercise responsibility and thus prepare for adult life. Indeed pupils may sit on all the councils and committees that must be set up in a secondary school — not only the administrative council, but also the class council, the standing committee and the disciplinary council, the respective functions of which are explained below. Pupils are elected by their fellows to all these bodies.

In secondary schools the administrative council must consist of 1/6 representatives of the school administration, 2/6 elected members of staff (of which at least 2/3 must be from the teaching staff), 2/6 representatives of parents and pupils, and 1/6 representatives of those interested locally in the activities of the school, such as the mayor. In technical institutions provision is made for representation of employers and trade unions. There may also be a number of coopted members. Thus in 1972 the administrative council of a large technical and commercial lycée in the Paris area comprised forty-seven members, made up as shown in Table 2.

Table 2.

Members as of right, including the "inspecteur d'académie" and "proviseur"	8
Teachers	7
Non-teaching staff	3
Parents	5
Pupils	5
Local representatives	4
Employers' representatives	3
Union representatives	1
Coopted	11

Meetings of the council must take place at least once a term. Its main tasks relate to the approval of the school rules, one of the most important of which is that religious or political propaganda within the school is strictly forbidden; the improvement of school facilities and the use of budgetary funds; the promotion of extra-curricular activities through the "foyer socio-éducatif"; and discussion of matters (not unknown in English schools) relating to the school canteen. All these topics seem comparatively innocuous, but appear to raise great controversy. A recent report, the Rapport Goguel, criticized the functioning of the administrative council because, it was alleged, it led too readily to personal and ideological confrontations, so much so that members outside the school ambit proper, in particular employers and trade unionists, tended to lose interest. It is clear that the main cause of friction arises from the presence of teachers on the one hand, and parents and pupils on the other. Moreover, parents are elected through national associations of parents, the main ones of which hold widely different political viewpoints. Thus politics is nevertheless brought into the school. Moreover, at present teachers feel inhibited at discussing before a group including parents and pupils the cases of other pupils who may be experiencing difficulties. Thus the administrative council, although more representative than the governing bodies of English secondary schools, seems more "politicized".

In practice the council appoints a standing committee ("commission permanente"), meeting once a month and on which both parents and pupils must be represented, to act in the day-to-day business of the school. The standing committee may also act as a "disciplinary council" ("conseil de discipline"), in which case its membership is enlarged to include, but only in a consultative capacity, the school social worker, the school guidance counsellor, two teachers who teach the class of the pupil who is accused of a serious offence, together with two pupil delegates from the same class.

Another important "participatory" institution within the school is the "class council" ("conseil de classe"). This consists of all the teachers teaching the pupils under discussion, led by the "principal teacher" ("professeur principal"), and since 1969 (Décret of September 16, 1969), at the discretion of the administrative council, representatives of parents and pupils. (This representation has been much contested: some teachers have refused to speak at meetings which parents and pupils are allowed to attend.) The role of the class council is defined as "examining the school situation of each pupil" and "all educational questions concerning the life of the school". The leadership of the "principal teacher" is vital in this task. His job is to coordinate the team of teachers who teach the class for which he is responsible, to note their comments on the pupils and to consult with the school psychologist and medical officer in difficult cases where pupils are not making progress. He calls meetings once a month —

teachers are paid overtime to attend them – and has the duty of improving the quality of teaching. (Teachers, being individualists, may, however, not pay much heed to his suggestions.) The post of "principal teacher" existed until recently only in the lower secondary school, but has now been created for certain classes in upper secondary education as well, although the role here is more one of "tutor" to pupils and as a mediator between them and adults.

The pupils themselves have their own representative body, the "council of responsibles" ("conseil des responsables"), composed of two elected delegates per class. Its function is to represent pupils' interests to teachers and administrators, either directly or through the other participatory bodies operating in the school.

The teachers likewise form "teaching councils" ("conseils d'enseignement"), each one of which comprises all the teachers teaching the same subject. These bodies aim to harmonize teaching methods and content and also decide how the grant allocation for teaching equipment should be spent.

The role of parents' associations is an important one. The associations are national and political. The two largest associations are fiercely competitive for membership.[4] The largest, the Fédération des Conseils de Parents d'Elèves des Ecoles publiques, usually known as the Fédération Cornec, after its president, was founded in 1946 by the primary teachers' union and the Ligue de l'Enseignement. Anti-clerical, sometimes Communist, it is the largest association, representing 1,196,690 families. In the 1972–1973 elections for administrative councils it gained 60.53 per cent of the three million votes cast. The main strength of this association lies in the lower secondary schools. The other main association, the Fédération des Parents d'Elèves (known until 1974 as the Association Armand, after its president, who has just retired, and now known as the Association Lagarde) was founded in 1926 and is strongest in the lycées. It is secularist, but not militantly so. It represents 650,000 families and in the most recent elections polled 27.14 per cent of the votes cast.[5] There are three other smaller parents' associations, more conservative in outlook, as well as parents' pressure groups such as Défense de la Jeunesse Scolaire.

[4] G. Tournis and R. Clarys, *Nouveau vade-mecum de la Direction de l'école*, 3rd edition, Paris, 1972, pp. 171–172.
[5] Figures taken from: *Le Monde*, July 21, 1973.

(This last organization is more militant: whilst the Sixth Plan was in preparation, for example, it complained bitterly that education, once assigned "the priority of priorities" had now been reduced to an infinitesimal role.) All these organizations conceive their task as to campaign for assistance for pupils — they are continually urging that free school transport and free school books should be provided — and also to act as a shield for the pupils against the authorities. Because they often represent highly articulate middle-class voters no government can afford to neglect their views. But, as in England, the mass of parents remain indifferent to attempts to organize them: in the elections of 1972—1973 for the administrative councils only 39 per cent of parents entitled to vote did so.

The development in the administration of French education is clear. From being purely bureaucratic — which to a large extent it remains — the administration has resisted the assaults of the new technocracy, but accepted a measure of participation and autonomy. What remains to be seen is whether the proliferation of bodies that are required to reconcile these frequently opposing principles can operate effectively. One can but agree with the judgement of Crémieux-Brilhac:

> The foreign observer is ... torn between lack of understanding and admiration: despair in the face of a cumbersome bureaucracy, in the face of dilly-dallying and ... an exemplary "administrative viscosity"; admiration at the feats of departments which, in spite of the shortcomings and the ball-and-chain which weigh them down, in the end accomplish so much.[6]

The Ministers come and go, but the administrators remain.

[6] Crémieux-Brilhac, *L'Education Nationale,* Paris, 1965, pp. 701—702.

CHAPTER 5

Planning and Budgeting

Since 1946 the French have accepted indicative planning of the economy as an integral part of the process of government. The decree setting up the Commissariat Général au Plan was signed by de Gaulle as the head of the first post-War provisional government. The First Plan, which ran from 1946 to 1953, took no account of education and was devoted to restoring the key sectors of the economy. The Second Plan (1954–1957) accorded only a limited attention to education, although a committee for the provision of education was set up within the network of planning bodies attached to the Commissariat Général. The committee dealt specifically with the building of schools and other educational institutions. During this period educational priority had to be given to the primary sector, because of the post-war boom in the birth rate, the effects of which were just beginning to concern education. The Third Plan (1958–1961) and the Fourth Plan (1962–1965) were concerned, as regards education, with secondary and higher education. The educational objectives of the Fifth Plan (1966–1970)[1] were defined as the maintenance of existing educational institutions at the existing level and at the same time to take measures to deal with the expected rates of increase in school attendance and to continue the reform of secondary structures, particularly at the lower secondary level, where colleges of secondary education were now beginning rapidly to supplant existing provision.

In elaborating the Sixth Plan (1971–1975), which has just closed, the Commissariat Général au Plan began by drawing up a number of options, which resulted in the detailed elaboration of a plan phased over the period. The Education Commission (which had now been established with wider terms of reference) was one of twenty-eight commissions collaborating in the drawing up of the plan. Its report dealt with the part that education

[1] For a brief account of how the Fifth Plan was prepared cf. P. H. Coombs and J. Hallak, *Managing Educational Costs*, London, 1972 pp. 16–20.

should play in the overall planning; working papers set out objectives and rough costings were made as to how these were to be realized. An innovation was the establishment and the listing of these objectives in an order of priority. The means of achieving these goals were looked at globally, expenditure was divided into capital equipment and current account estimates which went in some detail into the various pedagogical, administrative and legislative procedures that were involved.

The general objectives set out by the Education Commission were defined as the strengthening of the links between education and the economy and the reinforcing of general education. Quantitative and qualitative disparities of all kinds were to be eliminated. Priority was to be given to occupational and technological training. Better general education was to be achieved by the completion of the conversion of lower secondary schools to colleges of secondary education, improved methods of teacher training and a refurbishing and modernization of teaching methods, including the greater use of educational technology. An effort would be made to achieve greater equality of opportunity through the provision of better facilities for nursery education, an extension of adult education, the improvement of facilities for the handicapped and for social welfare.[2]

The Education Commission worked through three sub-commissions, dealing respectively with objectives, with means and with measures to synthesize proposals, Each sub-commission had a number of working groups attached to it. The Education Commission as a whole also worked in close cooperation with the Employment Commission for those matters which related to future training and employment requirements; with the Commission for Sports and Leisure; and with the Commission for Cultural Affairs. The final educational Plan is summed up in the overall Rapport for the Sixth Plan, which sets as the prime aims of its educational component the achievement of greater equality of opportunity and of better preparation for employment. At a time when recurrent education is a concept still viewed with much scepticism this side of the English Channel what the Rapport has to say about "éducation permanente" may be of some interest: "It is not possible to accept that the whole of knowledge can be transmitted irrevocably by the age of twenty and that the whole future of

[2] Cf. Le VIè Plan, *La Documentation Française illustrée,* No. spécial, pp. 269–270, Sept.–Oct. 1971.

a man can be determined by that age."[3] The figures in Table 3[4] show how the quantitative growth of the education system was envisaged between 1970 and 1975, by level of education.

Table 3. 1970–1975

	1970	1975
	(thousands)	
Special education	150	250
Pre-school	1890	2100
Primary	4125	4000
Lower secondary	2275	2600
"Short" upper secondary technical	491	650
"Long" upper secondary	660	750
Higher education	647	785
Total number of pupils and students	10,238,000	11,135,000

Whereas between 1966–1970 total numbers grew by 11.4 per cent, between 1971–1975 it was reckoned that the growth rate would slow to 6.9 per cent, although even so this represented an increase of 897,000. The deceleration in the rate of increase, it was reckoned, would afford an opportunity for an improvement in the quality of education, which had necessarily had to suffer in the 1960s when the emphasis had been on the astronomic growth in numbers.[5]

In monetary terms the accomplishment of these objectives would require an "envelope" for capital costs of 17 milliard francs (1970 francs), of which priority would be given to a sum of 4½ milliards for technical education, 300 million francs to "éducation permanente" and 450 million francs to agricultural education.[6] The total sum has been criticized as being too small, particularly if one of the twenty-five objectives of the overall Plan was to be achieved. This objective was stated as: "to double

[3] *Le VIè Plan de Développement économique et social, 1971–1975, Rapport Général: Les Objectifs généraux et les actions prioritaires du VIè Plan,* Imprimerie Officielle, Paris, n.d., p. 60. In the same report, cf. Chap. III, L'Emploi et la formation professionnelle; Chap. IV, L'Education, le développement culturel et scientifique; Annexe A4, La Formation professionnelle; Annexe Cl, L'Education.

[4] *Ibid.,* pp. 57–58.

[5] *Le Mouvement éducatif en France, 1971–1973,* INRDP, Paris, 1973 (Brochure No. 2032).

[6] *Op. cit.* in Note 3, pp. 57–58.

between 1970 and 1976 the extent of post-school education and to reach
the point where no child leaves the educational system without a sufficient
general education, combined with the rudiments of vocational training."[7]

The general principles behind French planning are apparent. The overall
purpose of the Plan is to establish an inventory of future public investment
within a given time span, detailing the works that have to be undertaken
and the property that has to be acquired or built. This inventory has to be
submitted by the Commissariat Général au Plan to the government and
accompanied by a reasoned exposition of the necessity for each type of
investment proposed. In educational planning the concentration is upon
medium-range investment needs. Unfortunately the "lead time" for the
production, through the education system, of trained manpower is perhaps
a dozen years. The output of the system is therefore less immediate than
in other fields. Forecasts are thus liable to greater fluctuation.

The Sixth Plan, as it related to education, dealt less with installations
and more with functions, as was denoted in the change of name of the
Commission, formerly merely a "commission of educational equipment",
to the Commission of Education. In formulating its final objectives the
Commission was subject more than most to a tight framework of
constraints — economic, demographic, social and legal, as well as political.
The facilities required are worked out in close co-operation with another
Commission, that of manpower.[8] Final costings are made after a study of
the administrative, technical and human resources involved. Even then,
since all planning is merely indicative and not mandatory, the government
can scale down the cost of the overall Plan. It is then the task of each
separate Commission to modify its projects accordingly, and this often
leads to the establishment of new priorities.

Despite the scepticism expressed regarding manpower planning, manpower forecasts still continue to be made in educational terms. The
inexactness of human resource predictions, now acknowledged by many
economists, has rather stultified the value of the elaborate procedures that
have been followed. The French were affected by the example of the
"dirigiste" economy forced upon them during the German Occupation and
also by the post-War ideas of Monnet, who may be said to be the father of
modern French planning. Thus they have attempted to correlate categories

---

[7] *Op. cit.* in Note 2, p. 8.
[8] J. Hayward, *op. cit.*, pp. 82–183.

of employment, years of education and formal qualifications ever since the Fourth Plan. Such omissions as the lack of selection for higher education and the inability to channel students into particular areas of study (with the exception of medicine) have militated against the rational distribution of highly trained people within the economy. Nevertheless the "grid" that has been used to collocate educational and manpower qualifications is not without significance (see Table 4).

Table 4.

Level	Average no. of years of study beyond age 13	Level of educational qualification	Category of employment
I	11	First degree; doctorate; engineer's diploma	Commercial and administrative cadres; engineers
II	9	as I	as I
III	7	University diploma of technology; non-graduate teachers' certificate	Other commercial and administrative cadres; industrial designers; teachers
IV	5	Baccalaureate; "brevet de technicien"	Foremen; clerical workers
V	3–4	Certificate of vocational aptitude	Clerical and skilled manual workers
VI	To school-leaving age	nil	Unskilled manual workers and labourers

An example given from the previous plan, the Fifth Plan, shows how this system of planning is used. Using the categories above, it was computed that in an age group of 840,000 the needs of the economy until 1970 would be:

Levels I and II combined, 67,200 (8 per cent);

Level III, 108,000 (12 per cent);

Level IV, 126,000 (15 per cent);
Level V, 378,000 — 420,000 (45 — 50 per cent);
Level VI, 126,000 — 168,000 (15 — 20 per cent);
Total, 840,000 (100 per cent).

Although such predictions have in the event proved inaccurate, the French quite reasonably argue that it is better to make some estimate of numbers than to make none at all.

Some educational planning has, however, not been without success. One example of this has been the long-awaited project to "decongestion" the Paris area. By the creation of a "crown" of new "academies" round Paris, such as those of Amiens, Rouen and Orléans, each equipped with its own university, and by the reorganization of universities within Paris itself, some relief for the hard-pressed capital has been obtained. Another example, this time of education co-operating successfully with the economy, is that of Western France, where the educational system has systematically supported the renovation of agriculture. Likewise in the depressed areas of Northern France, where staples such as the textile industry have been superseded, education has played its part in helping new industries to establish themselves.

Planning has also played a major part in the scheduling of new educational institutions. Over the past decade the Ministry of Education has been the largest building constructor in France. Industrialized building techniques have been adopted since 1964 and have produced rapid results. After a building operation has been decided upon, a period of three to five months normally elapses before finance is made available. Within a month construction can begin and in a maximum period of seven months the building is completed. In effect this means that about half the buildings planned can be executed within the same year and the rest at the beginning of the following year.[9]

However, in higher education building progress has not been so successful, mainly because of the dysfunctions of the planning system already mentioned. For example, the Fifth Plan had envisaged that in 1972–1973, 47 per cent of places would be needed for "literary" subjects and 63 per cent for "scientific" subjects. In the event the figures showed that 66 per cent of students were studying "literary" subjects, as against 33 per cent studying "scientific" subjects, with the result that laboratory

[9] Information given by M. Billecocq, speaking in the Senate, June 16, 1970.

space and valuable scientific equipment were left lying idle. Given the indicative nature of French planning such a mistake was perhaps difficult to obviate. On the other hand, in another sphere of planning for higher education the planners made a fundamental error. The model they adopted for new universities was that of the American campus, which had of necessity to be developed outside large towns. This has resulted in the construction of large complexes of teaching areas and student residences, ill adapted to "pedestrian living", often remaining construction sites for several years and lacking recreational space. Students have complained that such complexes are far from town centres, so that they inhabit "déserts d'ennui" and feel themselves as "towndwellers in exile". The anonymity of human relations on such a living plane creates tensions, so much so that now a deliberate policy has been adopted of at least not building new universities of gigantic size — a capacity of 8000 students is to be the norm.

Something must be said of the internal financial planning of the Ministry of Education and its associated agencies. Since 1973 within the Ministry itself the principle of management by objectives has been implemented.[10] The budget is established by *programmes,* each one of which is devoted to a particular area of the Ministry's activities. Any decision to enlarge one particular activity will consequently require extra finance. This acts as a constraint, enabling priorities to be established as between programmes. Objectives are set up for each programme and the measure of their attainment is by indicators that may be physical or financial. For example, a physical indicator might be the number of extra teachers required to implement a programme, as distinct from the financial cost of the programme. The overall time scale extends over three to four years and programmes are revised yearly in a process of "rolling reform".

The total budget within the Ministry is drawn up by a procedure of arbitrage. A first stage comprises the drawing up of draft projects in which the objectives and the different variables are expressed in quantitative terms and the costs evaluated. Each draft programme is then submitted to arbitration, in which costs and advantages are compared. The directors of objectives within the Ministry then pronounce on those projects and programmes that are to be given priority, although it is incumbent upon

[10] "La gestion par objectifs à l'Education Nationale", *L'Education,* Jan. 25, 1973 (pages roses).

the Minister to make the final decision. Meanwhile the total sum available for education has been decided upon by the government and programmes may have to be redrawn to take this into account, which in its turn means that the list of priorities may have to be revised. It is then the responsibility of the group of directors of ways and means to ensure that the physical resources required are made available. It is hoped eventually to calculate unit costs for all programmes (private estimates of these have already been made: Table 5).

The procedures for arriving at the total sums available for education within a given planning period have already been described. The total sums are not allocated as between the various years in which the Plan is current; it is now customary to operate a system of authorizations of expenditure which may be spread over a number of years. This system does not, however, preclude the drawing up of an education budget, within the National Budget, on a yearly basis. Since 1952, after allowing for inflation (but not for the increase in numbers) the sum spent yearly — roughly 17 per cent of the overall National Budget — has more than doubled in real terms. Fournier[11] attributes this additional cost in part to the lack of productivity of the system, although he adduces no evidence to substantiate this. It is certain that the "expenditure explosion" has also occurred because of the greater costs incurred in secondary and higher education, where the increase in numbers has been phenomenal.

Table 5.

School education	
Primary (6 years)	7000 F
Lower secondary (4 years)	16000 F
Upper secondary general education (3 years)	21000 F
Short technical education (2 years)	12000 F
Long technical education (3 years)	18000 F
Post-school education	
Law (4 years)	17000 F
Humanities (4 years)	22000 F
Science (4 years)	60000 F
Medicine (9 years)	103000 F
Pharmacy (5 years)	57000 F
Technology (in IUT, 1 + 2 years)	21000 F
Engineering schools (2 + 3 years)	80000 F

(1£ = approx. 10 F)

[11] J. Fournier, *Politique de l'Education,* Paris, 1971, p. 185.

The figures for 1970 (Table 5), the result of an enquiry by Professor Eicher,[12] show the unit costs per pupil or student by level of education. Unit costs for the period of compulsory schooling in England and Wales are somewhat lower,[13] but the difference is probably accounted for by the higher salaries enjoyed by French teachers. Most probably the costs of attending a grande école such as the Ecole Nationale d'Administration or the Ecole Polytechnique will even exceed the cost of training a doctor in France. The same enquiry computed the cost to' the State of training various categories of people from the beginning of their primary education to the obtaining of their final qualification. A primary teacher's training cost 58,000 F, a graduate teacher in the humanities cost 72,000 F, and a graduate with a technological qualification 65,000 F. These represent the public costs alone; to include the private costs of education another 20 per cent must be added. In general the higher the level of education and of the qualification sought, the higher the cost. Soaring costs have meant that in recent years educational expenditure has reached a plateau, as priority has increasingly been given to other welfare elements in the National Budget.

As an example of the incidence of costs between the various entities concerned the figures for the total expenditure on education in 1968 may be given (Table 6).[14]

---

[12] The enquiry was carried out by Professor Eicher, of Dijon, for the Institut de Recherche sur l'Economie de l'Education and reported in *Le Nouvel Observateur*, Oct. 7, 1974, pp. 69–72.

[13] The comparative computation is as follows:
Costs in England and Wales (1971–1972 figures):
Primary schools £239 p.a.
Secondary schools (pupils under 16) £211 p.a.
Therefore the cost for six years of primary education (£1436) and for five years of secondary education (£1022) give a total cost for *eleven* years of education of £2456. In France the cost of six years of primary education (7000 F) and for four years of secondary education (16,000 F) give a total cost for *ten* years of schooling of 23,000 F. To this figure, in order to equalize the number of years compared, must be added the notional cost of one extra year of lower secondary education: 4000 F (16,000 F divided by 4). The comparable cost is then 27,000 F, which is approximately £2700. It is interesting to note that the unit cost in France of primary education is considerably lower than in England (approximately £116, as compared with £239 p.a.), whereas the opposite holds good for secondary education (approximately £400 as compared with £211). The figures given for England and Wales are drawn from: *Statistics of Education*, 1972, Vol. 5, *Finance and Awards*, HMSO, London, 1973.

[14] Extracted from: *Rapport Capelle*, Document 136, Assemblée Nationale, première session ordinaire de 1970–1971.

Table 6.
(in tens of millions of francs)

	Amount	%	Amount	%	Amount	%
Ministry of Education	2052	78.6				
Other ministries (e.g. Labour, Agriculture)	225	8.6				
Common charges (e.g. pensions)	334	12.7				
Total *State*	2611	100.0	2611	90.3		
Local bodies (net)			286	9.7		
Total: *Public expenditure*			2897	100.0	2897	84.8
Families			350	67.5		
Industrial and commercial firms			168	32.5	518	15.2
Total: *Private expenditure*			518	100.0	518	15.2
Grand total of expenditure on education					3415	100.0

The general principle regarding the distribution of the financial burden of education as between the State and local bodies has been that the higher the level of education the greater the charges shouldered by the State. For primary and nursery schools, which are the responsibility of the communes, the State disburses a lump sum, the size of which varies according to different criteria such as the wealth of the commune and the extent of the geographical area in which it is situated and for which it has responsibility. In this way it is hoped to achieve an equalization of facilities. In general the proportion of local finance required for pre-primary and primary schools in the period of the Fifth Plan has been calculated at 31 per cent. For secondary education, although in some cases local authorities are technically responsible for buildings and equipment, in the main they have handed back the task to the State, because of the savings in cost made possible in this way by industrialized construction techniques. Local authorities are in any case liable to pay half the cost of the land on which it is proposed to build new secondary schools. In the realm of higher education, apart from some minor exceptional charges which amount only to some 2 per cent of the total, the State bears all the cost. Despite the attempt at equalization it is clear that the system of allocation of costs becomes inequitable as between local bodies and the State when, for special reasons, a particular locality has unexpectedly to provide a large number of primary school places. Thus when discussing the alleged centralization of French education the incidence of costs, which may bear heavily on some localities, must be borne in mind.

In higher education financial aid to students has traditionally been largely given indirectly through cheap student restaurants, reduced travel rates, hostel accommodation and minimal fees, although some students have received grants. In 1974 it was estimated that only one student in six received a grant, the value of which for undergraduates varied between £224 and £530. However, a new policy of giving more direct aid has been announced recently by the Ministry of Higher Education.[15] At secondary level also some costs have usually to be borne by parents, and the extent of these varies from area to area. In some localities, for example, bussing facilities are free, whereas elsewhere charges are steep. Pupils' textbooks have up to now had to be bought, although an extensive loan system is being organized. Economists of education now acknowledge that the pupil from poor parents will not stay the secondary course and enter higher education unless there is at least adequate support financially from the State when he has reached the end of compulsory schooling. They urge that this is where the emphasis should be directed if "democratization" of higher education is to become a reality. At the university itself the possibility of part-time or even full-time employment is always open.

[15] Reported in the *Times Higher Education Supplement*, Oct. 18, 1974.

PART III

SCHOOLS, TEACHERS AND SOCIETY

CHAPTER 6

Pre-school and Primary Education

The focus of interest in France, as elsewhere, has now shifted away from secondary and higher education to the nursery and the primary school, as the importance of these institutions in determining the future career of children has become recognized. The genuine pride that the French show in their nursery schools is matched by the keen interest they have manifested in the ideas behind British primary schools, with the result that "open-plan" structures, and concepts such as "family grouping" and the "integrated day" are filtering into French primary schools. In the field of nursery education, however, the British have much to learn from the French.

The first nursery schools were opened in the Vosges by Pastor Oberlin as early as 1771. Later the communes opened "salles d'asile" for children whose parents could not look after them during the day. All these institutions came under the aegis of the Ministry of Public Instruction by 1836. Thus by the time their existence was formalized by Jules Ferry, nursery schools of one kind or another already catered for 600,000 pupils. Today such schools may be private or public. Communes are required by law to open nursery schools, attendance at which is free, if their population exceeds 2000 inhabitants. These may be independent institutions, or attached to primary (and, occasionally, even secondary) schools, or constitute a special infants' section in an existing primary school. At present over two million children are enrolled in nursery schools or classes of one kind or another. In 1970 already the average enrolment rate for children aged between 3 and 6 (when compulsory schooling begins) was 84 per cent, a proportion exceeded within the OECD countries only by Belgium. Although figures are not strictly comparable, since compulsory schooling begins in Britain at 5, the percentages that follow illustrate how far the British have still to go in order to catch up: in 1970 only 11 per cent of British 2–4 year old children were in nursery schools; in France the percentages were: 2-year olds, 18 per cent, 3-year olds, 61 per cent, and 4-year olds, 87 per cent. By the age of 5 practically every French child is already in school. It is hoped that by 1977 this total attendance will be attained for all children from the age of 2. In 1975 the target for nursery education was set at three million pupils and it was proposed to provide 30,000 new nursery teachers.

Pre-school provision has been insufficient in the rural areas, in new suburbs and large housing estates. In Paris and the larger conurbations the position has been deemed to be satisfactory. To fill the need in the countryside a number of expedients are being tried. In some areas a nursery school is attached to a number of grouped primary schools, although this is not entirely satisfactory because it entails the bussing of numbers of small children. A second solution has been to introduce part time nursery education and to have one teacher divide her time between two localities. A third expedient has been to group all children aged between 2 and 11 in one primary school, in the charge of the primary teacher, with a peripatetic nursery teacher coming to the school once a week.

The renewed drive for nursery education dates from 1973, because it is looked upon as a vital factor in the equalization of opportunity. It has been remarked that "it is at three years old that preparation for the Ecole Polytechnique begins".[1] Indeed, the whole function of pre-school education has changed its emphasis. In the immediate post-War period nursery schools provided care facilities for children whose mothers went out to work — a higher proportion than in England. This custodial need of course remains, but it has been reinforced by a consciousness of the social value of the nursery school and by a belief that it will lessen educational disadvantagement. The value to children, particularly deprived children, of associating with others is recognized. To this social aspect the French have linked the pedagogical one. In the last year of nursery education, and indeed even before, the trend has been to begin formal learning, so that an initiation into the three Rs has accompanied the usual range of physical, manual and aesthetic activities. Moreover, interesting experiments are at present in progress to teach these infant pupils modern mathematics and foreign languages, particularly English and German. In the latter respect

[1] P. Nourry and P. Bois, "Français et égalité des chances: I. — La maternelle", *Le Figaro*, Oct. 27, 1970.

the link between France and West Germany has become very important, since it has developed into a regular exchange of nursery teachers.

The question as to who should take charge of nursery classes has been a matter of some dispute. When he was Minister of Education M. Guichard considered it unsatisfactory that ordinary primary teachers should be asked to run nursery classes unless they had had special training. On the other hand, he did not wish to fall back upon the play-group leader or the child-care worker. He proposed that some kind of auxiliary teacher would be the most appropriate person. In this he was opposed by the most eminent of all French experts in nursery education, Mme Herbinière-Lebert, despite the fact that she was employed by the Minister as an inspector. The new Secretary of State for pre-school education, Mme Lesur — the creation of this new post is an indication of the importance that the French attach now to nursery education — has attempted to resolve this dilemma by a compromise. For children aged between 2 and 4 a dual system is being established: teaching periods under the control of qualified primary teachers will be followed by spells of leisure activities organized by nursery assistants specially trained for their task. Furthermore, for children over 4 an important aim will be to ensure that the transition to primary school is made as easy as possible, since the number of those "repeating" the first grade of primary school is alarmingly high. Children who are capable and whose parents consent will begin reading, writing and arithmetic. But strict division by age groups will be abolished and children will be grouped according to their stage of development. Other measures decreed stipulate that nursery schools in towns are to open from 7.30 a.m. and not close until 8 p.m. — perhaps an indication that the number of working mothers is increasing. In remote areas, where formal nursery education cannot be provided, it is hoped that TV and radio programmes will help to fill the gap.

Before dealing with primary education proper, something must be said about special education for the mentally sub-normal, those with psychological difficulties, and the physically handicapped. From 1965 to 1972 the number of children that fell into these categories and for whom special treatment was provided approximately doubled, rising to 263,000. This figure probably represents a better diagnosis than any real increase in numbers. At the primary level such categories are dealt with usually in special classes attached to ordinary schools, although — and this applies to the secondary level also — special boarding schools exist for difficult cases. In the secondary school physically handicapped children of normal intelligence are taught in special classes in order that they receive more favoured treatment to make up for their physical disadvantagement. Those with slight mental defects also attend special classes attached to colleges of secondary education and may remain in them until the age of eighteen if necessary. Up to now a more stringent policy of segregation has been followed than, for example, in Britain, although this is now to change so that as many handicapped children as possible can be kept within the normal school system.

By law every commune is obliged to open and maintain a primary school. A school reserved for girls only' need not — but may be — opened in communes of under 500 inhabitants, nor a nursery school in communes with less than 2000 inhabitants. If such schools as these are opened they must be operated entirely at the expense of the commune, including payment of the salaries of any teachers employed. But the Law of October 30, 1886, as modified in 1936, stipulates not only that every commune must have a primary school, but that every hamlet separated from a village by more than 3 kilometres and containing at least fifteen pupils of school age must also be provided with a school. Primary schools for boys and girls must be separate, or at least the classes must be single-sex, although this stipulation has been modified in practice since 1964. Nursery schools, on the other hand, are always mixed.[2] This aversion for co-education is probably a vestige of the views formerly held by Catholics upon this subject.

The French child enters primary school proper at the age of 6 and leaves at the age of 11. Although the school has lost much of the prestige attached to it, since all pupils now move on to a secondary school, a certain penumbra of past glory, coupled with the fact that it has greater local roots than the secondary school, attaches to it. Founded on the three principles of obligatory attendance (Law of 1882), non-payment of school fees (Law of 1881) and religious neutrality (Laws of 1882 and 1886), the primary school was the showpiece of the Third Republic just as the college of secondary education is that of the Fifth Republic to date. As in England, attendance at a State school is not compulsory, and schooling

---

[2] R. Guillemoteau and P. Mayeur, *Traité de Législation scolaire et universitaire*, Vol. 3. *Enseignements élémentaire et pré-élémentaire*, Paris, 1970, pp. 91 et seq.

can take place in a private school or even in the privacy of the family. In fact the law requires the child to be educated rather than *schooled.* Originally compulsory schooling extended only from 6 to 13. In 1936 the leaving age was raised to 14 and in 1959 to 16 for those entering school in that year. The principle of religious neutrality must be strictly observed within the primary school. Originally one day a week — Thursday, now Wednesday — was allowed off from school so as to give parents the opportunity to send their children for religious instruction outside the school. Today a certain liberty is allowed the primary teacher to permit children to leave school early on other days in order to attend the catechism given by the parish priest. In the primary school the crucifix must not be displayed, as indeed befits the secular nature of this most Republican of institutions.

In former days the primary school enjoyed a good reputation because it was there that the valuable qualification of the Certificate of Primary Studies ("certificat d'études primaires"), which gave access to a number of subordinate jobs such as that of the postman or village constable, was obtained. As secondary education became generalized this qualification dropped into disuse and the status of the primary teacher who was responsible for it diminished. It was due finally to be abolished in 1962, although there is some evidence that it survived until 1970. The certificate was awarded on the strength of a one-day examination, the various parts of which were marked as the day progressed. To sit for it candidates had to journey to the chief commune of the canton, reporting by 7.30 a.m. Locally it was quite an occasion. At the end of the long day the results were announced and:

> In the evening the happy [successful] candidates, like conscripts, bought badges of honour and the tears of the vanquished were forgotten in the clamorous joy of the winners returning to their villages with flags and fireworks, whilst in the cafés there lingered on examiners, candidates, parents and grandparents, laureates and victims — emptying till late in the night the glasses of friendship and educational harmony.[3]

Such halcyon days are gone for ever. Moreover, in another respect the status of the primary school has gone down: it is no longer the institution where the difficult "entrée en sixième" (11+) examination was prepared, determining entrance to the lycée.

---

[3] H. Wadier, *op. cit.,* p. 114.

The disappearance of these examinations has nevertheless freed primary education from some of the constraints under which it had laboured. Although the school retains a predominantly intellectual tincture (which English primary schools do not), in 1969 sweeping changes were made.[4] The timetable was modified so that the total number of lessons per week was reduced from 30 to 27. Not only was the mid-week holiday retained, but children were dispensed from attendance on Saturday afternoons, as a result of the decrease in the number of lessons.

The present pattern of lessons within the primary school is as shown in Table 7.

Table 7.

1.	*Basic subjects*	
	French	10 lessons
	Arithmetic	5 lessons
2.	*"Curiosity-awakening" activities*	6 lessons
3.	P.E. and sport	6 lessons
	Total	27 lessons

The predominant position accorded to French is notable. In 1963 a special commission had been set up under an inspector-general, M. Rouchette, to make proposals for the reform of French teaching in the elementary school. The commission was particularly requested to take into account recent developments in linguistics and teaching methods, including the fact that the mass media were now exerting great influence over the development of linguistic ability. Hitherto French teaching had been rather rigidly divided into reading, writing, spelling, grammar, vocabulary, composition and recitation. The Rouchette Report, published in January 1971, instigated certain changes, but was not considered entirely satisfactory. Another commission, presided over by Pierre Emmanuel, had been set up in March 1970 with the task of reviewing French teaching throughout the school system. The regulations of 1969 had already indicated the direction it was thought that change should take: the language should be taught as above all an aid for the child to communicate and think.

[4] By the ministerial "arrêté" of Aug. 7, 1969 and the subsequent circular of Sept. 2, 1969.

In 1972, as a result of this rethinking, and after a number of experiments had taken place, definitive instructions for the teaching of French were laid down.[5] They conceive of it as the achievement of certain balancing elements:

> A balance between written and oral work: one of the first objectives of the teaching of French at the primary school is to help the pupils to be able to formulate and express their thoughts orally. Moreover, the understanding of the written language is linked to progress in oral expression and it is by favouring at one and the same time both written and oral expression that the teacher will help the child to communicate and think.
> A balance between theory and usage: the pruning of the grammar syllabus has been carried out and the manipulation of grammatical mechanisms has counted for more than an abstract knowledge of terminology.
> A balance between spontaneity and elaboration. The most common fault has been to show oneself too mistrustful of the child's spontaneity. It is by taking into account the natural and spontaneous movements of children that the teacher will assist in the development of language and will help the child to master a more structured language.
> A balance between intellectual training and the flowering of the sensibility: a basic dimension is given to poetry in school life.
> A balance between tradition and innovation: the basic principles of modern teaching method are recalled: the pedagogy of encouragement, of motivation, of activity; a pedagogy which at the same time is individual and calls into play group working methods, having as its aims the development of the pupil's personality. At the same time the use of exercises, as is traditional in the school, is recommended.

Whilst the above is somewhat minutely prescribed, great freedom is allowed in the methods to be employed. This in itself represents a minor revolution in the teaching of the mother tongue in France, although it is doubtful whether the somewhat over-free efforts at composition, where accuracy is sacrificed to imaginative quality, would be tolerated in France.

"Curiosity-awakening" activities are defined as including moral instruction, history and geography, observation exercises, art and crafts, singing and "directed work", which may consist of projects or exercises carried out in a group and which may arise from suggestions made by the pupils. The object of lumping these activities together is to allow teachers to plan their work more freely and integrate one element with another. In view of the current speculation about moral education in England, where it has traditionally been linked with religious instruction, the way in which this difficult subject is tackled is interesting. On beginning school the pupil is

[5] *Le Mouvement éducatif en France, 1971–1973,* INRDP Brochure No. 2032, Paris, 1973, p. 26.

initiated into moral ideas by the teacher recounting stories to which a moral is attached, or retailing the lives of great men. Later, talks regarding minor events in the life of the school are discussed. Later still a practical effort is made to inculcate in pupils "the reasoned practice of the principal individual and social virtues such as temperance, sincerity, modesty, goodness, courage and tolerance, and to inspire in them the love of work, a desire to co-operate, team spirit, respect of one's word once given, understanding of other people, love of one's native soil, the duties towards the family and towards one's country".[6] This is a truly formidable catalogue of virtues. History consists at this stage of short talks about famous Frenchmen of the past, followed by a rapid survey of some outstanding periods in French history, using local resources wherever possible. Geography is mainly a study of the locality. "Observation exercises" are the means of studying elementary scientific phenomena.

This much simplified timetable, constituted of three main elements only, allows for great flexibility. A system known as "le tiers temps pédagogique", tried out experimentally since 1964, is now being generalized. Under it French and mathematics are largely taught in the mornings, and the "curiosity-awakening" activities and physical education are reserved for the afternoons. Although homework has been forbidden in the primary school since 1956 — a prohibition which is still sometimes ignored by teachers — the practice of regular class tests ("devoirs") still continues.

It is officially recognized that the present refurbishing of programmes and methods cannot be accomplished without the retraining of teachers. During his teaching career the teacher will be allowed to take off a total of thirty-six working weeks — i.e. one teaching year — for in-service training.[7] In order to speed up the process, as a first step every primary teacher will be required by 1978 to have followed a six-week or three-month course. Similar "re-tread" courses have been organized for teacher trainers and primary school inspectors ("inspecteurs départementaux").

The question of discipline in primary schools — as indeed for secondary schools — is strictly stipulated. The regulations governing legitimate punishments date from 1887, were partially modified in 1919 and still

[6] *Horaires et programmes de l'enseignement du premier degré,* SEVPEN, Paris, p. 13.

[7] Ministerial circular of June 20, 1972.

control practice today. Corporal punishment is strictly forbidden — as indeed it is in the overwhelming majority of European countries — and the only sanctions allowed are the attribution of bad conduct marks, the reprimand, being kept in for part of the recreation time, or detention after school under the supervision of the teacher. For serious offences a pupil may be temporarily suspended.[8]

During the initial phase of the de Gaulle reforms primary education was temporarily neglected, because of the more urgent needs of the secondary school. However, as it is increasingly believed that by 11 the die is cast as regards equalization of opportunity, attention is now redirected back to nursery and primary education.

[8] Guillemoteau and Mayeur, *op cit.,* p. 251.

CHAPTER 7

Eleven to Fifteen: Educational Structures and Pedagogy

Lower secondary education in France begins theoretically for children at the age of 11. They then leave the primary school where they have spent the first five years of compulsory schooling and enter an institution giving a four-year course known as a "college of secondary education" ("collège d'enseignement secondaire" — CES). This is a comprehensive school which is divided into "tracks" from the beginning. There are three such tracks: Modern I and Modern II, and Transitional III. Modern I includes those pupils who under the former system would have embarked upon a lycée course at 11. Modern II represents less gifted children who are nevertheless considered capable of following an academic curriculum. Transitional III is reserved for those children — about a quarter of the total — who have fallen behind in the primary school either because they are not clever or because of some other reason. After the first two years some reshuffling of pupils goes on between these three tracks. The object of this resorting is primarily to ensure that as many children as possible can be transferred from the Transitional group to Modern II. Those pupils who are intellectually not capable of being promoted in this way remain in the lowest track and are placed in what are known as "terminal classes" ("classes de fin d'études"). It is likely that many will remain in the CES until the school-leaving age. The others continue in Modern I or Modern II and follow a curriculum with an academic bias. At 15, at the end of the lower secondary course, decisions are made regarding future schooling.

For the sake of completeness the general pattern of upper secondary education will also be described here, although full details will be given later.

The options at present available at the end of the CES course are two: the lycée, which leads to the baccalaureate examination giving access to higher education; and the college of technical education ("collège d'enseignement technique" — CET), which offers prevocational and vocational training. The lycée, a truncated version of the prestigious institution started by Napoleon, may be classical, modern or technical. All three types enjoy parity of esteem; the technical lycée indeed offers courses that may be more demanding than the other two more traditional forms. Three-year courses lead either to the baccalaureate or to a "technician's baccalaureate" which is a qualification leading on to other technical institutions or directly to skilled employment. The other option, the college of technical education, offers a choice of courses lasting two or three years. These courses are industrial or commercial, or relate to the "service" occupations of the tertiary sector.

Broadly speaking, therefore, the French secondary system comprises a common institution for all children from 11 to 15, followed by a bipartite system from then onwards.

This educational pattern did not emerge immediately, and it is necessary to go back to 1959 to see how it has evolved. Before the advent of de Gaulle the secondary system could be described as a bipartite one. The brighter minority of children entered the lycée at 11; the others continued in the primary school until the age of 14. There were some advanced primary schools, the "cours complémentaires", which continued the education of some children also to the age of 16. The Berthoin decrees of 1959 did not effectively transform this system. They merely instituted a "phase of observation and guidance" for all children aged between 11 and 13, regardless of the institution to which they had been allocated at the end of initial primary schooling. The decrees also stipulated that at a future date, which eventually turned out to be 1969, the leaving age for all children should be raised to 16.

Later a distinction was drawn between "long" and "short" secondary courses. In sparsely populated areas, where the setting up of full ("long") secondary courses was impracticable, colleges of *general* education ("collèges d'enseignement général") were set up in which modified academic courses were given. These colleges of general education are now being phased out as the new lower secondary school for all children, the college of *secondary* education, created in 1963, becomes generalized over the whole country and the network of lycées and colleges of technical education for upper secondary courses becomes more dense. The college of secondary education, a compromise between a fully comprehensive school and an élitist system, is perhaps the most solid achievement of the de Gaulle reforms, and the least contested.

This vast framework of new structures could not come into existence overnight, with the result that in some parts of the country traces of older institutions continue to exist. Thus there are still a few classes for pupils aged 11 to 14 existing in the primary school, which used to take pupils up to 14. Some of the lycées (now truncated and reserved, it will be recalled, for upper secondary pupils) retain, like the remaining English grammar schools, a selective character and accept pupils from 11 to 18. Such anomalies are, however, rapidly disappearing.

The college of secondary education, destined to receive all pupils for the first four years of secondary schooling, traces its lineage back to the "école unique" postulated by the Compagnons in 1918 and advocated in the Langevin-Wallon Plan of 1947. It was created by a circular of October 17, 1963. Administratively it has the advantage of housing all children under one roof. Pedagogically this has the great merit, in theory at least, of enabling pupils to move from one track to another with ease and of mixing together different categories of teachers. The new schools have a social aim of equalizing educational opportunity and of raising standards. They have been set up with great rapidity. By 1964, one year after their creation, 209 already existed (at a time when there were only 195 comprehensive schools in England). By 1972 this figure had increased to 2666. Not all these were housed in new buildings. They are designed to house either 600, 900, or 1200 pupils, although recent reports suggest that in future the optimum size will be 900. School conditions vary according to the area in which the school is located. In areas of low population density the school is limited to 600 pupils and facilities exist for boarding if bussing facilities are inadequate. In medium-populated areas the bussing time must not exceed 45 minutes. In thickly populated areas zoning takes place, with certain primary schools acting as "feeder" institutions for their local college of secondary education.

The cardinal principle dominating this reform of secondary schooling has been that of "orientation" or, to use a more familiar terminology, "counselling and guidance", pointing the direction in which the pupils should go, according to their needs and abilities. The principle dates back to the reforms introduced experimentally by Jean Zay in 1938. At the time when the French began to apply the principle, although the concept of *vocational* guidance was widely accepted, that of *school* guidance in a systematic fashion was hardly known in Western Europe.

Its adoption has eliminated the traditional formal examination that marked the "entrée en sixième", the French equivalent of the 11+. (In France, "sixième" is the first year of secondary schooling, corresponding to the first form in Britain and to the sixth grade in North America; subsequent classes are numbered in descending order down to "première", corresponding to the eleventh year of schooling; the final year is designated as "terminale".) The process of "orientation" into the secondary school begins in the last year of primary education. The wishes of the parent and pupil as to the particular track of the lower secondary school into which entrance is desired are first ascertained. The primary teacher then compiles a complete dossier on the pupil. This shows not only his scholastic record, particularly marks in class tests in French, spelling, reading and mathematics, with class positions, but also other personal details: the child's interests, his aptitudes, his behaviour in and out of school, his medical history, and, if possible, a report by a professional school guidance counsellor. These individual dossiers are scrutinized in May by working parties consisting of primary and secondary teachers, a guidance counsellor and representatives of parents' organizations. The local primary inspector and the headmasters of the schools concerned arbitrate decisions in doubtful cases. Moreover, if the track to which the pupil is ultimately allocated is unacceptable to his parents, they have the right to request a formal examination. Such a formal examination has in any case been compulsory until recently for pupils coming from a Catholic primary school and seeking entrance to a State secondary school. The decisions made upon the results of such an examination are final.

The process of orientation, following similar procedures, is continued throughout the four years of lower secondary education, which constitute the phase of "observation and guidance". Important milestones are reached at the ages of 13 and 15. At 13 the pupil may be shifted from one track to another, depending upon his progress. At 15, at the end of the course in the college of secondary education, a decision is taken whether to "orient" him towards "long" or "short" upper secondary education, viz. to a lycée or to a college of technical education. These procedures are the result of a systematic observation of all pupils. At regular intervals all teachers who teach a certain class meet under the chairmanship of the headmaster or the "principal teacher" ("professeur principal") of the class and in the presence of both parents' and pupils' representatives consider the work of each individual pupil. Careful records are kept. At 13, particularly, those pupils originally placed in the lowest stream who now show signs of academic improvement are moved to the Modern II track and may be given special remedial teaching — extra classes of "directed work" ("travaux dirigés") in French, mathematics and a modern language. At 15 the examination of the case of each pupil, because much depends upon it, is very thorough and is carried out by an enlarged guidance committee.

This commendable procedure of orientation is, however, not continued beyond the age of 15. Some French educationists would like to see it replace the highly conventional baccalaureate examination and even be used at the end of higher education to "orient" graduates into the most suitable kind of employment, whilst leaving them the right to accept what is offered them. But these progressives have not yet carried the day.

This may be because the principle of orientation has not been accepted without misgivings. Ideally, according to a pioneer in the reforms, Roger Gal, the orientation process should "try to grasp how there may be developed to the utmost the forces latent in every unfinished personality and seek out in what direction each human being will achieve fulfilment.". Thus conceived, orientation resembles a turntable which may be adjusted to the direction appropriate for the pupil and send him off on the right track. It contrasts with the selection process, which may be compared to a filter through which all may not pass. But parents fear that orientation gives too much power to the teachers, despite the safeguard that the conventional examination offered as an alternative undoubtedly provides. Consciously or unconsciously, it is argued, teachers may misjudge children. There is some evidence that, as in England, teachers are infected by middle-class values to an undue extent and will orient those children whose social background reflects those values to the so-called "enseignement noble" which leads to higher education and ultimately to the top posts in society. Political critics of the system see orientation as a covert form of selection under a more acceptable name. The numbers oriented towards a particular track or institution may fluctuate not according to the interests and abilities of children, but are dependent on the future needs of the economy. It is alleged that this is one reason why Alain

Peyrefitte, who was Minister of Education in 1968, set up a National Office for Information and Orientation (Office national de l'Information et de l'Orientation professionnelle – ONISEP). Having declared that orientation was the backbone of all educational reforms the then Minister went on to say that, although it was desired to make the system as flexible as possible, there must be concern to reconcile the long-term national needs with the aspirations of young people, as well as with the necessity of continuing to impart a humanist education. If this argument appears inadmissible it may be countered by retorting that it is little use steering young people into blind alleys or to enter forms of education that lead to non-existent jobs. In any case, orientation may be viewed as a form of selection over time rather than a "sudden-death" choice. This argument does not, however, appeal to the critics who assert that, despite attempts to mitigate it, élitism continues to prevail.

There are, however, now some indications that orientation in lower secondary education is obsolescent. One tangible step on the road to acceptance of a more radical comprehensive system has been the recent (1974) freedom granted to head teachers in colleges of secondary education to decide whether the system of division into tracks should be adopted in the very first year of secondary school. An indication that the climate of opinion on this question was changing came during the brief tenure of the Ministry of Education by M. Fontanet. The Minister was of the opinion that the tracking system had been a demonstrable failure and proposed three alternatives to replace it:

1. *Mixed ability grouping with setting for certain subjects.* Classes in the "basic" subjects – French, mathematics and a modern language – would be setted by ability. Weaker pupils would have additional teaching in these subjects. The more able pupils would have extra classes in what are termed the "curiosity-awakening" subjects, such as social studies and biology, or would begin Latin in the first two years instead of the third year as at present.

2. *Semi-mixed ability grouping.* Pupils would be graded according to their ability in the three basic subjects. One class, for example, might include children good in all three subjects, or another children weak in all three, or yet another those good at languages but weak in mathematics, or vice versa. Extra tuition would be given where needed.

3. *Mixed-ability grouping in all subjects.* There would be additional teaching for the less able. This would mean a heavier timetable for those who needed extra tuition in order to keep up with the rest.

Whatever solution is ultimately adopted, the principle of supplementary or remedial teaching ("une pédagogie de soutien") seems to be accepted. A consequential step might also have to be a lightening of the overall curriculum load. That the French should even envisage the third solution, which most nearly approximates to the Swedish one for this age group, is itself a measure of how far thinking has evolved since 1959. As late as 1969 Guichard, the then Minister, maintained that heterogeneous classes would ultimately work to the disadvantage of the less able and thus be the opposite of democratic: "Collective teaching — namely, a teaching which sacrifices nobody — demands a minimum homogeneity."[1] He considered that "to place all pupils in identical classes is inevitably to accept that social origins are translated into the rankings of pupils".[2] This rather goes against the experience of some schools. Already in 1970 a director of one college of secondary education declared that his practice was to decide which pupils in an intake were fit only for the lowest track and then to place the rest in Modern I and Modern II merely by alphabetical order.[3] What is certain is that the system which dates back to 1959 has not proved its worth.[4] Setting, mixed ability grouping, remedial teaching and a move towards greater individualization of instruction are all options that the French are at present keeping open.

There are, however, practical difficulties in abandoning even slightly the present system. The relaxation of streaming announced in 1974 by the Minister, M. Haby, had to be accompanied by a concession to teachers. Qualified graduate teachers ("certifiés" and "agrégés") could refuse to teach in mixed-ability classes and insist on their right to teach only the cleverest pupils. He hoped that teachers would not insist upon this right. However, the professional organizations of graduate teachers are alive to

[1] Guichard, speaking in the National Assembly in a debate reported in *Le Monde,* November 14, 1969.

[2] Quoted in P. Nourry, "L'Enseignement secondaire et l'égalité des chances II. L'école moyenne a-t-elle trouvé ses murs?", *Le Figaro,* Dec. 16, 1970.

[3] *Ibid.*

[4] Cf. L. Legrand, "L'Organisation des premiers cycles secondaires et l'individualisation de l'enseignement", *Recherches pédagogiques* No. 41, IPN (SEVPEN), 1970, pp. 5–11.

the implications of the move, which could, from their standpoint, be viewed as an attempt to bring about a unified teaching force, with a consequent diminution of the present hierarchical grades and ultimately of salary differentials and other distinctions.

The whole question of the sorting of pupils is complicated by the practice of "grade-repeating", which is widespread. In 1968 two-thirds of all primary pupils had repeated a grade at least once; about one in three had been kept down for a further year at the end of the first class of compulsory schooling, a strong argument for the development of a different kind of nursery education – or for producing a less demanding curriculum. In the college of secondary education 13 per cent of pupils have to repeat a grade at least once and of 100 pupils entering the lycée at age 15 or thereabouts only thirty-seven pass the baccalaureate three years later.[5]

Pedagogically the difference between pupils placed in Modern I and Modern II does not become very apparent during their time in the college of secondary education. They follow the same syllabuses and have the same options. On the other hand, it is generally conceded that the pace with pupils in Modern II may be slower and the methods may require adaptation. But the demanding nature of the curriculum has aroused protests from parents.

However, the problem has to be faced of what course to offer to the 25 per cent of pupils who from the beginning of secondary education are deemed at present incapable of following academic subjects and grasping abstract concepts. Many of these children are already a year or two older than the normal age because they have been kept down in the primary school. The transitional classes in which they are initially placed have the limited aim of trying to remedy the deficiencies in their primary schooling so that at age 13 some at least can be integrated into the Modern II track. The official policy for these classes is that they should not exceed twenty-five pupils and should be taught by one teacher only, who should have had training and experience in the use of so-called "active" methods. No set curriculum or timetable need be followed exactly, although the official apportionment of time according to subjects should be roughly respected. So far as possible teaching methods should be individualized, although the class should also be encouraged to assume responsibility as a

[5] J. Fournier, *op. cit.*, p. 144.

group and thereby learn the virtues of co-operating with others. Many of the teachers, schooled in the style of the post-primary teachers of former days, are extremely dedicated, but feel themselves very isolated from their colleagues teaching the brighter children. Certain lessons take place in half-classes, where the object is to teach the children to work independently. Thus in French, for example, they learn how to use such simple tools as a dictionary, a grammar, or the table of contents and index of a book.

At 13 there is always the hope that some of these less bright pupils may be able to move to reception classes and thence to join their fellows in the Modern II track. A few actually realize this ambition. The problem remains of what to do with the rest, whose intellectual "failure", in school at least, now seems definitive. As arrangements have stood since 1972 the majority are placed in special prevocational classes where they follow a course in which eight lessons are given over to French, twelve are devoted to mathematics, science and technology, and three to manual activities. For French and mathematics the pupils are setted according to their ability. Pupils who do very well in these classes may be allowed after all to enter a college of technical education at 16 and take a three-year course leading to a qualification of "vocational aptitude" ("certificat d'aptitude professionnelle". Others may after a one-year course take a less demanding qualification, the "certificate of vocational education" ("certificat d'éducation professionnelle").[6] A minority — at present under 10 per cent of the total lower secondary intake — may be placed in special classes preparing for apprenticeship. These classes are designed for pupils who have usually already reached at least the age of 15 without going beyond the second grade level of secondary education. The one-year course that is followed consists partly of on-the-job training, but is school-based. Twelve hours of their time is devoted to general education, but they may spend up to a further 28 hours in various jobs outside the school in which the conditions of apprenticeship are simulated as far as possible. Despite the long hours spent in virtual employment, there is no fixed scale of pay, although some employers do reward the pupils with a small sum of about £15 per month. Eventually these classes will probably be integrated into

[6] For a description of these classes cf. H. Wadier, "Les Sections d'éducation professionnelle ou les bas-fonds pédagogiques", in: *La Réforme de l'enseignement n'aura pas lieu,* Paris, 1970, pp. 45–49.

the centres of apprenticeship established under the Law of July 16, 1971.

The advantage of this system, which applies to pupils who are generally the most restive because of their feeling of failure, is that the law stipulating compulsory education until the age of 16 can be flexibly applied. The link with school is not severed, although in practice much training goes on outside in employment. Indeed, a further exception to the compulsory school-leaving age is made for pupils of a slightly higher level of intelligence who, by the 1971 law, are allowed to leave school at 15 to take up a full industrial apprenticeship.

In a country where centralization has been the order of the day – a centralization which, the critic should remember, is held justifiable on grounds of equality, the vast number of educational experiments that occur in Britain, where every teacher can virtually be his own innovator, is not to be expected. The French argue that experimentation is at the expense of the children and must therefore be carefully controlled. Nevertheless, this is not to say that there has not been a long tradition of rigorous experimentation in France, starting with the Freinet innovations in the 1920s, continuing with the pre-War "orientation" phase started by Jean Zay, and with the "classes nouvelles" of the 1950s, where activity methods and the "centres of interest" approach were the main novelties. Today a number of educational experiments are flourishing. Among the most interesting is that centred on the experimental college of secondary education at Marly-le-Roi, which was purpose-built to try out innovations. These consist of the extensive use of closed-circuit television and other audiovisual equipment, a modular timetable and experiments with the size of teaching groups. Yet another interesting "educational and cultural centre" is located at Yerres. This owes something to the idea of community school and to the Cambridge village colleges. The centre comprises seven different kinds of institution: a college of secondary education, a sports centre, a youth centre, an auditorium which may be used as a theatre, a cinema, a place for exhibitions or public meetings, a social services centre, a public library and a crèche. The recent innovation of allowing schools to use 10 per cent of curricular time as they wish has also proved moderately successful. To the British, who take such freedom to innovate for granted, the rigorous control usually exercised over the French school may seem repugnant; on the other hand, it must be said that many Frenchmen regard the comparative liberty of the British school principal with equal distaste. The French view is that so far as possible programmes and teaching methods should be uniform, since this is a precondition for true equality of opportunity.

Although there is no formal compulsory examination at the end of lower secondary education, those pupils in Modern I and II who so desire may sit for the "brevet d'études du premier cycle" ("first phase diploma of study"). The results of this examination in no way determine the way in which the pupil is allocated to either a lycée or a college of technical education at 15. The formal examination consists of tests in French, mathematics and modern language, one other subject chosen by the candidate and an optional test in physical education. The papers are set and marked by inspectors and teachers. The school record is taken into account in determining the final result. Those who fail the examination the first time may redeem themselves by presenting themselves for a second series of purely oral tests. The pass rate is about 80 per cent. About 60 per cent of the whole age group achieve the qualification. For some it can be a terminal examination, because they are already 16 when they take it. It is a useful qualification because it is required for posts in the intermediate grades of the public administration, such as the post office or local government. It cannot, however, be compared with GCE "O" level (the equivalent of which was abolished in France, as in many other European countries, some years ago), since it is not a necessary qualification for higher education.

At the end of the four-year course in the college of secondary education a third sorting of pupils is made. Twenty-five per cent leave full-time education and enter employment; 40 per cent enter a college of technical education; and 35 per cent enter a lycée, which may be either classical, modern or technical. The orientation process is similar to the previous occasions. However, most children also attend a centre for guidance (attached to the Service d'Orientation scolaire et profession-nelle), where they are given tests of verbal, non-verbal, numerical and mechanical reasoning, and of spatial ability. The results are communicated to the school committee responsible for deciding upon the pupil's future. Although this committee must take into account any reports made by guidance counsellors, their recommendations are not mandatory upon the teachers, who may overrule them.

Although the French acknowledge there are many deficiencies in the structure and pedagogy that has been established for lower secondary education, not the least of which are the constant alterations that are being made, what has been done has much to commend it. Unlike the English, they have plumped for uniformity and compromise. A child moving between the ages of 11 and 15 is not liable to find himself in a totally different educational structure, as in England. Moreover, as between total "comprehensiveness" in structures, they have looked for the happy mean and allowed for the possibilities of development. In this way they have not — at least as regards lower secondary education — incurred the antagonism of parents nor excited unduly the extremists at either end of the comprehensive spectrum.

The subject-matter of what is taught in the colleges of secondary education is dealt with later. First, however, it is necessary to consider the next phase of schooling, which has been aptly named the "phase of determination".

CHAPTER 8

Fifteen to Eighteen: The "Phase of Determination"

Between the ages of 15 and 18 the die is cast for the majority of French youngsters. The structural unity preserved up to 15 in education now becomes bipartite. The college of technical education to which most children move leads after one, two or three years to employment. The lycée, for those that survive to the end of a very exacting three-year course, leads on to higher or further education or to teacher training. And there are those who have already reached the age of 16 before leaving lower secondary education and who will in the main enter employment.

The stress on the technological in the education system has already been mentioned. The background to this must now be sketched in. Today the technological form of education embraces a variety of terms: higher and lower technical education, vocational and prevocational education. The term "vocational education" ("formation professionnelle") used to be the most widely employed. Today it is used "to include all forms of preparation or further preparation for the exercise of a specific calling, ranging from the acquisition of theoretical knowledge to practical training and the transmission of the appropriate professional ethics or code of conduct".[1] Before going on to describe the work of the college of technical education, in which most pupils receive their first preparation for the world of work, the relevant legislation, which is considerable, must be outlined.

The Astier Law of July 1919 is generally reckoned to have laid down the foundations for modern vocational training in France.[2] It not only established the financial basis for State institutions of vocational training but also made grants to private training institutions, including Catholic ones, a procedure which was quite exceptional at the time. From 1925

---

[1] R. Grégoire, *Report on Vocational Education,* OECD, Paris, 1967.
[2] Cf. Ponteil, *op. cit.*., pp. 346–354.

onwards a special "apprenticeship tax" was levied on industrial and commercial concerns, the amount of which was fixed yearly in the finance act. Just as the Weimar Republic established in 1918 compulsory part-time day release courses for all young people up to the age of 18 who were not in full-time education, so did the French for young people employed in industry. In France courses have normally been obligatory for those who were not otherwise in school or had not obtained one of a recognized list of qualifications already. During the Vichy régime "apprenticeship centres" were started as a measure to counter juvenile unemployment and three-year full-time courses were developed. By the 1959 reforms these were transformed into the present-day colleges of technical education. A law of 1966 increased the rate of the "apprenticeship tax" and established a national policy for vocational training.

Since July 1971 three laws have regulated full-time and part-time vocational training both for young people and for others already in employment. It is convenient to discuss these laws at this point.

The Law of Orientation of Technological Education, the first legislative measure, was essentially a response to the priority given in the Sixth Plan to industrialization, a vital aspect of which was the training of skilled workmen, technicians and engineers. The intention was to upgrade the status of technical education so as to attract a wider clientele and at the same time to refurbish the content of the courses offered. In 1971 it was admitted that technical education continued only to accept the failures from courses of general education. A start in the rehabilitation of the technical aspects of education had been made by introducing technology into the top two grades of the lower secondary school and by the proposal that another course styled as an "initiation into economic life" should also be made compulsory. There is no doubt that massive prejudice existed, and perhaps continues to exist, in the minds of middle-class parents and pupils against technical education. What Recteur Capelle had termed a "Mediterranean mentality" associated general education with the high culture and technical education with a lower intellectual level. Hence its lack of esteem. Even the term "technical" had acquired overtones of the second-rate; thus a deliberate decision was taken to employ the word "technological" in the title of the law, as being a more dignified description, less bound up with soiling one's hands in manual labour. A France essentially increasingly technocratic in its form of government had perceived that an education in which there is no technological dimension runs the risk of becoming an anachronism in the modern world.

The Law therefore placed on an equal footing both general and technical education and for the first time recognized the transferability of qualifications. The baccalaureate, the qualification of the complete general secondary course, was declared to have as its equivalent the "technician's baccalaureate", the award of technical education. Holders of the two-year diploma of technology acquired in higher education were henceforth allowed to continue their education to obtain a full engineer's diploma, which could be obtained by easy stages through a credit-unit system. Such measures patently required an upgrading of teachers in technical education, and as a first step the length of the training period was increased. Links with industry were reinforced so that teachers were able to take study leave in order to update their knowledge in industry or commerce. The Law also stated that qualifications could be obtained through full-time schooling, through continued vocational training and through apprenticeship.

The Law on Apprenticeship, passed on the same day, envisaged the unification and reorganization of apprenticeship, which should lead to the qualification of skilled worker. The general conditions of apprenticeship were defined: "Apprenticeship is a form of education. Its purpose is to give young workers who have completed compulsory education a general, theoretical and practical training with a view to their obtaining a vocational qualification."[3] Such training would be given partly in the firm, partly in an apprenticeship training centre. It would take one of four forms: artisan, industrial, commercial or agricultural. The duration would be two to three years. There would be required a minimum of 3,440 hours of practical, "on the job" training, supplemented by a further minimum of 720 hours of education in an apprenticeship centre ("centre de formation d'apprentis") which should be both theoretical and practical. Only approved employers would be allowed to take on apprentices. They would be bound to present the apprentice at the end of his course for a technical qualification — either the Certificate of Vocational Aptitude ("certificat d'aptitude professionnelle" — CAP) or the Certificate of Vocational Education ("certificat d'éducation professionnelle" — CEP). During his period of indentures the apprentice is entitled to a wage. The apprentice-

---

[3] "La réforme de l'apprentissage", *L'Education,* Mar. 5, 1973.

ship centres may be set up by local bodies, official or otherwise, by professional bodies and private firms, on terms that have to be agreed with the State. They must be prepared to offer courses for apprentices which last at least 360 hours a year; the most usual arrangement is one day a week for forty-five weeks. Two-thirds of the time must be devoted to general and theoretical technological training and the remaining third to practical training.

(For the sake of completeness the third legislative measure is mentioned here, although it impinges only marginally upon school education. The Law organizing Vocational Education within the Framework of Lifelong Education ("Loi portant organisation de la formation professionelle continue dans le cadre de l'éducation permanente"), to give its rather cumbersome title, granted study leave to those already employed. Lifelong education — "éducation permanente" — had been constantly on the lips of educators for a decade or more, and this law attempted to realize that ideal. Under it all employees, whether young workers or not, are entitled to attend full- or part-time courses lasting up to one year. The order of entitlement will depend upon seniority within the firm and the lapse of time since the employee obtained a qualification or last attended a training course. The employer must pay full wages for the duration of the course. Not more than 2 per cent of the work force of a firm may be away on study leave at any one time.)

Such is the legislation upon which technical education has recently been founded. The qualifications obtainable can usually be sought either through apprenticeship or through the college of technical education.

Courses in the college of technical education may be of four main types: industrial, commercial, "administrative" (here used to designate preparation for employment in the tertiary sector) and, exceptionally, agricultural (see Fig. 5). A one-year course leads to the Certificate of Vocational Education. This is for the least bright pupils and merely entitles them to seek jobs as unskilled workers ("ouvriers spécialisés"), but in a particular field. A more exacting course is one lasting three years, obtainable either in a college of technical education or in a centre for apprentices and adults. The number of specialisms in these courses, which lead to the Certificate of Vocational Aptitude, is constantly being added to and modified. Recently, for example, the trades of signwriter and furniture remover were added to the list. The qualification gives the right

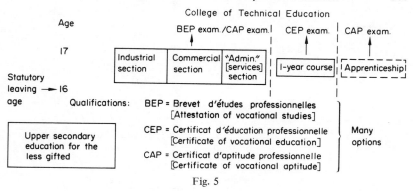

Fig. 5

to be classified as a skilled worker ("ouvrier qualifié") and also gives the opportunity of proceeding to other courses at a higher level. Some idea of how widespread the use of this qualification is may be gleaned from the fact that in 1971 there were 260 specialisms available nationally and another 86 locally, for occupations peculiar to an area. There were 341,000 candidates for the examination, of which just over 140,000 were girls and some 50 per cent overall were successful. Just over half had been trained for industrial jobs, mainly in the electrical and engineering occupations, and just under half for occupations in the tertiary sector, principally for secretarial work.

A specimen timetable for a three-year full-time course leading to a Certificate of Vocational Aptitude in an industrial section is given in Table 8.

A commercial division in a college of technical education may comprise four sections: shorthand-typing, book-keeping, clerical and retail distribution. A timetable for intending shorthand typists is shown in Table 9. It will be noted that the load is considerably lighter than for the industrial section, which is largely intended for boys. In both cases it will be noted that roughly half the curriculum is devoted to general education.

A different kind of qualification is a Vocational Diploma ("brevet d'études professionnelles") which is a more general qualification obtainable after a two-year course, leading also to employment as a skilled worker, usually after a further period of training in a specialized field.

Table 8.

Subjects	No. of lessons per week		
	Yr. 1	Yr. 2	Yr. 3
Civics, history and geography	3	2	3
French	3	3	2
Mathematics	3	3	3
Artistic education	2	1	1
Science and hygiene	2	2	2
Physical education	4	4	4
Total — non-vocational	17	15	15
Technical drawing*	2	2	3
Workshop and technology*	20	22	22
Grand total of lessons	39	39	40†

*Depending on the requirements for preparation for a particular occupation.

†In September 1974 it was announced that these timetables had proved excessive and that the weekly work-load was to be reduced to 36 lessons.

Table 9.

Subjects	No. of lessons per week		
	Yr. 1	Yr. 2	Yr. 3
General education			
French	5	5	5
Moral and civic education; labour legislation	1	1	1
History and geography	2	2	2
Modern language	2	2	2
Mathematics	4	2	2
Science and hygiene	1	1	1
Total — general education	15	13	13
Vocational education			
Commerce and accounts	4	2	1
Commercial correspondence	0	1	1
Business office techniques	0	2	3
Shorthand	3	4	4
Typing	3	4	4
Total — vocational education	10	13	13
Grand total of lessons	25	26	26

As from 1973 formal examinations have been abolished for these technical qualifications, which are obtained on a system of continuous assessment.

The preference up to now has been for full-time vocational and technical education at lower levels, which is less true of the English tradition. By October 1974 the colleges of technical education numbered 1312 and housed over half a million pupils in all. Strenuous efforts have been made to promote them. As yet, however, places are unevenly distributed over the whole country, with the result that in some areas selection has had to be the rule, whereas elsewhere there have been places to spare. This may happen for a variety of reasons. Pupils may refuse to travel long distances to the college or dislike becoming boarders, the other alternative frequently used in French secondary education; or the particular specialisms, notably in the commercial fields, which are more highly esteemed, may not be available locally.

What has been sketched out up to yet represents "short" upper secondary education. To complete the picture regarding technical education the "long" courses in technology offered at the upper secondary level must also be described. The first is the course given in a modern or technical lycée leading to the technological option in the baccalaureate. This will be dealt with later. However, other courses in the technical lycée, of a higher level than those offered in the college of technical education, also exist; some such lycées even offer courses which form part of higher education proper.

The specialized courses run in the technical lycées usually also require spells in industry or commerce. (See Fig. 6). The "brevet de technicien" (technician's diploma) is awarded after a three-year course in a variety of specialisms, such as those in the graphic industries, biological occupations, footwear, hotel-keeping and car engineering. A slightly higher qualification is also awarded, the "baccalauréat de technicien" (not to be confused with the *technological* baccalaureate already mentioned). This is a qualification awarded after three years' study in various branches: (a) industrial: mechanical construction, electronics, electro-technology, civil engineering and public works; (b) commercial: economics, administrative techniques, quantitative management techniques, computer science. Whilst it seems clear that some of these specialisms are of the same level as the Ordinary National Diploma in Britain, the difference would be that they all

"Long" General Upper Secondary Education

To Higher Education B.A.C.C.	Grade	Age	Section				
			A	B	C	D	E
	12 (Terminale)	18	Literary	Economic and Social Sciences	Maths and Physical Sciences	Earth Sciences Biological Sciences and Mathematical Applications	Scientific and Industrial Technology
	11 (Première)	17	Linguistic Philosophical				
	10 (Seconde)	16	A Literary	B Scientific		C Industrial Technology	

"Long" Professional Upper Secondary Education

		Leading to Technician Baccalaureate Options	Leading to Technician Diploma Options
Grades 10,11,12 Age 16 – 18	Industrial Education	1. Mechanical and Electrical 2. Civil Engineering 3. Laboratory Techniques 4. Computer Science	1. Industrial Techniques 2. Social Techniques 3. Hotel Techniques
	Economic Education	5. Executive Techniques 6. Quantitative Management Techniques 7. Commercial Techniques	4. Agricultural Techniques Note: In both Technician Baccalaureate and Technician Diploma many sub-options exist. Not all these give a qualification to higher education.

Fig. 6

comprise a strong element of general education and are not prepared for in further education, but as a normal part of a secondary course. Because of the greater State intervention it would appear that the complete network of technical and vocational qualifications seems to be more systematized. It may be that the award of such qualifications in full-time secondary education gives a purposefulness to the concluding years of schooling which seems to be lacking sometimes elsewhere.

Technical lycées also offer a post-secondary course known as the "brevet de technicien supérieur" (higher technician's diploma), also obtainable in various industrial and commercial fields.

So far as possible, in accordance with the principle of indicative manpower planning that France has attempted to follow since 1946, the various educational opportunities available and the occupational needs in various sectors of the economy have been roughly equated. A recent estimate has calculated these needs in educational terms as shown in Table 10.

Table 10. Percentage of Work Force to be Deployed

Research	1 per cent
Degree-level and above	7
Short courses in higher education	12
"Long" secondary technical education	15
"Short" secondary technical education	45–50
Education solely to school-leaving age	15–20
Total	100 per cent

As elsewhere, the academic secondary school, the lycée in the case of France, has long been the showpiece of French education. It was not without considerable heart-searching that it was converted from a secondary school catering for the age range 11 to 18 to one reserved for an élite of young people (which may nevertheless eventually rise to 40 per cent of the age groups) aged between 15 and 18. Because of the universalization of secondary education it can no longer be considered merely as a school for a privileged intellectual élite. Today it is analogous in some respects to a selective sixth-form college. There is, however, one vital difference: of those who enter and complete the course in France, about 80 per cent enter higher education, as compared with about half that percentage in England.

The more celebrated Paris lycées succeed in maintaining very high standards, particularly in the terminal classes. The Lycée Louis-le-Grand, for example, can only be compared scholastically with a school like Winchester. Like much else in French education it owes much to the high standards set in the old Jesuit "collège". Indeed, Louis-le-Grand was originally founded by the Jesuits in 1663 and acquired its royal name of Collège Louis-le-Grand in 1674. At the Revolution it was closed and turned first into a prison and then into a barracks (the description of the buildings of the old public school in England as monastic and of the lycée as barrack-like is indeed appropriate). The fact that such a noted anti-clerical as Voltaire and the "philosophe" Diderot had once been pupils did not save it from the Revolutionaries. Eventually, however, the school was reopened and underwent successive rebaptisms as the Revolutionary Collège Egalité, the Napoleonic Lycée de Paris, the Restoration Collège Royal de Louis-le-Grand, then the Lycée Descartes, before being named once again Louis-le-Grand in 1873.

If one strand in the lycée tradition originated from the Jesuits, it was Napoleon that wove a pattern that lasted over a century. He created one lycée in each chief town of a département, each under a régime that was largely military. It was he, moreover, who gave it that bookish bias that it has succeeded only with difficulty in throwing off. He declared:

> I wanted it [the lycée] to be strongly literary in character; I have a liking for the mathematical and physical sciences, for both represent a final, although incomplete application of the human mind; but literature is the human mind itself; the study of literature is a general education that prepares for everything, an education of the soul!

Even today, for the first two years of the three-year course, French is a compulsory subject for all pupils. At the end of two years it must be taken in advance as a subject for the baccalaureate and must be passed, just as a use of English paper had once to be for admission to English universities. Furthermore, philosophy is a compulsory subject in the last year for all pupils. It is therefore plain that the emphasis on the humanities has been retained.

When pupils enter the lycée at 15 they are allocated to either a literary, scientific or technical section. As has already been indicated this nomenclature does not signify that other subjects often reckoned, in the English context at least, to be incompatible, are excluded. The pupil placed in the literary section will still study science. The title of each section therefore represents a "bias" ("une dominante", or predominant field) rather than specialization in the English sense of the term. For the final two years of the three-year course the three options broaden out into five sections (sometimes six if an agricultural option is available): literary, social science, mathematics and physical sciences, mathematics and biological sciences, mathematics and technology. Although there is not an examination such as GCE "O" level, as in England, to be passed, entry to the top class ("terminale") is by the procedures of orientation already mentioned. The top class has, moreover, a number of sub-options within the sections; in the literary sections there are no less than seven of these, including an artistic one.

This structural differentiation is also reflected in the curriculum (see Table 11). For example, although philosophy is a compulsory subject in all

Table 11. Timetable for the terminal class in lycée [age 17–18]
No. of lessons per subject (in brackets, percentage of time per subject)

Subject		Section								
	A Philosophy and Letters		B Economics and Social Sciences		C Maths and Physical Sciences		D Biological Sciences		E Technology	
Philosophy	8	(28.6)	5	(17.2)	3	(10.3)	3	(11.1)	3	(8.8)
History, geography and civics	4	(14.3)	4	(13.8)	3	(10.3)	3	(11.1)	–	
Modern language	3	(10.7)	3	(10.3)	2	(6.9)	2	(7.4)	2	(5.9)
Mathematics	2	(7.1)	5	(17.2)	9	(31.0)	6	(22.2)	8	(23.5)
Physical sciences	–		–		5	(17.2)	4	(14.9)	5	(14.7)
Biological sciences	–		–		2	(6.9)	4	(14.9)	–	
Economics	–		4	(13.8)	–		–		–	
Construction (industrial design)	–		–		–		–		7	(20.6)
Workshop practice	–		–		–		–		4	(11.8)
Physical education	5	(17.9)	5	(17.2)	5	(17.2)	5	(18.5)	5	(14.7)
Compulsory options	[5–] 6	(21.4)	3	(10.3)	–		–		–	
Total	28	(±100)	29	(±100)	29	(±100)	27	(±100)	34	(±100)

Plus voluntary "interest" subjects.
Source: *Le second cycle long conduisant au baccalauréat d'enseignement du second degré: Horaires, programmes, instructions*, Ministère de l'Education, INRDP, Paris, 1975.

sections, the content of the subject will vary according to the particular section. Thus in the literary option the syllabus is fairly general; in the mathematics and biological sciences option the philosophy taught includes an element of physiology; in the mathematics and physical sciences option, there is some consideration of the philosophy of science. This raises an issue of some importance. In the English system the pupil studying classics at GCE "A" level, if he wished to study mathematics as well, would normally have to take an examination in mathematics exactly the same as that sat by the future university mathematician. In France the syllabus and level for compulsory subjects vary according to the section in which they are studied. Furthermore, by a system of "weightings" ("les coefficients") of marks some subjects count for more than others in the award of what is essentially a "certificate" rather than a "subject" examination. The total of "coefficients" is twenty. Thus, for example, in the literary section the mathematics paper has only a weighting of two, as compared with five in the mathematics and physical sciences section. Not only philosophy and mathematics are compulsory subjects in all sections. So also is a modern language. Mathematics in the social science section is biased to the applications of the subject to that particular field, with statistics and probability occupying a prominent position in the syllabus. Furthermore, in all except one section history, geography and civics, grouped as one subject, must be taken in the examination. There is also a test of physical education, except for the medically unfit.

Apart from French, which has nevertheless been studied right up to the end of the previous year, six subjects are therefore examinable for the baccalaureate. In the light of current discussions — one might almost write perennial discussions, because such arguments have been going since at least 1959 — concerning the reform of the GCE "A" level examination, this breadth of studies is notable. The principle of a broad general education is maintained to the end of secondary schooling because it is still believed that it will impart a "residue" of lasting value. One definition of "culture générale" has been: What remains when all else has been forgotten ("Ce qui reste quand on a tout oublié"). Yet the English system of specialization has at least the justification that it is followed by a shorter first-degree course than in most European countries. And the breadth of French secondary education may be impugned on the strength of the large "drop-out" that occurs at the end of the first year of university.

The content of the lycée syllabuses is discussed elsewhere, but a few general criticisms must be mentioned here. One move that has up to yet met with no success is the attempt to introduce interdisciplinarity. This has encountered opposition from specialist teachers, who may feel that their own subject is threatened. The "single-subject" approach has indeed been attacked, however, on philosophical grounds. It has been argued[4] that the syllabuses as they stand represent a predominantly nineteenth-century Positivist view of knowledge. Knowledge, according to this view, is synthetic, a matter of successive sense-impressions which, since they are a necessary condition for the formation of concepts, are best transmitted in a linear sequence. But the enforced constraint of linearity presumes strict boundaries to exist between disciplines. Hence, it is argued, the undue insistence upon the autonomy of each subject in French education and the consequent disregard of the connections that link areas in the structure of knowledge. Hence also the dogmatic nature of the programmes, to the detriment of a more modern view, allegedly more appropriate, that knowledge has become "relativized" and must be considered as only provisional in nature. Confusion is compounded by the encyclopedism that still characterizes many of the syllabuses, because the pupil is capable of apprehending only a part of the totality of knowledge. The process of the acquisition of culture is therefore dependent on the capacity of the pupil to absorb logical but independent sequences of facts and ideas in great profusion and as disconnected entities. Psychologically, it is held, this can lead to the establishment of "mental sets" which distort the vision of the world as it really is. Such a danger is, of course, not only apparent in France.

Encyclopedism has been condemned many times in regard to the lycée curriculum. M. Sarrailh, a former Rector of the University of Paris, once referred to "programmes démentiels", meaning not only the "over-burdening" that occurred in individual subjects but also the overall load of subjects. This, although it has progressively lessened, has not been entirely eliminated. Nevertheless, the French have set their faces firmly against specialization in the English sense. Table 12 represents a summary and approximate comparison of the percentage of time devoted to various

[4] Cf. Suzanne Citron, *L'Ecole bloquée,* 1971, pp. 36 et seq.

areas of the curriculum by French pupils studying in their final year in a section with an arts and science "bias" as compared with sixth-formers studying for GCE "A" level. (In the table relating to arts subjects the "humanities" in England are deemed to include "general studies" and most "minority time" options. In France the "humanities" are counted to include history, geography and civics as one subject, a modern language, and philosophy.)

Table 12.

	Arts (per cent)			Science (per cent)	
	France	England		France	England
Languages	52	40	Sciences	27	40
Humanities	32	40	Humanities	31	8
P.E.	8	8	Mathematics	35	20
Private study	–	12	P.E.	7	8
Mathematics	8	–	Private study	–	12
Total	100	100	Total	100	100

Table 12 seems to reveal a vital disagreement as to the kind of education most suitable for potential "leadership élites": "broadness" is opposed to "depth". Yet when a former Minister of Education, M. Fouchet, reformed the programmes in 1965 on the basis of what he termed the three main "axes" of modern culture, the humanist, the scientific and the technical, he was accused of over-specialization. The present arrangement is one that allows for a broad spectrum of knowledge, but the pupil has to pay special attention to one particular "colouring" of culture: the bias or emphasis required for a particular group of disciplines. Fundamentally the dilemma of the academic secondary curriculum at this stage arises from attempting to illustrate and exemplify as many different facets of knowledge as possible, whilst at the same time preparing pupils for the next stage of education or for employment.

CHAPTER 9

The Content of Secondary Education

Educational changes rarely proceed from one cause; nor are all their causes mutually compatible. This is particularly true of the reforms made in the content of French secondary education since 1959. Till then the emphasis in the curriculum had been overwhelmingly on the humanities. Science was accorded only a subsidiary role and technology, the phenomenon that most characterized the post-War world, none at all. French and the classics were granted pride of place, and a combination of subjects that also included mathematics with a modicum of the physical sciences was reckoned to be the ideal combination for the intellectual high-flier. Education was regarded as the training of the mind, the implementation of the principle of "learning to learn". Few concessions were therefore made either to the affective, aesthetic and physical aspects of education. The cult of the intellect remained the supreme goal. Comparatively speaking, despite constant transformations, this still holds good today. Any discussion of the curriculum remains primarily a discussion of the academic subjects of which it is largely composed.

Langevin had drawn attention to the gulf between the school and real life. The Fifth Republic had to redress twenty years of non-reform in the secondary curriculum. The technocrats of the régime, the former civil servants, industrialists and financiers who had become ministers, favoured an injection of "useful" elements into the pattern of studies. Pompidou, the teacher and banker turned politician, and even de Gaulle, son of a Catholic schoolmaster, embraced, albeit with some reserves, as will be seen, the saving virtues of a new educational Utilitarianism.

However, tradition is slow in dying. Although an effort was made to upgrade vocational and technical education at all levels, it was at first agreed that there should be no compromise on the maintenance of high intellectual standards. This position, which postulated that equality of opportunity meant principally the universal accessibility of the "high culture", has had to be modified. Not all pupils were capable of learning classical and modern languages: let some languages therefore be deferred or become optional. But the common lower secondary school would continue, at least for three-quarters of its pupils, to dispense a uniformly academic type of learning. Unlike many English comprehensive schools, with their proliferation of "soft options" for the less clever pupils, the equivalent school in France would offer no more than about a dozen subjects, and mainly intellectually demanding ones at that.

The position of the *classics* has already been touched upon. For Latin, after 1968 Edgar Faure made root and branch changes. The formal study of Latin was deferred until the third year of secondary education. Greek was reserved mainly for upper secondary education as an optional subject. Faure did, however, allow an "initiation" into Latin to be given in the second year, as part of the curriculum for the mother tongue. Equal place was given to the study of Roman civilization, whose values, it was alleged, informed our own; language was to be studied more to highlight French grammar. The deferment of Latin was greeted with approval by the teachers of French, who had felt that the mother tongue had always been put in the shade by the early start made on Latin. Despite the wistful regret of Pompidou himself[1] the classics therefore became the first casualties of "democratization" — a further proof that the school can no longer be held responsible for the inculcation of values in a society which no longer knows which values it possesses.

A second reform much called into question concerned the teaching of the *mother tongue*. The reform plan proposed by Rouchette (see p. 82) had been for primary education. In 1970 the then Minister, Guichard, set up another commission with a wider remit. It was headed by Pierre Emmanuel, the poet. The key position of the mother tongue was pinpointed by Guichard: "The teaching of French is at the heart of the difficulties of the new education and without its being reformed education itself will not be renewed."[2] The powerlessness of the "école du livre" against the overwhelming influence of the "école parallèle" (a term coined in the 1960s by the sociologist Georges Friedmann to describe the effects

---

[1] Pompidou is quoted as saying, "Translation from Latin is an almost incomparable exercise in reasoning", Cf. B. Girod de L'Ain, "Le Latin et la sélection", *Le Monde,* April 8, 1970.

[2] Cf. *Le Figaro,* Mar. 18, 1970, p. 12.

of the mass media upon the young) was seen as related to the teaching of French. This was too narrowly conceived as literature, too little related to communication, to the interests of pupils and to real life. In concrete terms Guichard wanted answers to such questions as the simplification of French spelling, the part that literature had to play, the place of creative activity as compared with the fostering of critical powers and, finally, the line that should be drawn between the acquisition of techniques of expression and cultural and aesthetic education proper. The minister's remit to the Emmanuel Commission was in two parts:

1. *Compulsory schooling.* How to give the pupil sufficient mastery of present-day French, both oral and written? How can the mother tongue contribute to the awakening of the intelligence, judgement, sensibility, taste and imagination? What is the place of literature in the scheme of work?

2. *Upper secondary education.* What answers should be given at this level to the questions already posed for compulsory education? How may creativity of expression be fostered? How should literature — and not solely national literature — be taught?

The reforms provisionally suggested had stressed oral expression, the study of contemporary literature and a move away from the teaching of formal grammar. Creativity on the part of the pupil should be encouraged at all costs, even if niceties such as correct spelling have to be sacrificed. These tentative proposals aroused a veritable furore. The traditionalist Association pour l'Enseignement du Français denounced the "obstinacy" and "fanatical proselytizing" of Pierre Emmanuel.[3] Disgusted at the inability of educationists to achieve a consensus the Commission, after two years' existence, resigned en bloc.[4] Some of its enemies had declared that it wanted to start a cultural revolution on the Chinese model. Nevertheless, despite great hostility, a score of lycées in 1972 adopted new syllabuses on an experimental basis. The programme offered a choice of writers, of which eight out of thirty-eight were of the twentieth century: Péguy, Apollinaire, Claudel, Valéry, Breton, Proust, Gide and Camus. Moreover, a thematic approach, which need not be chronological, was advocated. The essay was played down, and a new emphasis given to oracy.[5] To

[3] Cf. *Le Monde,* Feb. 2, 1973.
[4] P. Emmanuel, *La Révolution parallèle* (Preface), Paris, 1975.
[5] P-B. Marquet, "Quel français, demain?", *L'Education,* May 10, 1973.

traditional French minds, steeped in the intrinsic value of the formal dissertation and the "explication de texte", such innovations were regrettable and represented a watering down of standards.

A special problem is created by the large number of immigrant children. The Sixth Plan envisaged that immigrant families would be arriving at the rate of 20,000 a year. By now there are some 870,000 immigrant children to be educated. More than half these children come, in almost equal proportions, from Algerian and Portuguese families, and Spaniards and Italians, in almost equal proportions as well, account for another third. Thirty-two per cent of these children live in the Paris region, in cramped conditions in furnished rooms, temporary lodgings or "bidonvilles". Their parents are employed in menial jobs in the public services or in the building trade, mainly as unskilled or semi-skilled workers.[6] The problems of educating the children in French are numerous. Should the children be brought up with no formal training in their mother tongue, in order that they may concentrate on the learning of French, since this is the key to the mastery of all other subjects? Should the aim be integration with French children of their own age, or should their own national, religious and cultural identity be respected? At present the policy is for all such children to be kept in school with French children, under the age of 7. Between 7 and 13 the immigrants receive special teaching for 1½ − 2 hours a day in special classes, using materials supplied by semi-government agencies responsible for the teaching of French to foreigners, such as LEBELC and CREDIF.

The unity of the "hexagon" that is France has always been held to be absolutely dependent upon the monopoly of the French language itself. The politicians of the Third Republic had therefore banned the teaching of *regional languages* in schools on the grounds that official recognition of them would impair national solidarity. The experience of the immediate pre-War years when the Breton separatist movement "Breiz Atao" ("Brittany forever"), attracted a marginal number of supporters, and of the War years when a minute Flemish nationalist movement on French soil attracted a lunatic fringe in French Flanders,[7] and above all when Alsace

[6] *L'Education,* May 9, 1974.

[7] E. Dejonghe, "Un mouvement séparatiste dans le Nord et le Pas de Calais sous l'Occupation (1940−1944): Le 'Vlaamsch Verbond van Frankrijk' ", *Revue d'histoire moderne et contemporaine,* XVII, Jan.−Mar. 1970, pp. 50−77.

and Lorraine — the latter comprising many monoglot French speakers — were blatantly annexed by the Nazis on linguistic as well as historical and cultural grounds, demonstrated that the school ban on minority languages had been a wise one. Today, however, concessions have been made for Breton, Catalan, Basque and Occitan ("langue d'Oc") to be taught in schools. (Curiously enough, Occitan was the most popular language among these minority languages in numbers of candidates presenting it at the baccalaureat in 1971.) In Alsace the position is slightly more complicated. Although a German patois is freely used as the spoken language, the basic language, including that of the school, is French. This is a situation almost universally accepted.[8]

In the teaching of *foreign languages* the French have widely adopted the view that the spoken word must have pride of place, and audiovisual techniques, in which the French, with the CREDIF system as it was developed at St-Cloud, were pioneers in Europe, are widely used. A subjective impression is that the French have been more successful in language teaching than the English, in a situation where, in both cases, motivation is understandably low. Controversy has mainly centred round which foreign languages should be taught. Officially the French have tried to diversify their number, and have in particular promoted German as a countervailing element to English. Indeed, one of the most interesting and successful experiments in this field has been the creation of bilingual Franco-German sections in French lycées and German "Gymnasien".

Despite the divergent paths that *history and geography* now seem to be taking, the French have continued to link these two subjects in the school. In 1972 new programmes were adopted, the object of which was "to give an initiation into the contemporary world". At the upper secondary level this note of recency is particularly marked. In the tenth grade ("seconde") the aim is to situate the modern world in relation to the ancient world. The teacher is free to choose from a list of topics in history. In geography the emphasis is on human and economic subjects. In the top two grades the historical field is confined to the twentieth century, which should allow the historical and geographical approaches to be combined.

Civic and social education has always formed part of the curriculum in France, and often linked with the teaching of history and geography. The

[8] Cf. "Déclaration des quatre-vingt-douze universitaires sur le bilinguisme en Alsace", *Le Monde*, Mar. 21, 1972.

recommended method is the "concentric" approach used in geography, starting with a study of the local commune and working up to the study of the State and of international affairs. In the top classes of the lycée the subject is largely concerned with the organization of political life, and particularly with the workings of the Constitution and of democracy. Since 1968 pupils have been encouraged to participate actively in discussing questions. Nevertheless such a programme has been criticized as not being sufficiently related to matters that closely affect today, and in particular the pupil's personal life. One teacher, suspended for going too far in this direction, declared:

> Let us in fact really try to talk with the pupils, let us read with them something other than the compulsory (and debilitating) programme of the sacred humanities. . . . Let us tackle together the problems of today (madness, abortion, prison, sexuality, sport, immigration, military service, the family, etc.).[9]

Such discussion is feared, he said, because it might shake the edifice of the school. Yet in recent years there has undoubtedly been a great shift away from a purely descriptive and institutional approach to civic and social education, which is still continuing. The compulsory study of philosophy, in the top class of the lycée, would also seem to afford an opportunity for discussing many of the subjects that interest young people.

In *mathematics* proposals for reform have been put forward by the Lichnerowicz Commission. These have not aroused the same controversy as other suggestions for updating subject content. The commission adopted the standpoint that mathematics should be considered more as a language and less as a heteroclite collection of elements of knowledge. In order to ensure that this "language" should be appropriate it proposed a revision of the syllabuses every four years. The stress should be on the cultivation of the reasoning processes, leading on eventually to a "methodical apprenticeship to deductive reasoning". The translation into reality of these precepts has not always been favourably received. In particular the incorporation into the programmes of elements of modern mathematics has been criticized, since these tend to emphasize the abstract, treating the subject as a science of relationships almost akin to pure logic. The Ministry has yielded to pressure and admitted that modern mathematics "risks accentuating the tendency of the French mind to

---

[9] Letter to *Le Monde,* April 9, 1974, from M. Hennig, teacher at the Lycée Bichat, Nantua.

abstraction".[10] Exercises of pure arithmetic and relating to concrete situations have therefore been reinstated in the syllabus. There has also been a reconsideration of the place of mathematics in upper secondary education, with the result that as from 1974 mathematics has once again been made compulsory for all candidates, including those in the philosophical and literary sections, at the baccalaureate. This represents a victory for the concept of "culture générale" which held that mathematics, conceived of as a method of reason and order, was an integral part of the education of the cultured man.

In comparison with English schools, the role played by *science* still seems a diminished one. In the first four years of secondary education provision is made only for the biological sciences. The physical sciences are begun only in upper secondary education, and then only as one subject, not separated into physics and chemistry, with the former subject very much the predominant one. However, since 1970 *technology* has been introduced into the lower secondary school and, as teachers are being trained to teach this new subject, should by 1975 be general over the whole country. The subject has been defined as "the critical study of objects and simple mechanisms conceived by men for the satisfaction of their needs". Teachers have been warned against teaching it as a branch of the physical sciences or of applied mathematics. The object is to develop the scientific curiosity of the pupil, to enable him to apply reasoning to scientific and technical mechanisms and to bring his education closer to real life.[11] It is argued that technology is a way of organizing science for use, which is a mental operation requiring as much intelligence as the understanding of science itself. As such it is a part of a general culture for the present age.

Two recent curriculum developments are also worthy of note. The first was the introduction of a "sexual information" content into the programmes. This was in response to the growing concern regarding sexual matters that was felt, although the moral aspects of sexuality are still firmly held to lie within the province of the parents rather than the school. The other innovation represents a relaxation of the central control of the curriculum. As from 1973 all secondary schools have been free to allocate

[10] M. Fontanet, then Minister of Education, at a press conference on Sept. 4, 1973, reported in *Le Monde,* Mar. 21, 1972.
[11] *Educational Policy and Planning: France,* OECD, Paris, 1972, p. 121.

10 per cent of teaching time in any way they wish, instead of following strictly the nationally prescribed programmes. One object of this measure is to give the schools greater autonomy, and also to involve parents in discussion of the curriculum so allocated. Independent work, excursions, visits to places of local interest, remedial work for pupils that have fallen behind, drama: these are some of the ways in which this time has been used.[12]

There is, of course, the danger that having once enjoyed some freedom from central control of the content of education teachers may want more. But the arguments for uniformity remain strong. Ideally what is taught represents the best consensus that can be found as to what the content of education should be at any particular time. Curricular revision works by means of commissions on which many interests are represented, although to English eyes the role of the inspectorate in them appears too influential.

The pattern of the curriculum also presents strong contrasts with England or North America. In lower secondary education the outside observer is struck by the simplicity of the curriculum offerings. There is none of the wide variety of options that characterizes timetables in the English comprehensive schools. Whilst in upper secondary education the curricular pattern is drawn up either as a function of the future requirements of higher education or related to prevocational and vocational considerations, in the college of secondary education the majority of pupils follow an intellectually demanding, rather academically oriented course. It will be recalled that in this school tracks I and II are for the more able children, whilst track III is designed for those whose first necessity is to make up for the deficiencies in their primary education. Side by side with this vertical division is the horizontal one which splits subjects into "basic" and "curiosity-awakening" subjects. Table 13 shows the distribution of time in "sixième", the lowest class of the common lower secondary schools, for tracks I, II and III, and for "troisième", the top class in the same schools, for tracks I and II.

Several points seem worthy of comment. The English observer notes the absence of religious instruction, the one subject that by law must be taught in all English schools, and the one subject that is strictly forbidden to be touched upon in French State schools. One notes at the lower age

---

[12] Information collated from: *Le Premier cycle: Horaires, programmes, instructions*, Ministère de l'Education Nationale, SEVPEN, Paris, 1971.

Table 13.

		"Sixième"		"Troisième"
	Subject	I and II	III	I and II
I.	*Basic disciplines*			
	French	6	8	5
	Mathematics	4	4	3
	Modern language	4	3	3
	Technology	–	–	2
II.	*"Curiosity-awakening" disciplines*			
	History and geography	2½	–	
	Civic and social education,	1	4	3
	Biological sciences	2	–	1
	Art	1		1
	Music education	1	3	1
	Handicrafts	1		1
III.	*P.E. and sport* (includes one afternoon)	5	5	5
IV.	*Option: one* subject to be chosen from the following (3è only):	–	–	–
	Latin	–	–	4
	Greek	–	–	3
	A second modern language	–	–	3
	additional teaching in the first modern language.	–	–	2
	Total number of lessons*	27½	27	27–29

*A lesson lasts from 50 minutes to 1 hour.

the dominant position of the mother tongue and the diminished role ascribed to science.

Critics of the comprehensive principle in England have complained that the intellectual content of secondary education is being diluted. French inspectors who have visited English secondary schools have indeed been struck by the allegedly non-intellectual character of much that is taught.

In England the child that cannot do a foreign language will be offered European Studies. No such easy compromise is allowed in France. The French have patently tried a different formula. Within lower secondary education they have maintained traditional barriers but have tried to make lateral movement from one track to another easier. They have tried at the same time to preserve the high intellectual quality of their former élitist system. Time alone will show whether the programmes and methods they have used will justify their contention that this is possible. They have avoided offering easy options. At the beginning the teaching body were on the whole unsympathetic to the concept of the common school, but many are now reconciled to it as being a real step towards the democratization of the education system.

CHAPTER 10

The Baccalaureate

The climax of "long" upper secondary education in the lycée is represented by the baccalaureate examination ("le baccalauréat"), which at
present serves not only as a secondary school-leaving certificate but also as
a passport to higher education. In recent years the form and content of the
examination have been the subject of endless discussions and in the de
Gaulle era alone it underwent half a dozen changes (as compared with the
school certificate examinations in England which were last changed in
1951 and which, despite similar endless discussions, seem likely to survive
unchanged until at least 1980). But the baccalaureate has had a continuous
history of change ever since its inception in 1808, when it was started by
Napoleon. It has been traditionally the first degree of *higher* education,
conferring on the holder the right to style himself "bachelier-ès-lettres" or
"bachelier-ès-sciences", a right incidentally more frequently exercised by
proud writers of French textbooks in England than by those to the
manner born. As a title it has given some confusion in foreign countries. In
Napoleonic times the examination was entirely oral and candidates were
examined by a committee in groups of eight. Examiners voted for or
against candidates passing by means of black or white balls cast into a bag.
In 1821 an individual interrogation was substituted for the group oral
examination. In 1852 the Minister of Education of Napoleon III, Fortoul,
decreed that there should be written examinations in French composition
and in Latin translation and composition. Failure in French entailed
failure of the whole examination. Fortoul also divided the baccalaureate
into an humanities and a science option, the famous "bifurcation" which
aroused such controversy. But by then criticism of the examination was
frequent. In 1869 Cournot could already write prophetically of "the great
sickness of the baccalaureate which has had and will have such a disastrous
influence on the studies of our country".[1] A few years later Sarcey, the

[1] Quoted in J. Capelle, *Contre le baccalauréat.* To this work and its companion
study, *Pour le baccalauréat,* by J. Cornec, both published as one volume (Paris,
1968), I am indebted for much of the information given.

123

dramatic critic, termed the examination "the death of studies in France". By then, however, it had become a national institution. Attempts to convert the examination into an internal test proved abortive. The schools were not trusted to be impartial; above all the secularists did not agree to delegating to Catholic schools the right to confer this "first degree" of the University. In any case the right to award qualifications of all kinds has been one of the jealously guarded privileges reserved to the State alone.

Before the last war the reliability of the examination had been much called into question by the findings of a special body, the Commission française de l'Enquête Carnegie.[2] Bonnard, the notorious Vichy Minister of Education, issued a circular regarding the baccalaureate which read almost like a counsel of despair: "No matter how great the effort one makes to reduce the element of chance which enters into . . . competitive examinations, this element inevitably remains to a certain degree, and merely corresponds to what is always found in the tests that life offers."[3] It is perhaps the only uncontested educational statement he ever made. After the war the Langevin—Wallon commission was plainly worried about the examination. Writing undoubtedly with the baccalaureate in mind its authors postulated a change:

> Examinations at all levels must be of a new kind which separates tests of knowledge from the evaluation of abilities. At the end of a course examinations must be a means of verifying the whole of the course and not give rise to a limited preparation based upon a limited syllabus. By repeated testing one must try to probe the whole of what the candidate has learned, as well as his abilities, by eliminating chance as much as possible.[4]

This statement is interesting, because it does not suggest the abolition of the baccalaureate, but its use in a dual role, diagnostic and prognostic, and because it seems to open the path to continuous assessment.

Yet although there has been a progressive elimination of formal examinations from French education and their replacement by the "orientation" process described previously, which is in effect a type of continuous assessment, the existence of the baccalaureate was not called into question in the 1959 reforms. The fact that it is a "certificate" rather

[2] Cf. R. R. Dale, *From School to University,* London, 1954, p. 141.

[3] Quoted in J. Cornec, *op. cit.,* p. 32.

[4] The complete text of the Langevin-Wallon Plan (1947) is given in: *Groupe français d'éducation nouvelle, Le Plan Langevin-Wallon de réforme de l'enseignement: compte-rendu du colloque organisé par le Groupe français d'éducation nouvelle et la Société française de Pédagogie,* Paris, 1964.

than a "subject" examination makes the process of change difficult organizationally, particularly with the enormous upsurge in the number of candidates. Critics of the standards achieved have been numerous, particularly in higher education: one need only cite Dean Zamansky, of the former Paris Faculty of Science.

In 1959 a small step towards equality of opportunity was taken when the "second chance" examination, held in September for those that had failed the previous June, was abolished (only to be temporarily reinstated in 1965 when the authorities yielded to the pressure of bourgeois parents). It was not unreasonably held that the interval of the summer holidays only permitted useless cramming, which favoured those rich parents who could afford to pay for expensive summer tuition for their children. In 1960 the scope of the examination was widened by the introduction of technological and social science options into the system. Until 1962 the examination was still, somewhat like the General Certificate of Education, in two parts, although only one year lay between them. Then the first part of the examination was abolished and replaced by an internal "probationary" examination. This was then also abolished in 1964 and for it was substituted an orientation process that takes place at the end of the penultimate year. It would seem that the way had been cleared for the total abolition of the examination as a whole.

This, however, was not to be. By 1964 the baccalaureate had become a serious political issue. Mme Durry, a Sorbonne professor and a former director of one of the "écoles normales supérieures", declared that the university "faculties were littered with incompetents" who had just scraped through the examination and had exercised thereby their right of access to higher education.[5] A few months later M. Pompidou, then Prime Minister, was to allude to "those badly licked into shape creatures who constitute the majority [sic] of those who pass the baccalaureate",[6] a statement which aroused indignation in the pre-1968 generation of students at the time. Already fears that selection was to be introduced had induced Fouchet, the then Minister, to appear on television to announce the abolition of the first hurdle, Part I of the baccalaureate, and the reinstatement of the "second chance" session previously referred to. These can only be considered as sops to the bourgeoisie, for whom the

[5] Reported in *Le Monde*, Aug. 23, 1964.
[6] Speech in National Assembly, May 19, 1965.

examination had become a sacred cow. The sociologist Georges Gusdorf characterized the situation as follows:

> It is clear that in the reality of French life and by universal suffrage the baccalaureate has indeed been raised to the dignity of a myth. This myth, at first particular to the middle bourgeoisie, is today claimed by society as a whole. For a classless society is, as we know, a society in which everybody is bourgeois, so that the present democracy tends to consider the baccalaureate as one of the sacred rights of man and of the citizen. The content of the examination itself matters little. What counts in the eyes of public opinion is the label. The teachers who confer this label try desperately to defend it against an inexorable devaluation. Their resistance — which is nonetheless useless — is very understandable: by defending the baccalaureate they are defending the very last remains of prestige which cling to them, in a society which accords them hardly any esteem. A strike action at the time of the baccalaureate represents the ultimate weapon of the teaching body, its only means of drawing attention to itself by provoking national catastrophe.

It has indeed been claimed that the baccalaureate had become one of the instruments of Gaullist political action, a weapon used by the government to placate the bourgeoisie. Indeed any attempt to remove the privilege of access to higher education that passing the examination confers is calculated to stir middle-class parents to wrath, as well as the students, who for once make common cause with "les croulants" of the older generation. There is little doubt that the French bourgeoisie have failed to appreciate the full educational consequences of what democratization means. It postulates that the road to success must be a meritocratic one. If the poor can "rise" in society, others must "fall". Since the leading positions in society are limited in number the scions of the comfortably wealthy must, if their talent is inadequate, content themselves with a lower rank in society than that of their parents. It is for this reason, because the baccalaureate holders are still overwhelmingly middle class, that any attempt to restrict access to higher education is regarded by that class as a serious threat.

This dual function of the baccalaureate as a secondary leaving qualification and a passport to higher education lies at the heart of the controversy that surrounds the examination. Ranged against its use as an automatic qualification for the university have been such eminent names as Pompidou, Zamansky, Raymond Aron, the sociologist and political commentator, Jean Capelle, the former educational administrator, and Bertrand Schwartz, an influential background figure in the formulation of French educational policy, and perhaps, de Gaulle himself. On the other hand, most primary and secondary teachers, grouped in unions within the powerful Fédération de l'Education nationale, which comprises more than 450,000 teachers and educational administrators, have consistently set their face against any form of selection. In November 1967 the Fédération passed a resolution declaring that "the democratic concept is not to select in order to exclude, but to help and evaluate in order to promote and orient. Moreover it is not possible to judge the abilities of holders of the baccalaureate before they have had any contact with higher education." SNESsup, the most important university teachers' union, as well as the student unions, have also made common cause against selection.

In the face of this opposition the room for manoeuvre for successive governments of the Fifth Republic has been small. However, one small limitation has been imposed: a total mark of twelve out of twenty (twenty is the usual marking maximum in France) is necessary to achieve university entrance; a mark of ten out of twenty is necessary to secure a secondary leaving certificate. Every minister of education since 1968 has attempted to grasp the nettle of this problem, but none has as yet succeeded.

Public interest in the examination is intense. Examination questions are published and commented upon in the newspapers. The results and their attendant scandals achieve banner headlines. In 1964 there were leakages of certain questions before the examinations in philosophy and biological sciences. The leakage was traced and a girl secretary in the baccalaureate office, who was passing the questions on to her boy friend, was jailed for ten months. A more comical incident occurred in Corsica. After the examination in Latin translation had begun, a group of young researchers not taking the examination were handed the question paper. They promptly went off to a café, made a fair translation of the passage, returned to outside the examination room where they chanted *in Corsican* a correct translation under the windows where their attentive comrades were working. Nevertheless, the examination on the whole works with great efficiency and speed. In 1974, as early as July 19 (a point which English examining boards might well bear in mind) the national results were published in *Le Figaro* under the headline: "Baccalaureate '74: a good vintage." The proportion of successful candidates was given as 64.26 per cent. This is a slightly lower percentage than the passes at G.C.E. Advanced Level. Like the English examination, it is extremely difficult to find any justification for such a low proportion of success as compared with West Germany, where some 95 **per** cent are successful in the equivalent examination, the "Abitur". **If so** many candidates come a cropper it must surely be either because the examination and the syllabuses for it are unsuitable, because the teachers are failing in their task, or because many candidates are not of the requisite intellectual calibre. However, as Alain Peyrefitte, the luckless Minister of Education who was in the saddle in 1968, said, the French suffer from "l'examinite", a colloquialism easily translated and readily understandable in English as "exam-itis". As another, more eminent French statesman, M. Herriot, once remarked: "Of all examinations, the most stupid is the baccalaureate." The French, like the English, feel the need to ascribe marks to everything. One observer, speaking of the compulsion to mark everything, avowed that he had heard of marks with a minus quantity, −10, −20, −30, even being awarded in Latin and English and concluded: "It's no longer education, it's a polar expedition." Moreover, just as in England it is notorious that some subjects in the General Certificate examinations are easier than others, so are seemingly some options in the baccalaureate. If the overall French national average of baccalaureate passes in 1973 was 62.80 per cent, in the letters and philosophy option in that year the success rate was considerably higher: 71.78 per cent; in the mathematics and physical sciences option it was likewise higher: 71.82 per cent. On the other hand, in one sub-option, that of earth sciences, in the biological sciences option, only 50.09 per cent gained the qualification. Fluctuations in popularity also occur between the five different examination sections. The philosophy option is now consistently attracting fewer candidates: 10 per cent less since 1969. The social and economic sciences option attracted a modest 12 per cent of those successful, although as elsewhere these subjects are gaining in favour. On the other hand, the technological option — sometimes alleged to be the most difficult of all — attracted only 3.3 per cent of the total number of passes. In contrast, the less esteemed "technician's baccalaureate", which is much more a vocational qualification, attracted increasing numbers of candidates, particularly in the administrative and commercial options. Likewise a computer option started only in 1970 has gained in numbers. Not only some options are palpably easier to pass, but so also is the examination in some academies: in the Caen area in 1973 only 62.1 per cent passed, as against 73.3 per cent in the Strasbourg area. Overall, however, in 1974 almost 200,000 young people satisfied the examiners, of whom some 80 per cent were knocking on the doors of the university in October.

Perhaps the most serious consequences of the open-door policy for higher education that has been persisted in during the post-Gaullist era relate to employment prospects. So long as university education is linked to preparation for employment a surfeit of students will ultimately mean a shortage of jobs. To train students for non-existent jobs, it has been argued, is a formula for revolution. If the university doors remain wide open, at the end of their course only those with the "right connections" will obtain the top posts, a situation which is the reverse of the principle of democratization.[7] Despite this, the percentage of "bacheliers" in the age group has progressively risen, as Table 14 shows.

Table 14.

Year	Percentage awarded baccalaureate
1946	4.1
1950	4.8
1960	11.3
1965	12.0
1975 (projected)	21.0

Although numerous different techniques of assessment have been proposed, the French have relied largely upon the traditional "essay-type" questions in the examination, supplemented by oral examinations and the consultation of the school record in doubtful cases. Thus in the home of intelligence testing, the country of Binet and Simon, there is as yet no multiple-choice test in the baccalaureate; this may appear strange, but is perhaps explicable in view of the stress that the French place upon logical thinking and clarity of exposition.

Where do those successful in the baccalaureate go when they have left school? The high proportion entering university — in 1972, some 85 per cent of the boys and 77 per cent of the girls — has already been indicated. Tables 15 to 20 set out the position in greater detail.[8] Predictably, the

[7] J. Capelle, "L'université face aux problèmes de l'accès à la culture et aux emplois", *Le Monde,* Nov. 30, 1969.

[8] Given in: Note d'Information No. 74—08 of Feb. 26, 1974, Ministère de l'Education Nationale, Paris, 1974.

particular section options followed in the last years of school determine the subject areas studied at university, although the English observer, caught up in the quarrel about "specialization", would do well to note that 5.4 per cent who had studied in the literary or social sciences options were nevertheless admitted to medical schools. As regards girls, it will first be noted that in 1972 more girls than boys passed the baccalaureate. One in ten of the girls whose "bias" in school had been towards science and mathematics nevertheless took up the humanities at the university. Girls holding a baccalaureate in technical subjects overwhelmingly preferred to embark on the study of law or the humanities at the university. The majority of boys entered university at the age of 19. Since 18 is the normal age for leaving school this suggests that some had had to "repeat" a class as they worked their way up to the school or have had to sit the baccalaureate twice. Girls, on the other hand, seem to have experienced less difficulty, since a majority enter the university at 18.

To understand the discontent in higher education that bubbled over in 1968 it has been necessary to look closely at the central function of the baccalaureate as a "sieve" for higher education. The meshes of that sieve seem to be becoming less fine with the result that, as the numbers of those successful continue to increase, the prospect of mass higher education on the American model comes nearer. Perhaps, however, the time has come for an overhaul of university entrance procedures. Eminent voices have been raised against the use of the baccalaureate. Capelle sums up what for him constitute the seven deadly sins of that examination: its instability, its ambiguity, its lottery-like nature, its exaggerated social prestige, the cramming that it occasions, the waste of school time that accompanies it and its inevitable association with the wealthy. Paul Valéry postulated the abolition of all examinations; yet it seems that the baccalaureate will continue to survive so long as Frenchmen continue to believe that the ideal of equality can best be achieved through competitive examinations.

Table 15. Candidates Successful in the Baccalauréat:
Percentage taking each option, 1969–1973

	Letters – Philosophy	Economics and Social Science	Maths and Physical Sciences	Biological Sciences	Technology	Total
1969	47.8	6.2	15.3	26.5	4.2	100
1970	46.5	8.1	15.5	26.0	3.9	100
1971	42.4	9.6	16.7	27.4	3.9	100
1972	40.4	10.5	18.2	27.4	3.5	100
1973	37.4	12.0	19.0	28.3	3.3	100

Table 16. Candidates Successful in the
Technician's Baccalauréat:
Percentage taking each option,
1969–1973

	F	G	H	Total
1969	52.5	47.5	–	100
1970	38.7	61.1	0.2	100
1971	38.8	60.7	0.5	100
1972	37.3	61.4	1.3	100
1973	38.1	60.6	1.3	100

Option F = preparing for employment in the tertiary sector and for technical industrial occupations;

G = preparing for employment in administration and commerce;

H = preparing for employment in the computer industry. (This option was only started in 1970.)

Table 17. "Destination" of Baccalaureate-holders, 1972

	Nos.	Short technological courses (IUTs, etc)*	Teacher training colleges	Preparatory classes for grandes écoles	University	Total entering higher education	Other "destinations" (employment, etc.)
					(per cent)		
Boys	84,134	18.1	3.5	14.8	48.8	85.2	14.8
Girls	100,065	12.5	4.0	5.3	55.0	76.8	23.2

* = Instituts universitaires de technologie (University institutes of technology).

Table 18. Choice of University Subjects in Relation to Baccalaureate

		University disciplines in 1972–1973: per cent					
Baccalaureate Section		Law	Economics	Humanities	Science	Medicine	Pharmacy
Humanities and Social Sciences	boys	36.9	15.8	40.5	0.7	5.4	0.7
	girls	22.7	5.9	65.5	0.5	4.6	0.8
Mathematics and physical sciences and Biological Sciences	boys	3.0	5.9	4.3	40.1	41.3	5.4
	girls	2.8	4.7	11.4	32.4	34.8	13.9
Technology and technicians' sections	boys	32.5	31.7	8.6	21.7	3.6	1.9
	girls	55.1	13.2	20.1	6.1	3.4	2.1

Table 19. Age of Entry to University, 1972: per cent

	17 and under	18	19	20	21	22 and over	Total
Boys	8.7	31.6	35.3	17.8	4.1	2.5	100
Girls	12.8	38.8	30.8	13.3	2.9	1.4	100

Table 20. Distribution between University Subjects According to Sex and Age

	Law	Economics	Humanities	Science	Medicine	Pharmacy	IUT*	Total
Boys:								
18 or under	14.3	7.9	15.3	24.9	23.4	2.4	11.8	100
19	15.6	10.1	15.5	16.3	18.4	2.6	21.5	100
20 or over	17.0	11.8	17.6	13.5	18.3	3.5	18.3	100
Girls								
18 or under	14.0	4.9	39.9	13.2	16.6	5.7	5.7	100
19	18.2	6.2	42.2	9.0	11.6	4.2	8.6	100
20 or over	19.5	6.2	42.6	8.4	9.9	4.2	9.2	100

CHAPTER 11

Pupils and Teachers

According to one French headmaster, M. Bazin, the French pupil is an "helot king, the prison slave to strict rules, submitting to work that he has not desired, yet a king to whom is served tastily prepared dishes". Certainly the régime to which he must submit appears severe by English standards. The comparative size of France means that some 20 per cent of secondary school children are boarders. Although their life is less rigorous now, it is still somewhat Spartan-like. Until recently, after the rising-bell at 6.30 or 7 o'clock, pupils would file into the classroom for an hour's private study. Lessons proper start at 9 o'clock and last until midday. A two-hour break is followed by further lessons until 4.30. Private study is supervised in the evening and bed follows at about 9 o'clock. The grim, forbidding nature of the older lycée buildings, reminiscent of a military barracks, has already been remarked upon, but the pupil has been allowed to escape from such surroundings on Wednesdays, Saturdays and Sundays. He sleeps in a vast dormitory and enjoys scant privacy. He may spend his leisure hours in the "foyer", a kind of general recreation room. If he is a long distance from home he has a local "correspondant" to whom he may turn if he is in trouble. If his parents so desire the parish priest may visit the school and give him religious instruction.

The authorities are very conscious that the gap in extracurricular activities requires to be filled. Hence the recent development of what are known as "school co-operatives". The co-operative is largely run by the pupils themselves and constitutes a kind of federation of school clubs, organizing the activities and preparing the budget for each of them. French educationists have recently perceived the pedagogical value of such a system and have revived some of the ideas of Freinet, who saw in the co-operative a means of inculcating a sense of collective responsibility. Freinet favoured the pupils running their own newspaper, not only writing the contents but also printing and publishing it themselves. Some of his other projects have now also been taken up. He wanted to foster national and international exchanges and to set up "children's parliaments" at local, regional and national level in order to educate the future citizen in the ways of democracy.

The day pupil is hardly much better off than the boarder. He may be in school from 8 to 5 o'clock. Although Wednesday is a holiday, as is Saturday afternoon, the older pupils may have to work on both these days. The very intellectual approach to education, which leads to high academic standards, means that the work load is heavy. In secondary schools class hours may average over 30 a week, as compared with a European "norm" of 24. Competition is acute. Each year a national competition, the Concours Général, is held to determine the best pupils in France in the respective subject disciplines. Public interest is great enough for the results to be published in the daily press, together with interviews obtained from the successful "lauréats".

To compensate for this hard grind, the holidays are longer than elsewhere in Western Europe. The Jesuit tradition of shutting pupils off from the world and supervising them closely during their waking hours was one that survived the Revolution.[1] But holidays, in contrast, may total fifteen weeks a year, with a very long break in summer. Although the school year ends in early July, May and June are often months of disorganized schooling. The "class councils" which decide whether pupils should move up into the next class the following September meet already in May, with the result that pupils afterwards feel that their fate is sealed and cease serious work. Some schools are designated as national examination centres, even for examinations which do not directly concern the school, and teachers may be called away to act as examiners in a different locality. The school is not officially closed but pupils may be sent to a room to work in private study ("en permanence").

Discipline is enforced in France by the special supervisory body now known as "maîtres d'éducation". Teachers who wish to punish a child report him to the "surveillant-général", who assumes responsibility for imposing a punishment and for enforcing it. Although school discipline seems over-strict, once outside the school gates the pupil enjoys great freedom. The teacher considers that his responsibility ends there and

[1] H. Boirard, *Contribution à l'étude historique des congés et des vacances scolaires en France du Moyen-Age à 1914*, Paris, 1971.

would not consider it his duty, for example, to intervene if he saw his tender charges smoking or drinking beer in the nearby café.

In the classroom procedures are more regulated than in England. Every teacher must keep a "cahier de textes" which records the work he has covered with a class and which must be produced to a visiting inspector. Likewise the pupil has a notebook in which he has to record the lessons he has been set to learn or the written homework he has to do. A "livret scolaire" is kept for every school pupil, in which is recorded officially a wealth of detail: prizes, congratulations, official commendations, warnings, "black marks" ("mauvais points"), health, absence, lateness and progress in each subject and in each class. This school record is a key document when the future educational or vocational course of the pupil is considered.

Although school libraries seem somewhat ill-equipped by English standards — the books may even be in locked bookcases — libraries within schools which are reserved for teachers are well stocked, containing equipment and teaching material of all kinds as well as periodicals relating to the teaching of particular subjects. This service is in the hands of a qualified "documentaliste", whose duties are extremely varied, from making available a tape recorder to even typing out occasionally examination papers — chores which in England often fall upon the individual teacher.

The French teacher is even more traditional in his teaching methods than is his English counterpart. A poll carried out as late as 1966 in the Paris area showed that over 70 per cent of teachers lacked all interest in methodological innovations. Rote memory work, blackboard and chalk, pen and paper, have been the sole adjuncts of the kind of magisterial exposition or Socratic questioning which constitute still widely used teaching methods. One French observer, Vial, declares that: "For the majority of classes, the methods have in practice hardly changed for half a century, and this is particularly true for upper secondary education."[2] But perhaps the same might be said of the traditional sixth form in England.

Despite the massive reforms that have taken place, the half million teachers, conservative as regards their profession although to the Left politically, have felt profound disappointment. They have seen their

[2] J. Vial, "L'Evolution des méthodes pédagogiques en France", *International Review of Education*, 1967, vol. 3, p. 316.

function changed from being the proud transmitters of knowledge and culture to one they consider inferior, that of mentor, guide and counsellor. This has led also to a loss of prestige, of esteem within the community. This is true of both primary and secondary teachers. The reasons for this, as will be seen, are social as well as professional.

The status of "instituteur" (primary teacher) really dates from the Revolution. In a measure of 1792, inspired by Condorcet, it was decreed that "les personnes chargées de l'enseignement dans les classes primaires s'appelleront instituteurs" (people entrusted with teaching in primary classes will be called "instituteurs"). Under the Napoleonic régime, because the Emperor had expressed little interest in primary schooling, the recruitment of the "instituteur" had remained very much a matter of chance and often he would carry out a number of other tasks, some secular, such as that of public crier, shepherd or cobbler, some sacred, such as that of cantor or lay cleric charged with teaching the catechism or plain chant, in addition to his school duties.[3] Even in 1833, when Guizot introduced the law reforming primary education, he was still performing two jobs, although he might by now be engaged in innkeeping or shopkeeping.[4] In any case, he was still regarded as an inferior person, intellectually reputed to be between the mayor and the parish priest, but lacking the prestige of either. It was the establishment of a national system of primary education in the 1880s that conferred status upon him. The primary teachers have often been described as the missionary order of the Third Republic, its "black Hussars". In a predominantly rural France the new teacher became the natural ally of the secular authorities, in particular the mayor, whose secretary he often became, against the Church, with whose school his own was often in competition. His pivotal position in village life made him the friend and counsellor of the local farmers and peasants. When only a few children advanced beyond the primary school he enjoyed power. It was he who would coach the poor pupil for entrance to the primary teacher training school so that he in turn might become an "instituteur" and — who knows? — rise even higher on the educational ladder than his teacher. It was he who prepared the less bright children for the all-important "certificat d'études primaires" ("certificate of primary education"), the leaving qualification which opened up minor posts in the

[3] Ponteil, *op. cit.*, p. 98.
[4] *Ibid.*, p. 204.

civil service and thus enabled the son of the agricultural labourer to escape from the drudgery of the land. Today this lever of influence has gone. All children go on to secondary education and a largely urban population wants for its children, not a lowly qualification, but the baccalaureate. Historically the very success of the primary teacher in training a literate population has diminished the esteem in which he has been held.

The downward decline in the influence of the "instituteur" may be traced back to the Second World War. It was alleged that whereas in 1914 he had set an example of patriotism and courage, in 1940 he had turned and run in the face of the enemy.[5] This charge, sedulously put about by the Pétain government, was made plausible by the undoubted fact that pacifism and anti-violence had indeed characterized the attitudes of the primary teachers' union, the Syndicat National des Instituteurs, between the two wars.[6] Despite this, some "instituteurs" played an outstanding part in the Resistance during the Occupation.[7] Notwithstanding the cloud that somewhat unjustly hung over them the primary teachers staged something of a comeback in the Fourth Republic. In the 1951 elections 126 "instituteurs" comprised 3.8 per cent of all candidates — 12 per cent of all Socialist and 10 per cent of all Communist ones. Thirty-one of them were elected to the National Assembly and comprised 5.7 per cent of the total. However, the 1958 elections marked their political eclipse, when the population rallied to de Gaulle and a Centrist, if not a Rightist, view of politics. From being a force invariably consulted by politicians when major decisions had to be taken, the Syndicat National des Instituteurs was left out in the cold by de Gaulle, as when, for example, a settlement of the Algerian question was in the offing. This diminution of prominence in political life has perhaps been accompanied by a corresponding diminution of interest in politics by the primary teacher. Of his residual political beliefs, probably secularism is the predominant one: even though he may be a Catholic, "a primary teacher cannot but be secularist without placing himself outside the collective body of primary teachers".[8] Thus, from being the protectors and guardians of Republicanism, many teachers have

[5] H. Amoureux, *La Vie des Français sous l'occupation,* Paris, 1961, vol. II, pp. 339–340, note.

[6] R. Paxton, *op. cit.,* pp. 37 and 155.

[7] P. Delanoue, *Les Enseignants: la lutte syndicale du Front Populaire à la Libération,* Paris, 1973, pp. 191–310.

[8] J.-L. Crémieux-Brilhac, *op. cit.,* pp. 567–568.

become indifferent and have abandoned the "Hugolean doctrine of the upward march of humanity". Their voice no longer counts in affairs as much as it once did.

This may also be in part because the primary teachers are on the whole a disunited body. There are, it seems, "clans among the different generations, between qualified and non-qualified teachers, between those who have been to a teacher training college and those who have not, between those who teach the little ones and those who teach the older ones".[9] The division between trained and untrained is indeed significant.[10] It was reported that in 1973 some 80,000 teachers (both primary and secondary) were unqualified, recruited as "auxiliaries".[11] In primary education there are many peripatetic teachers, women "remplaçantes", who may, after four years' service and after having taken a part-time teacher's certificate, be recognized as qualified. Likewise there is the category of women "suppléantes", who act as supply teachers and are paid by the day. The increasing feminization of primary teaching – today it is estimated that 73 per cent of all primary teachers are women[12] – may also account for the disarray of the profession.

Yet the role of the young female primary teacher in many of the isolated communes of France remains a key one. At the age of 19 or 20 she may arrive in a remote village, feeling very lonely. She may face an all-age, one-class school. She must be on her feet all day, the sole person to look after the children during the recreation and at lunchtime. In the evening she may also run an evening class. She will also have to fill in a mass of documentation. Far from home, she must watch her behaviour

[9] Ida Berger and R. Benjamin, *L'Univers des instituteurs: étude sociologique sur les instituteurs et institutrices du Département de la Seine,* Paris, 1964, pp. 94–95.

[10] The content of the training course for primary teachers is at present being changed. Under the new system, intending teachers enter the école normale (teacher training college) after having passed the baccalaureate, at about age 18, and follow a two-year course. At present this comprises periods of teaching practice, general and special teaching methods, psychology and history of education as well as a range of courses in the subjects taught in the primary school. The course leads to a "certificate of end of teacher training studies" ("certificat de fin d'études normales" – CFEN) which gives exemption from the "certificate of pedagogical aptitude" ("certificat d'aptitude pédagogique" – CAP). The complete qualification is known by the acronym: CFEN – CAP.

[11] *France-Soir,* May 10, 1973.

[12] *The Times,* Dec 8, 1974: article by F. Gaussen in the "Europa" Supplement, p. xv.

carefully, because it will be severely judged.[13] In return for this austerity of life she receives a modest salary. Similar modest accommodation is provided for her. The obligation on the commune to provide lodging dates back to the Organic Law on education of October 30, 1886. Thus she may find herself, according to the terms prescribed, provided with "a kitchen-cum-dining-room and three rooms with a fire . . . either a cellar or a lumber room serving as a wine-store or a log-store, as well as the use of a lavatory", the whole attached to the school, which itself abuts on to the "mairie".

The primary teacher's career is more restricted than that of the secondary teacher. He may normally only be appointed within the department in which he has been trained, and will remain in that area for the duration of his professional life, unless special circumstances arise. As with secondary teachers, promotion is by "échelons", or "steps", to each one of which corresponds an index number from which his salary is calculated. The space between "échelons" is variable, so that there is no uniform annual increment. Seniority does, however, give rise to periodic promotion from one "échelon" to another. Quicker promotion than by seniority can be achieved upon the recommendation of the departmental primary inspector. (This is known as "promotion aux choix" and is explained below in greater detail in relation to secondary teachers.) Promotion also means that the teacher can be promoted to a post in a town, instead of remaining in an isolated village. Many primary teachers regard this transfer to an urban area as a very important move, principally because it will bring greater educational opportunities within the reach of their own children.[14] With both feet at last on the bottom rungs of the upward social ladder, they wish their children to rise even higher. Indeed the village primary teacher may aspire, with great expectation of success if he is intellectually gifted and determined enough, to rise through the ranks of primary and secondary schoolteaching to become a university teacher. (The Minister of Education in 1975, M. Haby, was once a primary teacher and finished his academic career as a university teacher.) Because intellectual merit is still an overriding factor, the career is open to the talents far more so than in England.

[13] G. Allan, *Instituteurs et Professeurs,* Paris, 1964, pp. 39–44, quoting from an article by Mme Grappin, published in *Avenirs.*
[14] Crémieux-Brilhac, *op. cit.,* p. 569.

Because of the creation of the college of secondary education a number of former "instituteurs" were recruited to teach the least gifted pupils in secondary education. Although their status has since been regularized, it has now been conceded that non-graduate teachers should teach side by side in this institution with the graduate teacher. The traditional secondary teacher has not looked upon this arrangement with much favour. It represents in his eyes a further devaluation of his prestige. This is in some way connected with the predominance of women teachers, so that the male teacher feels his position particularly threatened. Today 53 per cent of all secondary teachers are women,[15] but the feminization in secondary education has not gone so far as in primary education.

It has been said that secondary teachers are suffering from an identity crisis. When they taught only in the lycée they were accorded the same sort of status as that enjoyed by the local solicitor, the small factory-owner and other local bigwigs. They prepared the children of the local bourgeoisie for the baccalaureate, which was reserved for a social élite. Today, with mass secondary education a reality, with their salaries falling way behind that of their intellectual equals, when it is envisaged that by 1980, 31 per cent of pupils will be passing the baccalaureate, they have lost caste. Secondary teachers no longer have scarcity value. Whereas in the early 1960s a generation born in the war numbered only about half a million per age group and from this number had to provide sufficient teachers to teach an age group of about 800,000, this situation no longer applies. The watershed of teacher shortage is now past. Large numbers graduating from universities now find the way to schoolteaching barred to them.

Paradoxically, the categories of secondary teacher have multiplied. The case of the former instituteur, now teaching the less gifted in a college of secondary education, has already been noted. He is usually seconded for a trial period to this type of school and after a year takes a test of practical teaching. If successful, he may then take a further examination which gives him a qualification to teach this rather special type of pupil.

A second category of non-graduate teacher is known as "professeur d'enseignement général de collège". He becomes qualified to teach the lesser of the two academic tracks in lower secondary education. Those eligible to apply for these posts are students from a teacher training college

[15] Cf. Note 12.

who would otherwise become primary teachers; primary teachers who have already had three years' teaching experience; and students who have successfully completed one year of higher education. Thus the minimum entrance qualification is the baccalaureate. Training takes place in a special "centre de formation", one of which is to be found in each academy. The course lasts three years, two years of which are spent following courses in higher education, usually concentrating on two literary or science subjects, and one year of which is spent on teaching practice and theory. The final qualification awarded, the CAPCEG ("certificat d'aptitude pédagogique à l'enseignement de collège"), enables them to teach two or three subjects in a college of secondary education.

The two remaining categories of secondary teacher are reserved for graduates. These follow very different programmes of preparation for teaching. A few sit a competitive examination after one year at the university, success in which admits them to a secondary teacher training institute (IPES: "Institut préparatoire à l'enseignement secondaire"). They are then paid a salary, but are also committed to serve as a teacher for ten years. If this engagement is broken they have to refund at least a part of the cost of their training. They continue their studies for a degree, have some preparatory teacher training courses and prepare for the same examinations as those graduates who seek to enter teaching at a later stage. The degree course chosen must be in one of the subjects approved for secondary teaching (philosophy, classics, French, history and geography, modern languages, mathematics, physical sciences, biological sciences and social sciences). After graduation they sit for the first part of the examination for "the certificate of aptitude for secondary teaching" (CAPES: "certificat d'aptitude pédagogique à l'enseignement secondaire"). This is a purely academic examination, usually taken a year after the degree, in the same subject. But it is highly competitive: in 1974, 45,954 candidates entered for it and only 4022 (8.75 per cent) were successful. If this hurdle is successfully overcome the student enters a "regional teacher training centre" ("centre pédagogique régional"), in which he spends a year before taking the second, practical part of the CAPES examination. During the year he has three successive "practice supervisors" ("conseillers pédagogiques" – usually highly qualified teachers with much experience), spending nine weeks with each one teaching in a school. At the same time he follows a number of lectures and courses relating to school organization, his teaching subject and special topics. He undertakes the observation of one or two school pupils, assisting in counselling and guiding them and in compiling their school records. He has also to write a report on his practice in the various schools.

The last category of secondary teacher, one who stands at the pinnacle of teaching, is the "agrégé". The "agrégé" will have passed the "agrégation", a State competitive examination reserved for those who have already a master's degree. This is an extremely stiff test: in 1974, out of 24,027 candidates only 1096 (4.56 per cent) passed. The best method of preparation for it is to enter the Ecole Normale Supérieure, one of the grandes écoles,[16] although it is also open to graduate teachers in service who have the necessary initial qualifications. The examination consists of an eliminatory written test, followed by an oral examination and the teaching of one or two model lessons before an examining board. Until recently success in the examination entitled the agrégé to be appointed for life to a particular lycée without any further teacher training. Since 1970, however, the successful agrégé now undergoes some on-the-job training during his first year of teaching. The gap in practical knowledge typified the view that once was widely held that teaching required high academic quality; the rest — training of any kind — was mere "dressage", a term used to describe the training of circus animals.

So great, however, is the demand for agrégés, who have likewise to sign an engagement to serve the State for ten years, that today few of them enter school teaching, except to teach in the special post-baccalaureate classes preparing candidates for the "grandes écoles". Those with a scientific qualification may be offered posts in the Centre National de la Recherche Scientifique to undertake research. Others may enter universities as assistant lecturers with the hope that after obtaining further qualifications they may receive a permanent appointment there. In fact, in 1973—1974 out of a total of 240,483 full-time secondary teachers only 12,142 (5 per cent) held the "agrégation" qualification.

Those who hold the CAPES qualification or the agrégation — "professeurs certifiés" and "professeurs agrégés" — usually teach in the lycée.

A special category of teacher is employed in technical education. Recruitment and training follows a similar pattern to that for general education. The higher teacher training institution for technical education

[16] Cf. Chapter 16.

(ENSET: "Ecole normale supérieure de l'enseignement technique") offers a four-year course leading to the agrégation for the most highly qualified technical teachers.

Despite the keen competition to enter the higher categories of secondary teacher, there are large numbers of unqualified teachers employed. One teacher in four employed in the lycée is unqualified in the sense that he has not the CAPES qualification – although 84 per cent of these unqualified, known as "adjoints d'enseignement", do hold a degree in the subject they are teaching. One teacher in two employed in colleges of secondary education and one in three in technical education also lack the final teaching qualification. The "adjoint d'enseignement", like the "maître auxiliaire" and the "contractuel" (two other categories of temporary teachers) have few rights. Such teachers have no guarantee of tenure – the Ministry can dismiss them one day and take them back the next – no paid holidays generally, no pension rights, although some may have been teaching for years. Their salary in some cases is only half that of their established colleagues: they may earn less than an unskilled worker in the Renault car works.[17] They are often given the most difficult classes to teach and may have to teach subjects in which they are completely unqualified.

In the 1960s the unqualified teacher fulfilled a very useful role. In the 1970s he is rapidly becoming supernumerary as the numbers wishing to enter teaching increase – largely, it must be admitted, because more attractive possibilities of employment have diminished. Many are, of course, trying to achieve a qualification in their spare time by taking the necessary competitive examinations. Some two-thirds of all unqualified teachers have no more than three years of teaching experience. The main professional association, the Fédération de l'Education Nationale, is trying to improve their lot by persuading the authorities to allow them paid leave to prepare for the examinations. The situation whereby there are many wishing to become qualified teachers, when the schools still lack *qualified* teachers, and when would-be entrants are nevertheless rejected after examination, can only be described as paradoxical. The explanation would seem to lie in the high academic standards that are implacably imposed, coupled with a belief that any open "back-door" entry to the teaching profession would offend against the principle of equality.

[17] *Le Monde*, May 1, 1973.

Meanwhile there is much dissatisfaction with the methods of training teachers. The Caen Colloquium of 1966 wanted a form of training that would comprise three main elements. The first element would deal with communication skills: how the teaching "message" should be put over effectively. An analogy was drawn at the time with the special courses offered in the "grandes écoles" for future business and industrial executives on communication skills. A second element would comprise selected topics from the psychology and sociology of education: teaching techniques, special subject method, group dynamics, evaluation and educational technology; child development, class organization and pupil guidance; the aims and history of education and comparative education. The last element would comprise professional training proper and include a year spent in various types of school. The framework for such a course would be provided within the university, in an institute of educational studies. The present system of admission for graduates through an academic examination was condemned. Some practical experience should be required of would-be entrants, and young teachers who later proved unsatisfactory should be dismissed. An enquiry made in 1964 in the Seine area[18] had reported that 60 per cent of male and 45 per cent of female primary teachers had admitted that they had taken up teaching as the profession of "last resort". It was argued that more rigorous conditions would prevent this occurring.

The Amiens Colloquium of March 1968 took up many of the recommendations of the 1966 meeting.[19] It went farther, however, in that it recommended that the teaching profession should be unified: all teachers, whatever their academic origins, should be trained in the university, whose training centres should also concern themselves with in-service training. Theoretical courses, whilst necessary, should be subordinated to in-the-classroom training. Even nursery and primary teachers should undertake two years of higher education, followed by two years of professional training. In the early 1970s many other projects for the reform of teacher training have been mooted. (One has been adopted: the age of entry to a teacher training college for primary teachers,

[18]Cf. Note 9.

[19]*Association d'Etude pour l'Expansion de la Recherche Scientifique: Pour une école nouvelle: formation des maîtres et recherche en éducation. Actes du colloque national d'Amiens*, 1968, pp. 317–321.

formerly set at 15, has now been raised until after the completion of the baccalaureate.) The Fontanet proposals of 1974 suggested that training for lower and upper secondary education should be distinct. This idea has been retained in current proposals (1975) formulated by the Minister, M. Haby.

Such recommendations and proposals have not been universally welcomed. Professional associations have been intent on preserving a hierarchy of ranks, signified by differences in working conditions and salary. The highly-qualified agrégé not only receives a greater reward than his less-qualified colleagues but is required to teach only 15 class-hours a week — only 12 if he teaches the post-baccalaureate classes in which pupils are preparing for entry to the grandes écoles. His graduate colleague, the professeur certifié, is required to teach 19 class-hours, as against the non-graduate "professeur de collège", who teaches 21, and the primary teacher who must teach 28. In addition, there are comparatively large differentials in salary scales. The basic salaries for the various classes of teacher, at their maximum, in 1972 (chosen because it was the last "normal" year before inflation occurred) were as follows:

Primary school teacher	£2189 p.a.
Lower secondary teacher (non-graduate)	£2526 p.a.
Qualified graduate teacher	£3389 p.a.
Agrégé	£4294 p.a.

(Conversion rate, 1972: £1 = 11.50 F.)

In addition all teachers receive a residence allowance, the value of which depends on the area; for the agrégé living in Paris it was about £63 per month. Thus the latter, with no responsibility save that of teaching his subject to a very high academic standard for 12 to 19 hours a week, might have had a gross income of some £5050 p.a. — considerably better than a university lecturer in this country in 1972. In addition, if he had children, he would be drawing the very generous family allowances that the State provides for all families. Although teachers are forbidden (under the Law of 1886) to engage in other paid employment or other activities for profit, even during their holidays, they may teach adult education classes and also give private lessons, which are a very lucrative source of additional income.

Since 1972 the statutes governing secondary teachers have followed more closely those applied to other public servants,[20] and thus make them

[20] "Décrets" of July 4, 1972. Cf. also: Y. Daudet, *Les nouveaux statuts des enseignants du second degré*, Paris, 1974.

subject to administrative law. Uniform rules have been established for the recruitment, assessment and promotion of teachers, transfer between posts and the application of a disciplinary code.

Significantly also, the interpretation of the teacher's role has been widened by the statutes. The largest secondary teachers' union, the Syndicat National de l'Enseignement Secondaire (SNES), claims that the new statutes devalue "the concept of teaching and the transmission of knowledge in favour of tasks relating to the 'animation' (of pupils) which lack academic content".[21] Nevertheless, the Joxe Commission,[22] which dealt with the status of secondary teachers, reaffirmed that teachers should play a considerable part in management and organization, extracurricular activities, educational and vocational guidance, and the running of documentation centres and school libraries. The union has continually reiterated that if this is to come about there must be adequate safeguards for the teacher. Overtime must be paid where the hours of duty exceed the normal, and such tasks in addition to the teaching load should not be performed at the expense of standards. Thus class norms should be respected: if a teacher taught a class of over forty pupils his hours of service should be reduced by 1 hour, although the union did accept that where a class fell below twenty pupils the teacher could expect to perform an extra hour's duty without additional salary.

Another important change effected by the statutes has occurred in relation to recruitment. Hitherto the competitive examinations for the agrégation and the CAPES have been the only way in which to enter the cadres of agrégés and certifiés, who enjoy considerable material advantages in comparison with their non-graduate colleagues. Now these non-graduates, under certain conditions, may apply for the status of certifiés without sitting the requisite examinations. Furthermore, the professeur certifié may apply to be promoted to the rank of agrégé without examination. These forms of promotion to higher grades are – and will doubtless remain – very much the exception. But the effect of such changes in recruitment procedures is both to devalue the hierarchy, hitherto accessible only to an intellectual élite, and at the same time to reinforce it – a reinforcement which, incidentally, the Joxe Commission

[21] *L'Université syndicaliste*, p. 7 (Nov. 17, 1971).
[22] *Rapport de la Commission d'Etudes: la fonction enseignante dans le second degré*, Paris, 1972, 104. (Hereafter, the Joxe Report.)

had sought to eliminate by proposing a single cadre of secondary teachers.

The statutes also reasserted the principle of periodical assessment of teachers. The notion that teachers should be "marked" sounds faintly comical to English and American ears. But this marking procedure applies in France to all civil servants, teachers included. In fact, a graduate teacher is awarded two marks. The first, out of forty, is termed an "administrative" mark, and is awarded by the Rector of the academy upon the recommendation of the school principal. The teacher has a right of appeal against this mark. There is no appeal, however, against the second mark, termed the "pedagogical" mark, which is awarded by the general inspectorate and has a maximum of sixty points. The total percentage mark, which is communicated to the teacher, is important for his promotion.

The question of promotion is dealt with in the statutes. The system is one of "échelons" or "steps", and promotion from one "échelon" to another, with a consequential increase in salary, is by merit or by seniority. Promotion by seniority is not so rapid as by merit. There are two merit categories: "au grand choix", which signifies early promotion on merit, and "au choix", which enjoys a lower priority. For the agrégé the échelons of promotion by the three methods are shown in Table 21.

Table 21

Echelon	"Grand choix"	"Choix"	Seniority
From 1st to 2nd	–	–	1
2nd to 3rd	1 year	–	1½
3rd to 4th	1	–	1½
4th to 5th	2	–	2½
5th to 6th	2½	3	3½
6th to 7th	2½	3	3½
7th to 8th	2½	3	3½
8th to 9th	2½	3½	4
9th to 10th	2½	3½	4½
10th to 11th	2½	3½	4½

For salary purposes each échelon represents an index coefficient the unit value of which can be changed by the government according to circumstances. This use of an index is common to all French civil servants and thus ensures a constant relationship of teachers' salaries to those of others. The Ministry draws up a promotion list every year, in the three categories set out above. Thirty per cent of teachers receive early promotion on merit, fifty per cent are placed in the second merit category and the remainder move up only after they have acquired the necessary seniority. Thus an agrégé promoted solely by seniority would take thirty years to reach his maximum salary, whereas one who received early promotion on merit could reach it after twenty years. Since the school principals and, above all, the general inspectorate are the final arbiters of the various categories, it can be seen what power these officials wield in a centralized system.

The new statutes place teachers under the same disciplinary code as all other civil servants. The protests of teachers and, in particular, the largest association of teachers' unions, the Fédération de l'Education Nationale, have been most vehement against this. Ever since the Law of February 17, 1880 the education system had acted quite competently as its own disciplinary body. The code of discipline is quite explicit as to the procedures and sanctions that may be taken. Thus, whilst teachers may hold what personal, political or religious beliefs they choose, they are slightly more restricted than English teachers in expressing them. The new code means that, as civil servants, they have theoretically to be more restrained in their criticism of the government. It must be said, however, that this stipulation has not inhibited them unduly.[23]

The malaise felt by secondary teachers has already been touched upon. They are a disunited body in many respects, divided according to their political allegiance, the type of academic discipline they profess and their position in the hierarchy. The men regard the women teachers as privileged. A married woman, for example, can do all her teaching in the first three days of the week and then be free until the following Monday, if the "censeur" in the school, who draws up the timetable, is sympathetic. The secondary teacher feels very much that he has gone down in the world. At one time he was a "professeur", a title he shared with his university colleagues, one who, with tenure conferred by the passing of the agrégation, was immovable from the chair that he occupied in the lycée, whose main responsibility was to teach his subject to a high level. He would perhaps be working for the prestigious State doctorate, a far superior qualification to the Anglo-Saxon Ph.D., which after a decade of

---

[23] Cf. R. Magnuson, *Law and the Teacher in England and France, Comparative Education* (Oxford), vol. 2, June 1970, p. 91.

hard work would take him into university teaching. The Société des Agrégés would like to keep up these traditions and preserve the élitist position of its members. Although they are continually reproached for their long holidays, the graduate teachers feel that they work hard for an inadequate reward. Apart from teaching, their biggest chore is the correction of pupil's work, particularly in subjects such as French, philosophy and mathematics. Indeed, this occupies 6 to 10 hours a week; the same amount of time is spent in lesson preparation.[24] Although about half give remunerative private lessons, just over a third spend another 6 to 10 hours a week reading to keep up with their subject. A survey showed that their average working week totalled 49½ hours. Nor are they otherwise professionally idle: one in four has published at least one article relating to their subject or to their teaching — a high figure indeed by English standards. As well as being underpaid, they feel little satisfaction in their work. Yet in entering the profession many confessed themselves to be idealists. In enumerating the points they valued in their task, 46 per cent placed their work above all else; 21 per cent valued principally the human relationship with their pupils. Material considerations came much lower in the order of priority: only 8 per cent mentioned security of career, 3 per cent the long holidays and 4 per cent the relative freedom in the use of time.[25]

The lack of assurance is felt most strongly by those who teach in the lycée, particularly among those who teach the "literary" as opposed to the "scientific" subjects.[26] Their uncertainty has been termed "une crise de l'acte pédagogique". Teachers cast themselves in an unfavourable light, accusing themselves of harbouring undesirable traits such as an infinite capacity to entertain illusions, and a lack of realism and practical sense. It must be said that this unfavourable view of teachers is shared by their charges, who reproach them with being too self-satisfied, too formal and lacking in understanding.[27] It is alleged that this disparagement is also shared by the general public. In post-war films the "professeur" is viewed as a comic figure, a "pauvre type", a pathetic figure of fun, as in the role played by Fernandel in "Le Caïd". On other rarer occasions he is

[24] Vincent, *op. cit.*, pp. 82–83.
[25] Joxe Report, p. 31.
[26] Joxe Report, p. 25.
[27] Vincent, *op. cit.*, pp. 45–47.

portrayed, as in the "Quatre Cents Coups", as a consummate bully of the young.

Thus many secondary teachers feel themselves to be a bunch of "déclassés", living in a sociological ghetto. Indeed they are shown to be a group living in a "closed world".[28] In the small town their life is scrutinized with the same severity as that reserved for the young primary teacher in the remote village. Twenty years ago the local professeur was stigmatized if he drank his apéritif on the café terrace. Even today the young female teacher who frequents the same "bal populaire" as her older pupils is looked at askance. This social isolation is often reinforced by their origins: 23 per cent are themselves the offspring of teachers. Twenty-six per cent marry within the profession.

Status is, of course, an amalgam of many considerations. The secondary teacher feels a certain humiliation at being "marked" for teaching ability by the general inspector, despite the very high mark that is often awarded — up to 100 per cent for the very good teacher. On the other hand, a mark that is merely 64 per cent is felt in some way to be disgraceful.[29] The lycée teacher would not, for example, feel hostile to receiving in-service training, but would prefer this to be given by his colleagues rather than by inspectors or experts in educational psychology. He accepts the system of promotion to senior appointments by promotion from his own ranks, but rejects an idea that has been floated in ministerial circles of appointing schools principals and their seconds-in-command, the "censeurs", from managerial cadres without any experience of teaching. The rank and file teachers likewise object to appointments in the Ministry of Education going to non-educationists drawn from the ranks of the Inspection des Finances.[30] They are acutely conscious that their numbers have swollen unduly. In 1900, 6500 agrégés comprised the whole secondary teaching force. In 1972 that same force comprised 10,000 agrégés, 55,000 other graduate qualified teachers, 70,000 former primary teachers, and 35,000 temporary teachers, making a total of some 235,000.

In matters concerning their profession they feel that their opinion counts for too little. They are a shade less secularist than they once were: only 24 per cent think the State should have a monopoly of schools,

[28] Crémieux-Brilhac, *op. cit.*, p. 575.
[29] Vincent, *op. cit.*, p. 245.
[30] *Ibid,*, p. 244.

although 42 per cent think that Catholic schools should be denied State subsidies.[31] One of their bitterest resentments is that much of the process of reform, particularly during the de Gaulle era, was carried out without their being consulted. Even today their attitude to the Ministry that controls them is ambivalent: they protest when the central administration takes decisions and criticizes it when it fails to do so. They are against any infringement of "traditional liberties". They will unite against "inadmissible intervention" by parents' associations in school affairs; against primary teachers, whom they accuse of "imperialism" by seeking to gain a foothold — as they have in fact succeeded in doing — in the secondary schools; against their colleagues in higher education when there is any suggestion that the post-baccalaureate classes preparing candidates for entrance to the grandes écoles should be taken out of the lycée and made part of higher education. Yet they enjoy more autonomy in their teaching than the foreigner thinks: the many ministerial circulars they have theoretically to obey can be interpreted liberally, and often are.

On the whole, they remain conservative in educational matters, whatever political colour — and this is usually tinged with red — they wear out of school.[32] This conservatism has been remarked upon many times. Raymond Aron characterizes it as having causes which are "manifold, psychological, sociological".[33] Their conservatism is linked to their reluctance to accept any devaluation in the difficult qualifications they have so laboriously acquired, which they interpret as an attack upon "standards". They are, in fact, the prototypes of "la culture universitaire" which "expresses a clinging to abstraction, which is not only a refuge from the 'harsh imperatives of real life' ('la vie concrète') but also a protest against the rise of the technological producers of wealth, a disputation with the new order".[34] This conservatism is therefore their hallmark, although only 8 per cent of their number are politically active. A few, particularly those associated with two well-known periodicals, the *Cahiers Pédagogiques* and *L'Education*, are reformist. Today, however, more teachers are becoming aware of their lack of contact with real life. They have complained that one of their new duties is to steer pupils into the

[31] *Ibid.*, p. 216.
[32] R. Brechon, *op. cit.*, p. 28.
[33] Raymond Aron, 'Quelques problèmes relatifs à l'enseignement', *Archives européennes de la sociologie*, 1962, p. 121.
[34] Vincent, *op. cit.*, p. 237.

right kind of employment, but that they lack the expertise to do so. Thus since 1971 a pilot scheme has been operated for teacher volunteers to spend a period of up to a year working in factories and businesses.[35]

The decline in the political influence of the secondary teacher parallels that of the primary teacher. In pre-war politics men such as Herriot and Daladier, both secondary teachers, rose in the Radical party to the highest office. Later, other teachers — Mollet, Bidault and Tietgen — were to achieve equal distinction. Indeed the Parliaments of the Fourth Republic included just under a hundred secondary teachers, half of whom were Socialist or Communist and about a quarter Christian Democrats.[36] Despite the eminence reached by Pompidou, the Fifth Republic has not looked so favourably upon its secondary schoolmasters.

Before concluding, it is necessary to touch upon the position of teachers' unions. These had a struggle to establish themselves. The Law of 1884 granting certain categories of workpeople the right to organize themselves in trade unions did not include civil servants and thus also excluded teachers. Although teachers formed local groups to discuss professional matters it was not until the Law on Associations (1904) that civil servants were granted the right to create groupings of professional interests. This gave the seal of approval to the development of the local groups of teachers, known as "amicales" — "friendly societies" — which had now begun to organize nationally, particularly after the Dreyfus Affair, in order to spread the doctrines of secularism and Republicanism.[37] By 1924, during the Prime Ministership of Herriot, civil service unions were legalized fully. After the interlude of Vichy, when all trade unions had been banned, this right was embodied in a law in 1946. The pre-War Fédération Générale de l'Enseignement changed its name to the Fédération de l'Education Nationale (FEN), a change that signified its intention to recruit not only teachers, but all those employed in the educational system.[38]

Today the FEN comprises some forty unions, including teachers at all levels of education as well as other categories such as cooks or nurses who

---

[35] Enseignement: retour à la vie,' *L'Express,* Nov. 7, 1971.

[36] Vincent, *op. cit.,* p. 301.

[37] Crémieux-Brilhac, *op. cit.,* pp. 599 et seq.

[38] For an account of the origins and development of teachers' unions cf. J. M. Clark, *Teachers and Politics in France. A Pressure Group Study of the Fédération de l'Education Nationale,* Syracuse, New York, 1967, pp. 1–21.

are also employed in the educational field. Total membership numbers 450,000, which makes the FEN the largest member of the trades unions' central body, the Communist-dominated Confédération Générale du Travail (CGT). Within the FEN the largest union is that for primary teachers, the Syndicat National des Instituteurs (SNI), with over 300,000 members. The political stance of the SNI is social democratic, described for historical reasons as "de tendance autonome" and dedicated to a policy which is not only democratic, but reformist, secularist, anti-Communist and educationally conservative.[39] Although the "autonomistes" within the SNI just command a majority, the next largest grouping, styled "Unité et Action", is more sympathetic to Communist ideas; there are also one or two extreme Leftist groupings. The second most important member of the FEN is the secondary teachers' union, the Syndicat National de l'Enseignement Secondaire (SNES), with 80,000 members, with a majority grouped within the caucus "Unité et Action" and, since 1967, reflecting a Communist-dominated alliance of the Left, united in opposition to the Gaullist and neo-Gaullist régime and, in particular, to its educational policies. Another "tendance" particularly evident in SNES is that of the "Ecole émancipée", which may be described as "gauchiste", i.e. as part of an extreme Revolutionary Left encompassing Trotskyites, the so-called "cercles rouges", the Ligue Communiste, Maoistes ("L'Humanité rouge") and the anarchists – the protagonists of Danny Cohn-Bendit and "le situationnisme". The "Ecole émancipée" is in the tradition of Revolutionary syndicalism and harks back to the early years of the century, when the pacifist position of the union incurred governmental hostility. There is also a considerable social democrat grouping within SNES. The third most important union within the FEN is the Syndicat National de l'Enseignement Supérieur (SNESup), which recruits teachers in higher education and is Communist-dominated. However, most teachers remain apathetic as regards the political activities of the union to which they belong. In a recent survey only 41 per cent of secondary teachers considered that unions should occupy themselves with national issues other than education, although there was overwhelming support for the view that unions should speak out about educational reform as well as defend the material interests of their members.

Other teachers' unions have different affiliations, although, somewhat

[39] J.-C. Guérin, *La FEN. Un Syndicat?*, Paris, 1973, p. 45.

surprisingly, the Catholic Syndicat National de l'Enseignement Chrétien is linked to the FEN and thus to the Communist CGT. The rival to the CGT, the Confédération Française et Démocratique du Travail (CDFT), attracts the allegiance of the Syndicat Général de l'Education Nationale (SGEN). The CFDT is Socialist in its orientation. The Syndicat National Autonome des Lycées et des Collèges (SNALC) is affiliated to the Confédération Générale des Cadres. There are also a number of small independent unions which are not linked to any wider confederation.

Within the members of the teaching profession, however, the FEN remains predominant. In the 1969—1970 elections to the "commissions paritaires", the bodies that discuss matters such as transfer of teachers from one area to another and are composed of union officials and government representatives, the FEN won 56 out of the 73 seats. It retains close links with other organizations that relate to teachers' welfare, as well as with the secularist Ligue de l'Enseignement. It is itself whole-heartedly committed to the secularist principle, which has become identified with the Republican ethos and ideology. Some Left wing critics have seen in this out-and-out secularism a prop of the capitalist system. Writing as far back as 1884 Jules Guesde declared:

> The alleged secularization of the school on which the bourgeois Republic prides itself is only the substitution of one religion for another. It is the capitalist faith which is to be put in the place of the Christian faith, for the greater security and profit of our economic and political exploiters.[40]

According to Clark, also subsumed under secularism are "rationalism, humanism, tolerance".[41] Certainly these characteristics pervade the dogmas of the FEN and hence the whole State educational system.

On certain matters the unions, regardless of their political leaning or nominal affiliation, will unite. Thus, at the recent "rationalization" of the position of the large body of unqualified teachers, the unions presented a united front to the Ministry. On the other hand, pupils' "strikes" tend to provoke discordant reactions. The Debré proposals of spring 1973, which at first threatened to change to the disadvantage of the student population their position regarding military service, looked at one time the occasion for a new 1968. The lycée pupils, although not immediately affected, struck. They refused to attend set lessons, but put on "counter-courses" in

---

[40] Quoted in Guérin, *op. cit.*, p. 44.
[41] Clark, *op. cit.*, p. 31.

their schools. The SNES, Communist-dominated, saw the causes of their action as relating not only to military service, but also to what they considered to be outdated syllabuses, old-fashioned teaching methods, the lack of "relevance" of the curriculum, shortages of equipment and narrowing job opportunities. The union therefore supported the militant lycéens, as it had done on previous occasions.[42] On the other hand another union, SNALC, condemned the "atmosphere of hatred, intolerance and physical and intellectual violence" that pervaded the schools: they considered the striking pupils to be motivated by a "red fascism". Thus there is by no means unity between the unions on all issues.

Nevertheless, the hostility of teachers generally to what must be styled the de Gaulle reforms has been one of the most striking facets of the last fifteen years. Politically most teachers were opposed to the manner in which the general acceded to power. They disliked his solution to the problem of subsidies to Catholic schools, one of the first issues that the new régime dealt with. They felt they were disregarded in the vast changes in the educational system that were set in train. Their status was, they felt, lowered, their salaries diminished relative to other professions. They did not like the kind of technocratic society which the new régime installed. They clung to their old ways. Some entered the political lists against him; others became embittered and then indifferent. The old order, reaching back to 1789 and then the idealism of Jules Ferry, was broken up in just under a decade. But the dreams embodied in the Charter of the Resistance and in the Langevin-Wallon Plan remained unrealized. Teachers felt cheated of their inheritance.

[42] *Le Monde,* April 13, 1973.

CHAPTER 12

Social Factors in Schooling

If political factors have been decisive in determining educational reform, the social factors to which they are linked have not weighed negligibly in the balance. Inequalities springing from a variety of causes have been acutely perceived, and have originated the demand for "democratization". The increase and distribution of population have profoundly affected schooling, as has the flight from the countryside and the increasingly urban lifestyle of Frenchmen. The result has been a revolution in social, cultural and economic attitudes which has modified traditional ways of education.

An enquiry carried out in 1964 by INSEE,[1] entitled "Formation, qualification professionnelle", presented a broad picture of the degree of social mobility as shown in Table 22.

In 1964 the picture was therefore one of comparatively little upward movement. Education had not yet become an agent of competitive mobility. Indeed under 20 per cent of established industrialists and big business executives had then received any form of higher education. Already, however, a new class of leading cadres, technicians and administrators was arising. Thus, among the under 30s, 78.4 per cent of engineers had a qualification of higher education; 89 per cent of heads of companies ("présidents de gestion") had a similar qualification, and over half of these had in fact graduated from a "grande école". Throughout the 1960s this tendency to require a university education for the leading positions in society was in fact accentuated. (It must be remembered, however, that, because educational success is so linked to social class, the insistence upon the "passport" afforded by higher education may in fact work against social mobility: the comparatively uneducated, who formerly qualified "on the job", are thereby excluded from access to élites.) Nevertheless, how far the broadening of educational opportunity has been

[1] Summarized in Fournier, *op. cit.*, p. 301.

Table 22

For 100 children from:	The new distribution is (%):		
	Upper	Middle	Working
(a) the upper class (5.4 per cent of fathers, comprising industrialists, owners of large businesses, higher administrative cadres, and members of liberal professions)			
43 per cent remain in it	2.3		
44 per cent pass to middle class		2.4	
13 per cent pass to working class			0.7
(b) the middle class (26.4 per cent of fathers, comprising white collar workers, lower army and police cadres, artisans, small businessmen, artistes)			
48 per cent remain in it		12.7	
11 per cent pass to upper class	2.9		
41 per cent pass to working class			10.8
(c) the working class (68.2 per cent of fathers, comprising farm workers and owners, blue-collar workers, including foremen)			
77 per cent remain in it			52.4
21 per cent pass to middle class		14.3	
2 per cent pass to upper class	1.5		
Totals (for a new generation)	6.7	29.4	63.9

paralleled by a broadening of social opportunity cannot as yet be exactly ascertained. Certainly, however, one condition for remaining or moving into the upper classes would seem now to be a good education. "Sponsored mobility" is no longer sufficient.

The "social demand" for longer schooling may reflect an awareness of this new condition of success.

Initially, however, the expansion of schooling owed more to demographic factors than to a greater desire for education. Sauvy is categorical that in this respect population increase was the key factor. At the March 1968 census France had 49.8 million inhabitants; its population had increased by 1 per cent annually since the war. Despite a fall in the birth rate since 1965, there have still been over 800,000 children born every year. The proportion of young people aged under 19 is about 32 per cent, and in 1968 approximately one-third of these were still in full-time education, a fraction that has continued to grow. These statistics show how difficult in physical terms it was to carry out sweeping reforms as well as provide the requisite number of school places. There was much overcrowding in schools. Sauvy,[2] however, maintains that this could have been prevented. He declares that the French have preferred to use their resources to bring about a rise in the standard of living here and now, to the detriment of the potentially greater rise that might ultimately have occurred if more provision had been made for schools. This may well be another straw in the wind indicating that the nation has taken a more instrumentalist view of culture than hitherto, since education must now compete for resources against cars and roads and other physical "goods".

The distribution of population has also affected the provision of schooling. The policy of the Third Republic of providing a primary school in every commune was certainly an ambitious one, but it was also wasteful of resources in modern terms. Today, of the 38,000 communes, two-thirds have less than 500 inhabitants and only about 3000 more than 2000 people. Although rationalization of primary education has occurred, in 1970 there were still 7000 rural schools with less than fifteen pupils on the roll. Some mayors are so worried that the local school may have to close that they deliberately recruit for local jobs, such as in forestry, men with large families. Despite this, the abandonment of the countryside continues. It is said that every Parisian remains a peasant at heart, but the young people who pull up their roots have no intention of returning to the farmsteads that their ancestors may have tended for generations. By 1968 over 70 per cent of Frenchmen lived in towns. Despite the measures of "deconcentration" the Paris conurbation, with over 8 million inhabitants, comprises just under one-sixth of the national population. Depopulation has occurred in the western parts of the Massif Central, whereas the Mediterranean coast, the Rhône valley, Haute-Savoie and the Haute-Garonne have become growth areas.[3] Whereas Napoleon could cover the

[2] Cf. A. Sauvy, *La Montée des jeunes*, Paris, 1959.
[3] W. D. Halls, "Les effets de l'urbanisation sur l'éducation française", *International Review of Education*, 1966, vol. 4, pp. 461–469.

whole territory of France by setting up one secondary school in each "département", the Fifth Republic has had to build many secondary schools at a time when the population has never been more mobile. Furthermore, urbanization creates a demand for longer schooling, so that the massing of people in towns has meant the need for better educational facilities.

The educational ecology of France has been transformed, moreover, by easier communications. When secondary schooling was given only in a distant town, the "chef-lieu" of the département, which the agricultural worker rarely visited, it was less likely that he would send his son — the question hardly arose for girls — away from home to board. Such a move would not only deprive the family of the child's company, but also of his labour in the harvest-field or on the farm or smallholding in general. At each holiday the parents would be increasingly aware of the social and cultural "distance" that was progressively separating them from their son. Today, such considerations hardly apply. Not only are schools strategically sited by the "commission de la carte scolaire" in Paris, but a network of school transport assures that virtually all children are within a 40-minute ride of a secondary school. The farmer, grown richer, increasingly resembling the industrialist or businessman, no longer shrinks from sending his children away to board, although he may well prefer a Catholic college to a State lycée.

Nevertheless regional variations, not always rationally explicable, still exist in the rates of school attendance. With the notable exceptions of the Paris area and Brittany, Northern France has less full-time attendance rates than does the area south of a line drawn from Besançon to La Rochelle. A tentative explanation may be that employment possibilities have always been poorer in the South, where parents prefer full-time schooling rather than unemployment for their children. Thus even sparsely populated areas such as the Hautes-Alpes have high attendance rates. And in Britanny this also holds good, where, perhaps because of the strength of Catholicism, larger families are the rule.

France as a whole did not become aware until the mid-1960s of the extent to which social, cultural and economic factors affect the progress of children in school. It is now acknowledged that the preponderant determinant in educational attainment is the quality of the home background, and that disadvantagement starts in the primary school. It has been shown that children of industrial workers are more frequent "grade-repeaters" than others. One survey reported that by the end of primary school 35 per cent of such children had already been kept down at least one year, and 16 per cent two years.[4] Likewise children from broken and disturbed homes tend to under-achieve in school. Indeed, the success of pupils at the end of primary education correlates highly with social class, as Table 23[5] shows.

It can be seen that on the basis of school record and assessment the percentage of excellent and good pupils, who constitute 41 per cent of the whole, is considerably higher than this figure among children with fathers who are employed in the liberal professions and the intermediate and higher cadres. Moreover, other statistics show that this success on the part of more fortunate children confirms strikingly the teachers' opinion of such children's abilities.[6]

However, some progress towards the equalization of opportunity has been made during the decade 1953–1962 (i.e. three years after the introduction of the Gaulle educational reforms) (see Table 24).[7]

Table 24 shows not only that the numbers entering academic secondary education had increased (from 30 per cent in October 1953 to 55 per cent in September 1962) but also that children from lower socio-economic categories had increased considerably in number — although proportionately they were still grossly under-represented as compared with more favoured social groups.

French research has also established that the extent of parental income as such affects a child's success in school less than does the cultural or educational qualifications of the parents. The child's level of attainment depends upon the assistance he can be given in the home — not so much upon the amount of help, as upon its quality, which is clearly dependent

---

[4] A. Sauvy and A. Girard, "Les diverses classes sociales devant l'enseignement': mise au point général des résultats", *Population* (Paris), Mar.–Apr. 1965, p. 230. Cf. also M. Gilly, "L'influence du milieu social et de l'âge sur la progression scolaire à l'école primaire", *Bulletin de Psychologie*, No. 257, 1967, pp. 797–810.

[5] A. Girard and H. Bastide, "La stratification sociale et la démocratisation de l'enseignement", *Population*, July–Sept. 1963, p. 439.

[6] P. Clerc, "La famille et l'orientation scolaire au niveau de sixième", *Population*, Aug.–Sept. 1964, p. 447.

[7] Compiled from A. Girard *et al.*, "Enquête nationale sur l'entrée en sixième et la démocratisation de l'enseignement", *Population*, Jan.–Mar. 1963, pp. 39 et seq.

Table 23

Father's occupation	Pupils' attainment (per cent)					
	Excellent	Good	Average	Fair	Poor	Total
Wage-earning agricultural	5	27	35	23	10	100
Independent agricultural	10	32	32	19	7	100
Industrial worker	7	27	34	22	10	100
Artisan, small tradesman	10	33	34	16	7	100
White-collar worker	11	33	34	16	6	100
Intermediate cadres	21	43	25	8	3	100
Liberal professions	17	38	33	10	2	100
Higher cadres	22	40	28	8	2	100
Total (per cent of working population)	10	31	33	18	8	100

Table 24

Father's occupation	Per cent entering branches of secondary education reserved for brighter children		
	Oct. 1953	Sept. 1962	Per cent increase
Wage-earning agricultural	13	32	19
Independent agricultural	16	40	24
Industrial worker	21	45	24
Artisan, small tradesmen	39	66	27
White-collar worker	45	67	22
Intermediate cadres	81	84	3
Industrialists and businessmen	68	85	17
Liberal professions	87	93	6
Higher cadres	86	94	8

upon the education that the parents themselves have had.[8] Such an "educogenic" family will also be more ambitious for its children, a fact which motivates their aspirations considerably. What Bourdieu has described as a certain cultural capital and ethos is transmitted from one generation to another in such families.[9]

The sociological findings from studies sponsored by the Institut National d'Etudes Démographiques and carried out in the early and mid-1960s corroborate conclusions already reached in other industrial countries. It is a moot point whether, if they were replicated a decade later, they would produce the same results, since conditions have changed considerably. But committed sociologists such as Pierre Bourdieu are sceptical that French schools, as at present constituted, can compensate for social disadvantagement. He regards the concept of the school as a "liberating force" as a myth. On the contrary, it is basically a conservative element, because it treats inequalities arising from social "facts" as natural. He seems to share Christopher Jencks' view that the school of itself cannot bring about a more equal society. Nevertheless, there are reasonable grounds for assuming that schooling now gives greater equality of opportunity, which, expressed in France under the clumsy term of "democratization", has been the declared goal of every reform since 1959 and is the express objective of the Sixth Plan.

In any case, democratization in France has expressed itself educationally in a very special sense. It has meant, as has already been seen, the attempt "to universalize the historical norms of a learned culture" which was formerly the prerogative of a very narrowly based social élite. According to Castel and Passeron, this insistence upon the transmission of the high culture has been one factor that has militated against the success of educational reform.[10]

In one important respect, the educational equality of the sexes, France seems to have taken the lead in Europe.[11] Although the Revolutionaries had posited that women should be treated equitably as regards education,

[8] See note 4, p. 215.

[9] P. Bourdieu, "L'école conservatrice: les inégalités devant l'école et devant la culture", *Revue française de sociologie*, vol. VII, 1966, pp. 325–347.

[10] R. Castel and J. Passeron (eds.), *Education, développement et démocratie*, Paris, 1967, p. 237.

[11] Cf. Michèle Tournier, "Women and Access to University in France and Germany (1861–1967)", *Comparative Education* (Oxford), vol. 9: 3, Oct. 1973, pp. 107–119.

it was not until 1861 that the first baccalaureate was awarded to a woman. In 1867 a woman first achieved a university degree. The law passed by Camille Sée in 1880 made secondary education more generally available to girls. After 1918 the most active educational feminists had been the young "Sévriennes", the "agrégées" of the Ecole Normale de Jeunes Filles de Sèvres, which had been founded in 1881. After the Second World War the social welfare laws and the shortage of teachers and administrators helped the feminists, although they were opposed by the "grand corps" of the civil service, by businessmen and the Church – the last had as its slogan "the mother in the home" ("la mère au foyer"). However, between 1945 and 1967 the proportion of women in the universities rose from 33 to 44 per cent. At a lower level, that of the baccalaureate, parity had almost been achieved between the sexes. The comparative Table 25 shows how far France is in advance of its neighbours in this respect.

Table 25. Qualification for university entrance

	Per cent	
	Boys	Girls
France	51	49
Belgium	61	39
Federal Republic of Germany	64	36
England and Wales	64	36
Italy	67	33

In 1970 the last educational bastion in France fell to women. The élitist Ecole Polytechnique threw open its doors to girls for the first time, this despite the fact that in higher education girls usually tend to choose literary and linguistic subjects rather than technology.

Bourdieu and Passeron,[12] despite the efforts at reform, regard the French educational system as merely one that reproduces the existing social structure, a view which is generally shared by the Marxist sociologists. It has even been argued that in a technocratic society such as exists in France and other countries of Western Europe this system of "reproduction" is inevitable. Touraine[13] conceives knowledge as a capital

[12] P. Bourdieu and J. Passeron, *La Reproduction: éléments pour une théorie du système d'enseignement*, Paris, 1970.
[13] A. Touraine, *Le Communisme utopique*, Paris, 1968.

good. As knowledge evolves only those with a high level of education can keep their knowledge up to date. The less well educated gradually see their stock of knowledge become outdated. The result is that only the educational élites can maintain their position in society. The others would require some form of lifelong education ("éducation permanente") in order to do so. Thus the controllers of the education system have the whip hand.

It could indeed be argued that facilities for adult education have been provided only half-heartedly, although the new laws on technological education passed in 1971, with provision for release from employment, go some way to remedy earlier deficiencies. In the past few years massive efforts have been made. The Ministry of Labour alone runs 165 specialized vocational training courses in 135 centres, and the Conservatoire National des Arts et Métiers has recently opened a further forty centres. In addition Radio Télévision Scolaire-Promotion runs some twenty-five further training programmes a week for adults. These and other measures may eventually break the cycle of "reproduction" of élites.

Yet other measures have been brought in to cope with specifically economic handicaps. In 1973 it was estimated that a child embarking on his secondary school career might cost his parents as much as 350 F. (then about £32). In the first two years textbooks might be supplied free, depending upon the area, but exercise books, a protective overall ("un tablier") which is worn as a kind of uniform, sport kit, school transport, lunches, art material and compulsory insurance must all be provided. However, financial awards are made to necessitous secondary children, and their value in real terms has increased over the years. It is realized that poor parents will be reluctant to keep their children beyond the compulsory leaving age unless they are compensated in some way for the loss of earnings this entails. Support of poor working-class children at the upper secondary level is thus recognized to be essential if a greater proportion of them are to enter the university later. The network of school transport is well organized: at present a million children take advantage of "le ramassage scolaire". But there are grumbles because it is usually not free and a third of the cost has to be borne by parents. On the whole, however, it may be said that financial considerations weigh less now than they did.

Nor have health aspects been neglected. There are now many open-air schools for delicate children; "lycées climatiques", located by the mountains or the sea, are one original feature of French education. The system whereby in the lower classes one-third of the time is spent in open-air activities has also paid dividends in improving health. There are also numerous facilities for normal children: "snow classes" ("classes de neige"), "countryside classes" ("classes vertes"), "seaside classes" ("classes de mer"), installed in appropriate centres, receive groups of children for a period of two or three weeks at a time. Progress on the medical front over the past fifteen years has been remarkable.

For "latch-key children" of secondary age, who would otherwise roam the streets until their parents returned from work, supervised private study facilities are provided after the end of lessons proper. Children of "travellers" and migrants can receive free tuition through the Centre National de Télé-enseignment. In primary schools no homework may officially be set, so that children from poor homes should not be placed at a disadvantage. In innumerable small ways attempts have genuinely been made to equalize opportunity. It is now realized that educational disadvantagement is likely to end up producing juvenile delinquents. In a study of young offenders placed in special institutions ("l'éducation surveillée") Guy Villars[14] found that few had attended a nursery school, many had entered compulsory schooling late and had been obliged to repeat at least a year of primary school. They then found themselves as Tritons among the minnows, placed among pupils much younger than themselves and rejecting school and its values. Eighty-six per cent came from "inadequate" families, over half of which lived in poverty, huddled together in squalid and overcrowded conditions. Villars concludes that "the school environment is the crucible in which react the amalgam of personal deficiencies and pathogenic family factors".

The social climate in France is of course no more favourable to education than it is elsewhere. It was a primary teacher who first used the term "parallel school" ("l'école parallèle") to describe the educative (and diseducative) forces of the mass media. The expression was popularized by Georges Friedmann in a series of articles in *Le Monde* in 1969. The press, cinema, television, radio, records, books and pictures exert great affective

---

[14] G. Villars, *Inadaptation scolaire et délinquance juvénile.* T.I. *Des écoliers perdus.* T. II. *L'Organisation du désordre,* Paris, 1972–1973 (Thesis for a "doctorat d'état").

power upon the young teenager. Whereas the school was once the sole provider of such stimulation, today the pupil has a wide choice, and sometimes a range of superior technical quality to choose from than he enjoys in school. This leads to discontent.

Such discontent may be rational or irrational. Dissatisfaction with the traditional forms of schooling found violent expression in 1968 and has been a constant source of apprehension to the authorities ever since. They find the pupils' tactics difficult to deal with, particularly since they are often supported by parents or teachers. Although the ringleaders may be suspended or even expelled, this does not seem to act as a deterrent. Dissidents may be required to sign a solemn pledge not to offend again before being readmitted to lessons. In extreme cases a school may even be closed for a week or two. The situation is more complex than in England, because some of the oldest pupils may be really well past university age. Furthermore, the lowering of the age of majority to 18 in 1974 conferred on certain pupils rights which are sometimes incompatible with the rules necessary for running a school.

How young people view the kind of society that they are growing up in is difficult to ascertain, because the evidence is conflicting. A report made by INSEE in 1970[15] speaks of the contradictions perceived by young people between what adults suggest is good for them and what is the reality of life today: the gap between the two is often too large for them to bridge. It is reported that among the under-25s there are 600 deaths by suicide each year. On the other hand, an earlier report[16] dating from 1967 paints a much rosier picture of the attitudes of young people. The overwhelming majority (96 per cent) are glad they live when they do and are pleased to be French (82 per cent). The multiplicity of their views on what would make them happier suggests that they labour under no insuperable disadvantages. In descending order, the following are mentioned as giving greater happiness: an interesting job (13 per cent), a better salary, improved leisure facilities, friendship, success in studies, more freedom, possession of a car, ability to travel more (3 per cent). The mention of the desire for a more interesting job may be connected with another fact reported: more young people were working as unskilled and

[15] Reported in: *Le Figaro*, Jan. 31–Feb. 1, 1970.
[16] *Rapport d'Enquête du Ministère de la Jeunesse et des Sports*, Paris, 1967. (Known as the Missoffe Report.)

untrained labourers than in the working population as a whole — although some may have been merely filling in time before doing their military service.

The overall picture that emerges of the social context of education is one that seems to typify industrial societies everywhere. The same causes of educational disadvantagement are apparent. The same malaise exists among young people. The same remedies are being tried. But in France, as elsewhere, no one has as yet found definitive solutions.

PART IV

THE POLITICS OF EDUCATION

CHAPTER 13

Politics and Education 1958—1968

The Constitution of the Fifth Republic promulgated on October 4, 1958 heralded a chapter of educational reform. The student revolt of 1968, which failed to become a revolution, marked after ten years a watershed in educational change. It was not till then that "root and branch" reforms became a possibility.

The "decade of the General" began and ended in an atmosphere of revolution. It was on an educational issue — the subsidizing of Catholic schools — that the rule of de Gaulle almost foundered before it had properly begun; it was a crisis engendered in the educational system — the pseudo-Revolution of May — that precipitated his final personal eclipse. Few domestic questions dominated the years between these events so persistently as that of education. We must first ask why this was so.

Ten years of non-reform lay between the Langevin-Wallon Plan and the foundation of the new Republic. An élitist two-track system had survived all assaults upon it. Most children benefited only from elementary schooling; the privileged few passed on to the lycée. Educational facilities in rural areas seldom went beyond the minimum legal requirement. Technical education was a neglected field. Catholic schools, which nevertheless educated a fifth of the nation's children, were deteriorating through lack of funds. The post-War "bulge" in the population had begun to affect the primary schools in 1952 and by 1958 increased numbers were reaching post-primary education. A new "social demand" for education contributed to what Louis Cros called "the explosion in the schools". Objectively — and this the technocratic-minded politicians that de Gaulle gathered round him saw clearly — the way to economic stability and future growth lay through the creation of a more highly qualified work force, which only education could ensure. Finally, de Gaulle himself, although no Jules Ferry dedicating himself to the education of the people, was after all the son of a Catholic schoolmaster and recognized the legitimacy of the rising level of aspirations.[1] The urgent need for action nevertheless precluded the working out of a coherent plan, with the result that despite later attempts to order reforms logically, successive Ministers of Education were forced to act empirically, reacting to situations rather than controlling them.

During the brief interregnum of absolute power before the 1958 Constitution came into effect de Gaulle governed by decree. Thus it was that the last Minister of Education of the Fourth Republic, M. Berthoin, succeeded in pushing through a modest reform which was nevertheless a basis for further changes. The Berthoin decrees of January 6, 1959 had not to be submitted to the National Assembly for approval — and Parliament had proved a stumbling block when reforms had been proposed on previous occasions since 1945. The measures as a whole did not arouse much hostility, or indeed much interest, at the time. The public's mind was occupied with other matters.

In contrast, the flare-up in the "religious question" did. After the interlude of Vichy the secular nature of the State had been reaffirmed and subsidies to private schools had been withdrawn once more. The Marie Law and the Barangé Law, both passed in 1951, gave modest aid to Catholic schools: the first extended to Catholic pupils' eligibility for State scholarships awarded to those in need; the second granted a capitation sum of 1000 (old) French francs per head to be spent on pupils in both Catholic and State schools. In the case of State schools this sum was paid into a special fund administered by the département. In the case of other schools it was paid over to parents' associations, whence it found its way into Catholic coffers.

By 1958 one and a half million pupils were being educated in private, mainly Catholic schools. They comprised 15 per cent of all primary children, 40 per cent of those in secondary and 45 per cent of those in technical schools.[2] Yet facilities in such schools were poor, particularly for the teaching of science, and many teachers lacked formal qualifications. The majority in the National Assembly, which had installed de Gaulle in power, were clamouring that something be done: the UNR, the Indepen-

[1] De Gaulle's views on education are given in his memoirs. Cf. C. de Gaulle, *Memoirs of Hope: Renewal, 1958–1962; Endeavour, 1962 –,* translated by T. Kilmartin, London, 1971. References are to the latter volume.
[2] *Journal Officiel (JO),* Dec. 24, 1959, sessions of Dec. 23, 1959, 3595–3635, gives the full debate.

dents and the MRP (Christian Democrats) were pressing for action. In the very first session of the new Assembly, Michel Debré, de Gaulle's Prime Minister, was taken to task because he had not referred to aid to private schools in his outline of future government policy. Outside Parliament such bodies as the APEL (Association de parents d'élèves de l'enseignement libre) and the Secrétariat d'études pour la Liberté de l'Enseignement, headed by Edouard Lizop, lobbied extensively. By May 1959 380 deputies — more than two thirds of the National Assembly — together with 160 senators, supported their cause. Ranged against them in Parliament were the Socialists and the Communists, supported outside Parliament by the Comité National d'Action Laïque, the main teachers' unions, and the traditional stalwart protagonist of anti-clericalism, the Ligue de l'Enseignement. By the end of January already the Association Parlementaire pour la Liberté de l'Enseignement had extracted a promise by Debré to propose legislation by the autumn. There was a sharp reaction: Bayet, the president of the Ligue de l'Enseignement, wrote to Debré declaring that aid to Church schools "would be the triumph of the spirit of Vichy over that of the Liberation and at the same time an attack on the secularism of the State and the unity of the Nation". The government set up a conciliation commission, presided over by M. Lapie, a Socialist and a former Minister of Education. Its report, published in October 1959, put its finger on the problem which, it said, "resides in the existence of two types of education, not only without contact with each other and ignoring each other, but sometimes in competition and almost antagonistic . . . It is this permanent opposition, too frequently exploited by partisan passions, which is contrary to the national interest." It proposed a system of "contracts" between the government and the private schools which would grant subsidies in exchange for certain controls.

On the basis of this report Debré published the text of a bill. André Boulloche, the Socialist whom de Gaulle had appointed as Minister of Education on January 8, 1959, promptly resigned. He could not accept the first article of the bill, which stated:

> . . . the State proclaims and respects liberty in education ['la liberté de l'enseignement'] and guarantees the exercise of it in private educational institutions which have been opened in accordance with regulations.
> It takes all necessary steps to ensure for pupils in the State educational system denominational liberty and the liberty of religious instruction.

In the private educational institutions which have subscribed to one of the contracts outlined below, education placed under such contractual regulation is subject to the control of the State. The institution, whilst preserving its own character, must give this education with absolute respect for liberty of conscience. All children without distinction of origin, opinion or beliefs have access to it.[3]

Boulloche felt that his conscience would not allow him to administer a law couched in such terms; what he had wished for was a measure that might be a first step towards the total integration of Catholic schools into the State system. Moreover, within the Council of Ministers other "laics" such as Jeanneney had reservations about the bill.[4]

Nevertheless, the bill was tabled in the National Assembly. The debate of December 23, 1959 was concerned with much more than the provision of aid to private schools and recalled the great arguments regarding the relationship between Church and State that had taken place in the same building in the 1880s. Debré urged that France must not be the prisoner of past prejudices; the concept of liberty must include "liberty in education".[5] He granted that in the nineteenth century the State had found it necessary to fight clericalism in order to rid itself of constraint. This was no longer necessary. To be a Catholic was no longer incompatible with being a good Republican. Catholic schools formed part of "the public service of national education" and to nationalize them was no solution. Biaggi, supporting the bill, declared that subsidies would enable these schools to function without charging excessive fees. Thus, as was just, children from poor Catholic families would be able to attend them. The right to teach should not be denied to any who were qualified to do so. Durbet, another supporter of the measure, appealed to the UNESCO Declaration of the Rights of Man, which assigns to parents the prerogative of deciding upon the education of their children. Such a right already existed in Alsace-Lorraine (the special educational régime which has its origins in nineteenth-century Prussian rule allows for the public primary school to be denominational and for some 2 hours a week to be given over to religious instruction). The right also existed in the Islamic territories of

[3] Law No. 59–1557 of Dec. 31, 1959. The text of the law is given in full in: Nicole Fontaine-Garnier, *Un Bilan: dix années d'application de la loi du 31 décembre 1959,* Paris, 1969, p. 337.

[4] J. Chapsal, *La Vie politique en France depuis 1940,* 2nd edition, Paris, 1969, p. 409.

[5] *JO,* 3596.

France — a reference to "metropolitan" North Africa.[6] Another speaker referred admiringly to the fact that subsidies to denominational schools in England had been raised from 50 to 70 per cent "without the slightest protest from the Labour Party".[7] One hard-liner used the debate as a pretext to attack secularism, "which is not neutrality at all, but merely a dogmatic teaching based upon materialism".

The reactions of the Communist and Socialist opponents of the bill were predictable. Billoux, the Communist, declared the measure to be anti-democratic, because "liberty in education is a liberty for the rich". To grant subsidies would mean creating "le peuple catholique et l'autre". For the Socialists Guy Mollet, himself a former schoolmaster, quoted an Encyclical of Leo XIII, Libertas Praestantissimum, which admitted that "the public authorities cannot accord such' a licence ('liberty in educa-tion') to society unless they scorn their duty".[8] To accept money from the State is to surrender part of one's freedom. Mollet quoted a speech made by the Abbé Lemire made in December 1921 in order to support this contention. He recalled the bitterness that still rankled in the Pas de Calais area some forty years later, when the owners of the coal mines had refused to take on miners who did not send their children to Catholic schools. Mollet claimed to be dispassionate. He argued that the Law on the Separation of Church and State (1905) categorically forbade financial aid: "The Republic does not recognize, remunerate or subsidize any religious denomination." The bill called into question not only the separation of Church and State, but the very neutrality of the State. "We are not anti-religious", he went on, "We have never sought to silence the song that lulls human misery". Debré, on the other hand, had harked back to the Occupation, when Jews and Freemasons, excluded from teaching in the State system, had been able to use the private schools in which to find a post and also in which to educate their children. Old enmities, echoes of the Third Republic and the ghosts of Vichy, were revived in the debate. At the end of the day, however, 427 votes were cast for the bill and only 71 against. On December 31, 1959 the bill became law.

The law set out a system of contracts. Schools which did not wish to be linked by contract to the State remained subject to control only in the

[6] *JO*, 3601.
[7] *JO*, 3609.
[8] *JO*, 3607.

matter of teachers' qualifications, compulsory school attendance, the observance of public order and morals, and certain details of health and social policy (Art. II). At the other extreme, schools that so desired could be fully integrated into the State system (Art. III). Primary or secondary schools could, on the other hand, sign a contract of association with the State.[9] Their timetable, the allocation of teachers and the number of teaching hours given must meet with State approval (Art. IV). The school must agree to respect the general regulations of the public educational system in respect of programmes, timetables and methods (Art. V). It must charge no fees, except to boarders (Art. IX). In return the State took over the payment of teachers' salaries (Art. X) and the appropriate public authorities assumed responsibility for the school's running costs. Primary schools, however, had the option of signing another form of agreement known as the simple contract.[10] This stipulated that the time devoted to class subjects must not be less by 20 per cent than the time allocation in the State system (Art. III). The State must approve the timetable, the allocation of teachers and the number of teaching hours given (Art. IV). The school agreed to harmonize its programmes so that pupils might transfer without difficulty from the State to the private system and vice versa (Art. V). In return the State undertook to pay teachers; it would be agreeable to the school charging fees, provided the amount was agreed beforehand (Art. X). The law was to operate for an initial period of five years, although it could be extended for a further three.

As will be seen, the simple contract, which tied the hands of the Catholics less, was the one preferred by primary schools, despite the fact that the contract of association was open to them. But this contract was also rejected by many secondary and technical schools who therefore remained unaffected by the law.

Indeed the new measure was hedged round with a number of qualifications and obscurities. Before a contract could be made with the State it had to be proved that a school had run for five years previously in an efficient manner. But during the period of validity of the law new types of private school were established, as educational structures changed in State schools, and as population shifts occurred. These new schools had

---

[9] The model for the contract of association is given in N. Fontaine-Garnier, *op. cit.*, Annexe VI, pp. 350 et seq.

[10] For the simple contract, cf. N. Fontaine-Garnier, *op. cit.*, Annexe V, 99. 346 et seq.

also to serve the five-year probationary period. Furthermore, Catholic schools had to be shown to be catering for a "recognized need" before they could ask for a contract, but the definition of need was obscure. In any case, even when all necessary conditions had been fulfilled, the law left it open as to whether the State was bound to agree to a contract. Finally, private higher education, such as that given in the various Catholic Institutes, was excluded from the terms of the law.

However, the great nineteenth-century debate about the relationship of education to religion, which had once again been revived, had been settled for at least a decade. It demonstrated that the political "frontier" of secularism had not changed. Gaullists, Christian Democrats and right-wing independent groups lined up against Socialists and Communists, with the Radicals, as always, split on this fundamental issue. The new régime, which claimed that its protagonists represented a "photograph" of the whole nation, had been shown to represent in its majority the traditional clerical and conservative Right. The Catholics accepted their new position with quiet satisfaction, although some extremist pressure-groups declared themselves dissatisfied. On the other side the Comité d'Action Laïque reacted sharply, declaring that the State school was being "assassinated". In the spring of 1960, after the passing of the law, a petition organized by the Front d'Action Laïque collected millions of signatures. Teachers had distributed the petition to their pupils for signature.[11] The advocates of secularism had hardly changed the substance of their objections, but they particularly resented money being handed to private education when State schools were already suffering financially. The Catholic approach had been less dogmatic than on previous occasions when the "religious question" had been raised. They were more inclined to insist on more mundane matters such as the question of social justice for the teachers in their schools and to point out the public utility of the existence of private schools at this juncture — for it is certain that, had not the private system been given the means to continue, the State schools would have been overwhelmed by the influx of new pupils. For the new government the passage of the law was a triumph. They had acted, as Meynaud remarks, as they were to act in the future, on the basis of a Jacobin conception of power that implied the subordination of particular interests to the exigencies of the overriding national wellbeing. It was a conception that

[11] J. Chapsal, *op. cit.*, p. 410.

was to be applied time and again in educational policy.

But de Gaulle was not disposed to turn his mind again to educational matters until the new Constitution had been made to work and until he had settled the war in Algeria, which was a prerequisite for setting France on the road to economic recovery. The Pinay-Rueff Plan and the deflationist policies that were followed left little money for educational reform and this was only sufficient for schools to keep their heads above water and to cope with the rising tide of numbers. After the resignation of Boulloche, Debré himself took over the Ministry of Education for a short while. There followed a succession of Ministers: Louis Joxe (appointed January 15, 1960), Pierre Guillaumat (November 23, 1960, ad interim), Lucien Paye (February 20, 1961). It was a period of planning. A formula much bandied about at the time was "to ensure the selection of the best by the fostering (of the ability) of all" ("assurer la sélection des meilleurs par la promotion de tous"). It was soon realized that if democratization, which had by now become a vogue word, were to be effective, the creation of the phase of observation in secondary education could only be a first step. Indeed the fact that in the phase children remained in the schools to which they had been assigned at 11 — post-primary (elementary), higher elementary (the 'collège d'enseignement général', formerly the 'cours complémentaire') and the lycée, still in the eyes of many the true secondary school — militated against transfer between institutions at 13, as the decrees of January 1959 had envisaged. The lycée pupil — or his parents — would not accept returning to a form of elementary education; the child in the other schools was not able to cope with the work in the lycée if he were transferred, because he had already missed two years of the course. However, apart from the problem of transfer, other ideas were fermenting: there was felt a need to encourage more pupils to follow scientific and technical courses, courses which should be less theoretical, and less oriented to mathematics. At the same time there was for the first time a clearer perception of the problem caused for education by social disadvantagement.

The formation of the first Pompidou government on April 15, 1962 did not bring about any drastic educational changes immediately. But there was no doubt of the interest that the new Prime Minister felt in education. He had not forgotten his earlier career as a schoolmaster. A graduate of the Ecole Normale Supérieure, after passing the "agrégation" in French and classics he had been appointed to the Lycée Charles in Marseilles, one of the largest schools in France. In 1938, by a stroke of good fortune, he had been appointed to one of the most prestigious of all French lycées, the Lycée Henri IV in Paris, where he had spent the Occupation outwardly engaged in teaching. In 1944, by another trick of Fate, he had entered de Gaulle's Private Office. He was then aged 33. His sole political knowledge had been acquired through another qualification he had gained, the Diplôme de Sciences Politiques. When de Gaulle had entered the political wilderness in 1946 Pompidou had accepted a post in the Rothschild Bank. There he had had time to continue scholarly pursuits and also to keep in touch with his former political master. Despite his financial career, which had been followed by a return to politics, albeit as a "technocrat" rather than a professional, he had not forgotten his early teaching years and still held strong but somewhat conservative views on educational matters. In fact, it has been alleged that in the first Debré government he had been offered, but had refused, the Education portfolio.[12]

For his own first Education minister Pompidou chose Pierre Sudreau, who, however, resigned when de Gaulle proposed that in future the President be elected by universal suffrage.[13] Sudreau was followed by Louis Joxe (October 14, 1962). But this was another interim appointment for Joxe. He was succeeded on December 7, 1962 by Christian Fouchet, a Gaullist of the War era. Although Fouchet had always enjoyed the confidence of de Gaulle, the General had at first refused to consider him for the post of Minister of Education because he was not "a specialist". Nevertheless, he was to hold the office until April 8, 1967, a tenure of four years four months, and the longest stay in the Rue de Grenelle for a century, when Victor Duruy had been Minister. De Gaulle, writing in his Memoirs, states of the period: "I set about fixing the policy for education" by holding a special series of Cabinet meetings.[14] These were, of course, attended by both Pompidou and Fouchet, of whom de Gaulle writes that "he had no intention of being in turn unseated by his unruly mount", unlike his five predecessors since 1959. Despite industrial unrest and the necessity for a Stabilization Plan to combat inflation in 1963, the

[12] P. Alexandre, *Le Duel de Gaulle-Pompidou,* Paris, 1970, p. 80.
[13] *Ibid.*, p. 132.
[14] de Gaulle, *op. cit.*, p. 361.

key decision in the Gaullist educational reforms was taken by the creation of the college of secondary education in August 1963. This establishment of a lower common secondary school for all children was to have the most far-reaching consequences and entail massive expenditure. The proportion of the National Budget spent on education, which had remained stable at around 12–13 per cent since 1959, rose steeply from 13.72 per cent in 1963 to 17.30 per cent in 1968. Thus the "golden mean" of expenditure on education advocated once by Ferry had been exceeded.

Fouchet was indeed, if not a specialist, at least a technocrat. His first move was to reorganize the Ministry of Education into seven directorates, together with various specialist services, all headed by a new top civil servant, a Secretary General with little experience of educational administration. This step led to friction within the Ministry and ultimately to the resignation of some top civil servants. Fouchet pressed ahead with other reforms. Through the creation of the lower secondary school it became possible to rationalize educational provision throughout the country so as to take into account areas of population growth and decline. This was a logical step. But what Fouchet did not foresee was the confusion that would be created as the changeover to a different system of structures and levels took place. Pupils and teachers suffered as the changes increased. For teachers a further cause of resentment was the reform of the various educational advisory councils whose membership was broadened to include more non-teachers and less of their own number.

However, it is principally with reforms in upper secondary and higher education that Fouchet's name will be associated. Henceforth success in the baccalaureate examination would not give unrestricted access to all faculties so that, for example, a pupil the emphasis in whose studies had been on the classics would no longer, on the strength of the baccalaureate be admitted to a science faculty, although he would still have the right to a university place as such. Thus the course and the examination were parcelled up into a number of sections — five in all — each of which gave access to specified faculties only. The diminished position afforded the classics in the new programmes, and the stress on modern studies also gave cause for alarm in some quarters. Not only was it genuinely felt that the classical heritage of France was being seriously undermined, but also that an effective filter which had in the past efficiently debarred the less privileged from higher education was being removed. The prestige symbol of the baccalaureate and its role as a passport to the more lucrative posts in society were being undermined. The middle classes had not raised much protest at the creation of the common lower secondary school because "streaming" had been preserved and it was plain that at 15, when it was important, their children would still gain access to the truncated lycée. The expansion of higher education was then proceeding apace and, as in England, the children of the better-off were the principal beneficiaries. So long as the floodgates remained unclosed and no serious selection, beyond the baccalaureate examination, was imposed, the bourgeoisie acquiesced in the régime's educational policy. Yet this first step towards a limitation on university entrance was one that many university teachers and administrators, fearful for standards, had long advocated. At a time when France had great need for technologists and technicians the most popular faculties were law and letters. For a government whose avowed aim was economic growth, which had in practice revived the old slogan, "Enrichissez-vous", this seemed plain foolishness.

Fouchet introduced sweeping reforms also into higher education. The so-called propedeutic year in the university faculties, which was in effect an extension of secondary school, was a stumbling-block that caused too many failures. It was argued that if the system were ordered better and a 2 year course instituted as the first phase of higher education the considerable drop-out rate — as much as 40 per cent — would fall. Hence the introduction of two diplomas, one for arts and one for science, awarded upon completion of a two-year course. At the same time the degree structure in universities was reformed, with a three-year course leading to a "licence" (or bachelor's degree) and a four-year course leading to a master's degree. The master's degree was made a necessary condition for entrance to the "agrégation" teaching qualification for secondary teachers. In an effort to reduce the influx of students into courses with no immediate use in employment a new institution of higher education, the University Institute of Technology (Institut Universitaire de Technologie), was set up as from October 1, 1966. These new institutes would provide two-year courses in preparation for industrial and commercial careers, severely practice-oriented and allegedly intellectually less demanding. As a general principle in higher education a system of yearly in-course examinations was instituted. These reforms, instigated by Fouchet after a Ministry committee, the so-called Commission des Dix-Huit, had reported, represented a considerable advance on the old system whereby the accumulation of a certain number of certificates led to the granting of a degree.

In an effort to cope with increased numbers in all forms of education new academies had been created: Nantes, Orleans and Rheims in 1961; Nice and Limoges in 1965. To decentralize, first-year students were placed in newly founded university colleges ("collèges universitaires"), which however quickly developed into universities in their own right. Despite these measures the growth indices of higher education continued to increase. If numbers enrolled in higher education are assigned a base index of 100 in 1950, by 1955 this had risen to 113, by 1960 to 150, by 1965 to 292 and by 1968 to 394.[15] The problem of selection was therefore posed in its starkest form. There was no easy solution.

On April 8, 1967 Pompidou formed his fourth government and Alain Peyrefitte was appointed Minister of Education. After the complex and far-reaching reforms of his predecessor the education system required a breathing space. This was not granted it. Throughout the year that followed the difficulties multiplied. The demands for selection for higher education came more insistently from official quarters and were resisted no less stridently by students, their parents and many of their teachers. The administrative machine was overloaded. Speaking at the Amiens Colloquium, which brought together 600 people concerned with education only two months before the explosion of May 1968, the Minister referred to the enormousness of his task:

> ... National education is a vast undertaking: a personnel which consists of one civil servant in two, numbers undergoing education which represent one Frenchman out of four (the three others being of course parents of pupils or former pupils or both, the largest undertaking in Europe if one excludes the Soviet education system and the Red Army). It is a ponderous administrative machine. The conflict between requisites imposed by the intellect and those imposed by organization makes our task difficult. ...
>
> We must tread a narrow and uncomfortable path along the peaks, at equal distance from apostolic idealism and a management technocracy.
>
> This discomfiture, this malaise of national education is everywhere strongly felt. It expresses itself in criticism that is often violent, sometimes unjust. But self-criticism is preferable to self-satisfaction. The exaggerated statement of those who say today, "The French educational system is the most atrophied in the world" is to be preferred to the exaggeration of those who were wont to

[15] OECD: *Educational Policy and Planning: France,* Paris, 1972, pp. 20 (Table 5) and 23 (Table 6).

say, "French education is the best in the world." In short, it is easier to temper the ardent faith of the iconoclasts of today than to shake the deep-rooted certainties, the naïve beatitudes of yesterday.[16]

The analysis was a correct one, save in one vital respect: the iconoclasts would not moderate their demands. May 1968 broke upon a France where a slogan relating to de Gaulle was already gaining currency: "Ten years, that's enough!" ("Dix ans. C'est assez!")

Meanwhile the President held strong views regarding education. Musing in his retirement at Colombey-les-deux-Eglises, both in his memoirs and in his reported conversations with André Malraux, de Gaulle had much to say on it, both before and after 1968.

He recognized that education represented "a thorny task" for any government, because of the clash of pedagogical theories and political ideologies.[17] He boasted that the decree of 1963 which initiated the college of secondary education "initiated equality of opportunity", thus putting "an end to the long-established system of predetermination".[18] However, he accepted that "streaming" was a necessity.

The teacher, however, perhaps by some Freudian quirk, was his "bête noire", for whom he reserved some of his strongest vituperation. He admitted that the centralized nature of the administration was irksome for the teachers. Nevertheless they were also, he said, "disposed by the spirit of the age towards relentlessly critical and contentious attitudes". Their charges were hardly better. Indeed

> (The educational question) was a particularly lively one, because teachers' and students' organizations invariably indulged in the most extreme theories, advanced the most outrageous solutions, split up into every possible category of Marxism and anarchy, and agreed only in their desire to use education as a means to destroy present-day society.[19]

His own view of what education should be about was somewhat different:

> I, on the other hand . . . regarded education as an outstanding public service endued with exceptional importance and distinction. In my view the mission of the men and women who guide the young into the kingdom of knowledge entails a sovereign responsibility on the human level. The powerful influence they exert on our destiny by teaching the flower of the people constitutes a unique national duty.

[16] Reported in: "Association d'Etude pour l'expansion de la recherche scientifique: Pour une école nouvelle", *Actes du Colloque d'Amiens,* Paris, 1969, p. 385.

[17] de Gaulle, *op. cit.,* p. 359.

[18] *Ibid.,* p. 362.

[19] *Ibid.,* p. 359.

In a rare remark regarding his father he goes on to say that his own lofty ideal of the mission of the educationalist had been influenced by him.

Yet he is no airy idealist living in the clouds. He desired a form of education that would develop "powers of reasoning and reflection" but one that would also be "relevant to contemporary conditions, which are utilitarian, scientific and technical".[20] Like Napoleon before him he doubtless believed that "there will be no political stability as long as there is no teaching body based on stable principles". He returned again to the charge that the teachers were the villains of the piece. He accused them of sabotaging the principle of "orientation" instituted in the 1959 reforms. Although he had "personally taken steps to widen the scope of public education to the utmost" they had opposed his every move. He had wanted streaming and selection to be introduced "from top to bottom of the system", but his requests, even his orders had met with "a stubborn passive resistance".

> Once again it was brought home to me that, unless a clean sweep is made by dictatorship or revolution, no institution can really be reformed without its members' consent. This was certainly true of the teaching profession. While they readily accepted "democratisation" which corresponded to the basic ideological stance they had come to adopt . . . they were not in the least prepared to wield authority and accept the burden of responsibility.[21]

He accused the teachers of deliberately keeping up numbers for entry to higher education by lowering pass standards in the baccalaureate. They were not willing to "take the initiative in *closing doors*" [present writer's italics] for some of their charges.

De Gaulle's solution to the problem of recalcitrant teachers would be, he said, one day to rebuild the whole educational system so that all who used it — teachers, administrators, pupils, students, parents — would share directly in the running of the system. He believed in "participation" in education just as much as he believed in participation by workers and employers in the running of businesses and factories in a labour system that would be neither capitalist nor Communist. "Participation" was in fact the panacea proposed by Edgar Faure for education after 1968. The revolt provided de Gaulle with the pretext he sought: ". . . the educational system, under the guidance of the great ministers I was to call upon for that purpose [Faure and Guichard] would be reformed by law from top to

[20] *Ibid.*, p. 360.
[21] *Ibid.*, p. 363.

bottom on the hitherto unacceptable basis of participation".

He recognized that in higher education there was need for "linking the teaching in the faculties to the practical concerns of the modern world". To this extent he shared one of the concerns of the students. In general, however, he is dismissive of them. Many of them were unsuited for higher education. As for their political activities, he asks: "Who remembers today that L'Action Française once dominated the Sorbonne? Similarly the slogans of today — alienation, Malthusian forces, etc. — will be quickly forgotten".[22] The "enraged students" of 1968 were mere "misadventures"[23] with whom the statesman had to deal: the "drama of the students" was not really a "university drama", but rather "a crisis of civilization".[24]

A policy must be gauged by its success. In education this is always difficult to evaluate. The era of de Gaulle might be assessed educationally, it has been argued by Fournier,[25] by drawing up an index of "cultural level". Thus, whereas in 1959, at the beginning of the educational reforms, only 59 per cent of the age groups successfully completed lower secondary education up to the age of 15, by 1968 this had risen to 73 per cent. In the same period the proportion of the age group passing the baccalaureate rose from 9.3 per cent to 15.2 per cent and those obtaining a first degree from 2.1 per cent to 5.3 per cent. All in all, this does not represent an exceptional "inflation" in success rates and demonstrates how slowly educational reforms work themselves out in practice.

[22] A. Malraux, *Les Chênes qu'on abat,* Paris, 1971, p. 187.
[23] *Ibid.*, p. 228.
[24] *Ibid.*, pp. 203–204.
[25] Fournier, *op. cit.*, p. 285.

CHAPTER 14

The May Revolt

Bliss was it in that dawn to be alive,
But to be young was very heaven.
Wordsworth

They (the students) have much to learn from the French peasants:
balance, hard work, tenacity, respect for the public welfare.
Leading article in *L'Aurore*, December 16, 1968, p. 1.

Paris has always been the hub of the student world: since 1900 one-third
of all French students have been attracted to the capital. Here they have
often suffered from *anomie*, a loneliness accentuated by the fragmented
nature of the French university and the lack of a sense of belonging to a
community "of masters and scholars" in the English meaning of the term.
This alienation has sometimes led to the adoption of extreme positions.[1]
The years before 1905 had led students to an intransigent secularism and
Republicanism, which the "Dreyfus Affair" had reinforced. However, in
the years immediately preceding the First World War the pendulum had
swung towards nationalism and Catholicism. The turbulent 1920s were
marked by deep divisions among students: there were the Gideans,
individualist and sceptical; others adhered to the cult of the heroic, as did
Malraux, who was to become de Gaulle's closest political friend; politically
the Right was represented by the Action Française, the so-called Camelots
du Roi; and there were others who swung to the internationalist
Communist Left, marching ritually each year to the Mur des Fédérés. The
Second World War and its aftermath ensured the continued polarization of
the student body to Right or Left, with the latter by far the stronger
camp. For a while "engagement", "involvement" as understood by Nizan,
Sartre or Simone de Beauvoir, became the fashion. About 1960, however,

[1] For an analysis of student attitudes cf. P. P. Clark and T. N. Clark, "Writers,
literature and student movements in France", *Sociology of Education,* Fall 1969, vol.
42:4, pp. 293–294.

a disillusionment set in. Marxism, orthodox and pure, had lost its appeal. The writers, the traditional luminaries of the student Left, became "lost leaders", in a Wordsworthean sense. Their works ceased to be studied with the same avidity. Literary texts were supplanted by the new holy writ of sociology. In any case, influential students such as Danny Cohn-Bendit inveighed against the "personality cult" in any form. There was a symbolic rejection — symbolic because in practice the students continued as before — of the consumer society and the values it represented. The young intellectuals likewise resented a political system in which "ministers reigned like great Commissioners of State, imbued with the authoritarian tradition".[2] The atmosphere became ripe for revolt. Thus, after Berkeley, Columbia, Bonn, Berlin, Warsaw and Prague, it was the turn of Paris.

The first disturbances were at Nanterre, a bleak university campus not properly equipped, situated on the outskirts of Paris in a desolate, broken-down area. On March 22, 1968 less than 100 students occupied the campus. The "Mouvement du 22 mars", from such modest beginnings, was to trigger off a student reaction that shook France.

One must examine in greater detail why students were ripe for protest and revolt. The overall figure for university drop-out has been estimated at 40 per cent. But the overall figure for those that failed to pass their first year examinations was even more catastrophic in some subjects: in science, 57 per cent; in French, 48 per cent; in the classics 38 per cent; in law 50 per cent.[3] This colossal wastage was attributed by some students to bad conditions of learning and study. They wished for an end to overcrowded lecture rooms and libraries. They wanted teaching methods other than the traditional lecture, the "cours magistral", given in an amphitheatre before hundreds at a time. They wanted greater personal contact with their teachers. It was reported in November 1968, after the disturbances were over, that in the mathematics faculty at Toulouse the student/teacher ratio was 90:1; it was alleged that in the medical faculties for the whole of France there was only one biochemistry lecturer for·1000 students. Other reported figures give the more general picture of the student/teacher (the British figures are given in brackets for purposes of comparison):

> Letters and philosophy: 53:1 (Britain: 8.5:1)
> Law, economics and social sciences: 50:1 (9.3:1)

[2] Raymond Aron, *La Révolution introuvable*, Paris, 1968, p. 96.
[3] J. Papillon, *L'Ecole, pourquoi faire?*, Paris, 1965, p. 201.

Physical and biological sciences: 17:1 (7:1)
Medicine and pharmacy: 10:1 (6:1)

It is true that to improve the situation assistant lecturers were being appointed at last. These, it was reckoned, would act as a "transmission belt" between students and professors. This move was, however, resented because the students felt they were deprived of the constant and direct intellectual exchange with scholars. Indignation was heightened on this score by the alleged scandal of the absentee professor. Holding a chair at some provincial university, he would prefer to live in Paris so as to have access to the great libraries for his research. On Sunday evenings he would take the train to his university town, descend upon his students like an absentee landlord, give the statutory 3 hours of lectures that were required of him, see a few doctoral students, and by late Monday evening could be back in the capital, his teaching obligations discharged for the week — and this for only seven months of the year! In any case, teaching was often taken less seriously than research: the way to promotion lay through publication rather than by attending to students. Professorial attitudes were in any case deemed to be over-authoritarian: the professors were considered to be "les mandarins", pillars of the Establishment.

The students also called into question other matters. They wanted respect by the authorities of the "franchises universitaires" which they had enjoyed intermittently. These consisted of the right of assembly within the university precincts and the right to hold political meetings without police intervention. Immunity from police interference had been a right enjoyed at intervals ever since the foundation of the Sorbonne and had indeed been guaranteed by Napoleon in 1811.

Added to these grievances was a new uncertainty regarding the prospects of employment. Already in 1964 Georges Gusdorf had declared:

> The immense majority of students think solely of obtaining . . . as well paid a job as possible. It is clear that culture is not considered as a necessary and sufficient value; the time spent at the university corresponds to a technical apprenticeship.[4]

But job prospects in 1968, with 514,000 students, were not the same as they had been even four years earlier, when there were just over half that number. Zamansky, dean of the science faculty at the University of Paris, had posed the pertinent question: How does anybody think that French

[4] G. Gusdorf, *L'Université en question*, Paris, 1964.

society can absorb every year 3000 sociologists, 2400 psychologists and 750 archeologists? Zamansky's answer to the problem had been the imposition of a numerus clausus, but this had been rejected almost unanimously by the student body. There was no doubt that career prospects for many students were poor: history or philosophy graduates, for example, had no market value save in teaching. French industrialists and businessmen were not over-anxious to employ the arts and science graduates, whose studies really only fitted them for secondary teaching. Many indeed sought refuge in a teaching post. In an enquiry made by the Centre d'Etudes littéraires supérieures appliquées, attached to the Paris Faculty of Letters, it was shown that in 1968, although only 59 per cent of arts students had said at the outset of their university studies that they wanted to teach, in fact 69 per cent had eventually adopted this as their career. Table 26 shows the wide range of careers opted for by the remaining 31 per cent.

Table 26

	per cent
Social sciences, research	5.1
Economics, statistics	1.5
Translating, interpreting	1.8
Secretarial	1.7
Documentation, publishing, museums	4.8
Administration	4.2
Foreign Service	0.2
Journalism	0.4
Publicity	0.5
Commerce, tourism	0.6
Applied psychology	4.0
Medical occupations	0.5
Legal occupations	0.2
Artistic occupations	0.5
Other	5.0

As can be seen, the outlets for arts graduates in industry and commerce were few, as compared with similar prospects in Britain. Students in general also feared that they were being "processed" rather than educated, turned into cannon-fodder for the production line in a consumption-conscious society. Such a fear raised doubts about the nature of society itself.

The Fouchet reforms of 1965 had done nothing to allay such fears. The new two-year diplomas were seen by students as another hurdle deliberately erected to eliminate as many of their number as possible. They saw the introduction of yearly examinations that had to be passed, as against the old "certificate" system, as an attempt to restrict the time in which the degree might be taken. In the past this had been often as much as five or six years, because many students worked full-time and most at least part-time. The introduction of a "third-phase" doctorate, on the lines of the Anglo-Saxon Ph.D., to which students would be directed instead of the more prestigious State doctorate, was likewise regarded as an attempt to fob them off with the second-best. The new University Institutes of Technology were viewed as institutions expressly created to provide dead-end jobs in the middle cadres of industry. Thus the whole paraphernalia of the Fouchet plan for higher education was rejected by many students as one geared to the short-term growth needs of giant firms, as aiming to produce teachers on the cheap, possessing a cut-price degree, whilst leaving the route to research and the élite positions in society open mainly only to those who graduated from the grandes écoles. It was said that, all in all, it was a policy of Malthusianism.

The criticism of the University Institutes of Technology appears unjustified, since, by their own admission, students in the more traditional disciplines could not obtain jobs. In 1965 there had been a profound imbalance of students, with the faculties of letters and law accounting for 54 per cent of the total numbers, and science for only 31 per cent. The drop-out in science was in any case over half the number enrolled. It seems a little churlish on the part of the students to refuse to accept selection and also to reject the provision of training for employment in sectors where jobs *were* available.

However, some students had wider, political motives for revolt. Many were simply fed up with the paternalistic régime — "Dix ans, c'est assez!" Others had opposed de Gaulle from the beginning and particularly disliked the manner of his assumption of power. They were also in revolt against the modern bourgeois State. They felt themselves to be adults, yet condemned to live half as children up to the age of 23.[5] This was the perennial clash of the generations.

As the revolt strengthened, so did the demands of the "political"

[5] Aron, *op. cit.*, p. 53.

students increase. They wanted power within the university, which crystallised into a claim for "participation". They also wanted greater autonomy within the system. Courses, they said, should be interdisciplinary. A greater share of resources should be devoted to student welfare: thus the quality of student restaurants should be improved; students should receive free of charge the roneographed lecture courses which were sold at high prices and yet which were indispensable to those who could not attend lectures because they were working. Examinations should be abolished and replaced by a system of continuous assessment. (Some even argued that school pupils should participate in the marking of the baccalaureate examination.) They wanted to modernize the content of higher education. Since the faculties of letters and science had mainly prepared students for secondary teaching, the subjects predominantly taught in them had been those that had a place also in the lycée curriculum. The result was that other subjects had been established with difficulty. Thus ethnography and social anthropology, for example, had been taught at the Ecole Pratique des Hautes Etudes and at the Collège de France, but not in the university faculties. The students argued that much that was taught was in any case without relevance in the modern world. This assertion had some truth in it. Despite the reforms effected by Louis Liard at the end of the nineteenth century, the university had tended to be separated from the mainstream of national life. In fact, many institutions of higher education concerned with technology and industry had grown up outside the university proper. France had developed no counterpart to the red-brick universities of northern England. Thus participation, autonomy and relevance summed up succinctly the claims of the dissident students.

The deeper political motives lay behind these claims. The politicization of higher education – the introduction of the clash of politics into the day-to-day activities of the university and its student body – has been one of the most significant developments of modern times. At least student fervour in the past had not called the very existence of the university itself into question. The great anti-Fascist demonstrations of the 1930s, for example, had been carried out by students who had no desire to destroy the university itself. In 1968, however, some students saw matters in a different light. Their criticism was not only of the educational system and of the French bourgeoisie, but ultimately of all ideologies. They felt that the whole fabric of society was rotten. The school was an agent of social discrimination, which in turn was prolonged into the university. Students felt themselves vulnerable, insecure, even oppressed. They were, after all, the products of a secondary school system which possessed, often literally, all the disadvantages of an unfinished building site. The greatest edifice of the Third Republic was in process of demolition, and its reconstruction was piecemeal, incessant and not always acceptable. The moderates who believed in reform, as opposed to the revolutionaries and the nihilists, were convinced that the university was in urgent need of rehabilitation. They had come to mistrust representative democracy; for them the way of change was through another type of grass-roots, participatory democracy. They criticized the bourgeois university, which seemed too exclusively in the service of big business and capitalism, exercising a conservative function within society and dispensing a bourgeois culture. The competitive system which the university embraced favoured the rich and the already privileged. It might be urged that a certain meritocratic element had penetrated the walls of the university but by then the pass had been sold for the majority of the poor and disadvantaged, who had already dropped out. Those underprivileged who had penetrated the portals of the university were allowed to enter, not faculties such as medicine and law, which led to high positions, but the less prestigious one such as letters. But already in the field of the social sciences groups had formed which saw destruction as the only fate worthy of the bourgeois university. From these arose the leaders of the revolt. Indeed, there were no other leaders to hand. The Communists, seeking to establish their image as a "respectable" political party, would have no truck with the students in revolt, seeing in them spoilt scions of the bourgeoisie — "fils à papa". Intellectuals such as Sartre and Marcuse had become outmoded; indeed, the very silence on the intellectual Left was sometimes deafening.

What was left was anarchy and nihilism. "Who would give the primacy to reason?" was one slogan, in this late spring of slogans, daubed upon the walls of Paris. In this respect the movement of revolt was a flight to irrationality, the ultimate treason of the intellectual, the final denial of all that the university stood for. If it was, as Aron asserted,[6] the end of ideologies, it was because both socialism and capitalism had failed. The consumer society, the technocratic society, had become disgusting and obscene. It was, as the Catholic review *Esprit* remarked, a cultural crisis

[6] *Ibid.*, p. 158.

not just against the régime, but against an over-rigid form of society, from which the university remained alienated. The revolutionary students considered that the relationships between Frenchmen had become too authoritarian, too hierarchical. This was typified in the relationships between professors and students, a style of relationships (which, Wylie had once remarked, began in the primary school) between teacher and taught. Scathing comments about the Establishment, "le système", "le mandarinat" were freely bandied about.

Yet the extremist factions lacked any real programme of reform. Their first task, they naïvely considered, was to overtopple society. Everything — including knowledge, which had to be called into question in a new kind of "critical university" — had to be changed. Since the legal opposition had failed to achieve a radically new social order, illegality was the sole alternative. This way the most intransigent students were willing to tread. Indeed they saw themselves, somewhat arrogantly, as the spearhead of the masses who stood inarticulate and helpless in the face of a government from whom they were separated by an unbridgeable gulf.

A dangerous irrationality thus characterized these students. They were imbued with an "aesthetic nihilism". They acted like an "irruption of barbarians, unconscious of their barbarism".[7] The confusion of their ideas is aptly summed up in the strange, picturesque and occasionally obscene slogans that bedaubed the walls. The themes of these slogans were not only political, anti-Gaullist and anti-clerical, but were psychological and philosophical, full of symbolism, idealism and hedonism.[8] They expressed a vague belief that life should be happier. Gilbert Cesbron, whose novels betray a deep insight into the psychology of young people, has attempted to analyse one of the most striking slogans that appeared:[9] "Under the cobblestones [those same cobblestones thrown up to form the barricades and to attack the CRS], the beach" ("Sous les pavés, la plage"). Three meanings can be assigned to it: "the exhausting, stupid existence forced upon us by industrial society stifles happiness"; "if you chipped away the mean ways, the ruthless pursuit of profit and the hardness of heart of our contemporaries you would find love and tenderness"; and "behind the tumult of the barricades and the rubbishy meetings lies the festive

---

[7] *Ibid.*, p. 13.
[8] Cf. J. Besançon, *Les Murs ont la Parole,* Paris, 1968.
[9] G. Cesbron, "La Plage et la Grève", *Le Monde,* April 4, 1973.

occasion". If ever the Americanism of "crazy, mixed-up kids" were aptly applied it would be to the students of Paris in 1968.

At the time France boasted no less than ten student organizations, all highly politicized, ranging from the extreme Leftist "Gauche proléta-rienne" to the extreme Right-wing neo-Fascist "Action Française". Yet it must be emphasized in any consideration of the "events" of 1968 that *less than 10 per cent* of students belonged to any of these bodies. Moreover, the fulcrum of action was decidedly to the Left. The prime movers throughout the uprising were the so-called "Gauchistes", that left-of-Communist spectrum of ultra-red that included such strange and unlikely bedfellows as Maoistes, Trotskyites, Che Guevaristes and Castroistes, as well as a number of other "groupuscules". In a poll taken after the events it was demonstrated that only 12 per cent of the student body embarked upon what Raymond Aron has scornfully dubbed "la révolution introu-vable" with the firm intention of creating a new social order on the ruins of the old. In any case, although these young bourgeois acted as a catalyst for a deep-seated malaise in French society, they had not the slightest hope of making common cause, as they so earnestly desired, with the young workers of Flins and other factories. There was a world between the two. The Communist-controlled Confédération Générale du Travail (CGT), no less than the Communist Party itself, flatly rejected the overtures for an alliance. The Party was nourishing hopes of achieving power through the ballot box and was not anxious to see its image of acceptability as a plausible alternative government, painfully built up over the years, shattered by the excesses of a few spoilt bourgeois youths imbued with romantic ideas and, in particular, possessed by extreme Leftist heresies that the Party sternly condemned. The students' concerns were political, but what interested young workers more were social and economic improvements in their drab working lives.

The events that started at Nanterre came with startling suddenness, starting among the sleazy slums on the outskirts of Paris, far from the bright lights of the Left Bank. The "movement of March 22" began with the occupation of the university buildings. The ringleaders were eventually ordered to appear before the disciplinary council of the university. Agitation simmered throughout the month of April and on May 2 the atmosphere became so tense that all courses at Nanterre were suspended. The following day there was a meeting of students at the Sorbonne, from which the police later expelled the students. This intrusion of the civil power into an area held sacrosanct since the Middle Ages touched off a strike by the Union Nationale des Etudiants de France (UNEF), headed by Jacques Sauvageot. The strike was supported by the largest university teachers' union, the Syndicat National de l'Enseignement Supérieur, (SNESup), headed by its secretary general, Alain Geismar. The other students' union, the FNEF, which had been founded by Gaullist students in 1961 to counter the Leftist tendencies of the UNEF, took no part in the strike. The smallness of the numbers involved must again be stressed. The "movement of March 22" had involved only about 100 students; among the members of UNEF only some 10 per cent were active members; SNESup, despite being the largest university teachers' union, represented only about a quarter of them. The cardinal mistake of the authorities, however, was made on May 5, when some students were committed to prison. This aroused tempers even among the moderate students. The next day the disciplinary hearing took place at Nanterre. The Sorbonne was closed. The rioting that then occurred was directed against the police action at the Sorbonne and towards securing an amnesty for the imprisoned students. On May 7 it reached its peak. For 16 hours, right through the night, what had started as a student demonstration in the form of a march through Paris developed into a pitched battle between the riot police, the CRS, and the students. The outcome was 700 casualties, 109 arrests, and £100,000 of damage. According to some accounts there were some 10,000 students on the streets that night.

The government now became thoroughly alarmed. Peyrefitte, the Minister, speaking the following day in the National Assembly, declared: "If order is re-established, everything is possible; if not, nothing is". His appeal for order evoked a negative response. On May 10 Nanterre was completely occupied by students, more rioting occurred and for the first time barricades, the traditional Parisian symbol of incipient Revolution, appeared in the streets. This "night of the barricades" was followed by the return of the Prime Minister, Pompidou, from a visit to Afghanistan. On May 13, the tenth anniversary of the régime, a general strike of teachers and certain groups of workers occurred. This marked the beginning of what has been termed the "social crisis" and the real testing time for the government. The political parties swung into action. The Communists, who had been lukewarm at the turn events were taking, now realized they had to back the industrial strikers if they were to preserve their credibility. Together with the CGT, the Party decided to use the crisis in order to wring material gains for their supporters. But there was no thought of revolution. On the other hand, the Parti Socialiste Unifié (PSU), a small but significant party on the extreme Left, saw the situation as an opportunity to reshape the political and social structures of France. The Socialist party proper, however, remained comparatively inactive at this juncture.

The big Paris lycées were now also involved in the events. The PSU was instrumental in organizing pupils into the "Comités d'action lycéens", who, following the students' example, turned out on the streets to demonstrate. Even some 14- and 15-year-old pupils took part. The committees set up groups within the schools to consider the whole educational structure and curricula. They were joined by many of their teachers. The ephemeral literature of the time, which included "manifestos", pamphlets and broadsheets, contains many interesting proposals for school reform.

On May 14 a stay-in strike was staged by the car workers of Renault and in other factories. More lycées and universities were occupied, including the Sorbonne itself. The so-called "Commune of the Sorbonne" — the title is reminiscent of 1870 — involved both staff and students. Speaking that day in the National Assembly, Pompidou admitted the "symbolic value" of the occupation. He compared the desire on the part of some to destroy the University completely to the attitudes of the Sorbonne rioters in the fifteenth century. But he promised to set up a "comité de réflexion" to consider reforms.[10] However, he found himself under attack from all sides. Mitterand, the Socialist leader, accused the police of brutality. He read out a letter signed by a number of deans of faculties threatening to resign unless the government granted additional financial aid to alleviate conditions. Even the moderate Sudreau, himself a former Minister of Education, was moved to remark, "Le recteur napoléonien a vécu". The Communist deputy, Ballanger, accused the régime of wishing to train up a caste of technocrats instead of throwing open the University to society as a whole.

On May 18 de Gaulle cut short a State visit to Romania and returned to

[10] *Journal Officiel,* 1968, p. 1770. (Assemblée Nationale, première séance du 14 mai 1968.)

Paris, uttering the famous but inelegant phrase, "Reform, yes; mess, no" ("La réforme, oui; la chienlit, non"). On May 24 he went on television to announce a national referendum which would in fact be tantamount to a vote of confidence in the régime. The speech was a resounding failure. The government now realized that its prime task was to appease the workers — the students' hash could be settled later. Substantial benefits were conceded to the striking workers in the Grenelle Agreements of May 27, in which both trade unions and employers participated. Surprisingly, these concessions were at first rejected by the workers. The third and ultimate phase of the crisis, which had now become wholly political, had begun.

The Socialists now became alive to the political possibilities of the situation. In conjunction with the PSU, the students' and teachers' unions, they made plans to fill the vacuum of power if total breakdown of government occurred. If the government ceased to function or were to resign then it was proposed that Mitterand should assume the Presidency of the Republic and Mendès-France (PSU) should become Prime Minister.

At this juncture Alain Peyrefitte resigned and Pompidou himself took over the Ministry of Education for a few days. From this moment on, the whole crisis began to take a turn for the better, from the viewpoint of the régime. De Gaulle, who had spent a few days in Germany consulting French Army leaders there as to what military support he could muster in the event of armed rebellion, returned to Paris and, in a second but strikingly more powerful television speech, announced the dissolution of the National Assembly and the holding of elections. Thenceforth there was a gradual return to normality.[11]

On May 31 Pompidou appointed a technocrat, François Ortoli, as Minister of Education. In early June a return to work was voted in many places. From June 7 onwards schools began to reopen. During the week-end of June 7–10 there was, however, a new flare-up by students and once more the barricades were raised. This time, however, the government reacted with great firmness. In a few days the Odéon Theatre, which had been occupied by students for almost a month, was evacuated. On June 16 the Sorbonne was cleared by the police without resistance.

[11] There is a plethora of books on the "events" of 1968, mostly partial in their scope and judgements. Two short but interesting assessments are given in: J. Soustelle, *Vingt-huit ans de gaullisme,* Nouvelle édition, Paris, 1971, pp. 391–399; and A. Hartley, *Gaullism. The Rise and Fall of a Political Movement,* London, 1972, pp. 275–289.

The black and red flags of anarchy and revolutionary power were hauled down. On June 27 the last surviving bastion of revolt, the Ecole des Beaux-Arts, was evacuated. The elections that followed in late June resulted in an outstanding victory for the parties of the Majority. They won 358 out of 485 seats. The Gaullist party alone, fighting under the tendentious title of Union for the Defence of the Republic (UDR), had an absolute majority, without needing its electoral allies. The Centre voters had been thoroughly alarmed by the catastrophic perspectives that a revolt sparked off by a mere handful of students had opened up, and had also voted massively for the *status quo*. On July 10, 1968 Couve de Murville was appointed as Prime Minister and three days later Edgar Faure, a veteran Radical politician, who had been once Prime Minister during the Fourth Republic, was appointed by de Gaulle as Minister of Education, with instructions to clear up the mess.

The lesson of May 1968 is surely that modern industrial society is unusually unstable and fragile. It is also that, in France, it is still the bourgeoisie, or rather its sons, that makes or frustrates revolutions. The numbers required to bring about revolt are few. There is little doubt, for example, that the majority of students wanted only to reform the university, not to destroy it: they wanted changes made in its programmes, teaching methods and material facilities. They were anxious about employment prospects. The one issue on which they felt deeply was the lack of equal opportunity for those less fortunate than themselves. On the other hand, a minority raised other issues of principle. An interesting task for the future student of semantics would be to pinpoint the exact meaning of the terms that were bandied about during the spring of 1968. The Gaullists spoke of "order". Their opponents had a wider vocabulary: "reactionary", to describe the régime; "dialogue" and "contestation", as a means of achieving their aims. And there was a further vocabulary the precise implications of which both sides had now to hammer out: "participation", "interdisciplinarity", "autonomy", "shared management" ("co-gestion"). Changes in the university could no longer be delayed.

CHAPTER 15

The Reform of Higher Education: Problems and Solutions

The task of Edgar Faure in the reform of higher education was a formidable one. He was suspected by everybody — students, parents and political parties alike. He encountered hostility among those closest to de Gaulle, although it must be said that he was firmly supported in his efforts by the President himself. His own view of the situation was brilliantly summarized in the series of speeches and interventions he made at the time in the National Assembly.[1]

His point of departure was the outmoded character of higher education: "the Napoleonic conception of the centralized and authoritarian university is outdated", he declared.[2] The University (by which he meant the whole educational system) had spoken in no uncertain voice, just as had those, he said, who in another cause had once stormed the Bastille.[3] His analysis of the causes of the student revolt takes him into the realm of philosophical speculation. Man, who has at his disposal more power over nature than ever before, refuses to accept a passive role. This refusal is most marked among the students, who may be compared to colonial peoples aspiring to freedom.[4] Because of the easier means of communication young people have become more critical. They are intensely aware of the ever-shifting and expanding boundaries of knowledge and are anxious that what they learn should be up to date. The authorities, for their part, have the obligation to make an "agonizing reappraisal" of education in the light of the principle of "participation". The university, as part of the nation, must be subjected to the same process of democratization and renewal as the nation itself. The problem was partly one of numbers: in November 1967, 80,000 new students

[1] E. Faure, *L'Education Nationale et la participation*, Paris, 1968.
[2] *Ibid.*, p. 18.
[3] *Ibid.*, p. 48.
[4] *Ibid.*, p. 41.

entered universities which already housed double the number of students than did those of England, Germany and Italy. Despite this he (Faure) set his face resolutely against any selection, save for restrictions as to the particular *type* of higher education that the student might opt for. On these principles, which are a judicious blend of special pleading and expediency, but based upon a genuine desire for reform, Faure enunciated the broad outline of his work of "renovation".

On a number of minor points he was explicit. He wished for teaching to take place in small groups of not more than twenty-five students, although for practical work numbers might rise to forty, and for lectures, when these were necessary, an appropriate maximum might be 250 students. The concept of the professorial chair, with all the privileges that it implied, should be supplanted by that of the *department*. All this is clear, but on the major issues the detail is not spelt out so precisely. He wanted institutions to possess both freedom and responsibility for their own administrative organisation. There must be the possibility of inter-disciplinary teaching. Institutions must be able to determine the content, methods and assessment procedures of what they teach. But this autonomy could not be absolute. The right of the State to award all national qualifications must not be abrogated. And there is the necessary constraint also of finance. Participation there must certainly be, but how it was to occur would not be the same at all levels and in all fields. The three great themes that he hammered home to a perplexed Assembly were indeed autonomy, participation and interdisciplinarity. All sides were well content to let him proceed with reform, but criticized him severely as he did so.

Before this triptych of reform is considered, however, the problem of the democratization of higher education, to which Faure referred, must be considered. The evidence of social selection at work in schooling has already been discussed. Three studies, largely carried out in the 1960s, confirm that the same forces were at work in the universities. Over the decade figures would seem to show that, although the proportion of students from lower socio-economic categories did increase, they were still at a disadvantage as compared with their richer fellows.

In 1962, according to Bourdieu and his associates,[5] the chances of

[5] P. Bourdieu, C. Grignon and J. Passeron, "L'évolution des chances d'accès à l'enseignement supérieur en France, *Higher Education*, vol. 2 (4), Nov. 1973, pp. 407–422.

reaching a university varied from one in a hundred for the least favoured socio-economic category to fifty chances in a hundred for the most favoured one. By 1966 the range of opportunity was from 2 to 70 per cent. In fact, the total rise in enrolments for the age groups 18–21 had been roughly distributed between the various social classes in proportion to the original inequalities that existed in 1962. Where there had been slight progress towards equalization this had occurred with the children of industrial workers, whose chances had been raised from 1.3 to 3.4 per cent. This still compared vastly unfavourably with the chances of children from the higher cadres, 58.7 per cent of whom were in universities in 1966 as compared with only 38 per cent in 1962. The figures which relate to the grandes écoles show that children from the higher cadres and managerial classes are overwhelmingly in the majority. They are also able to pay the high fees demanded in private higher education by institutions training for careers in advertising and journalism. Even within the university poorer students have made only slight headway in penetrating the more prestigious – and ultimately more lucrative – areas of study such as medicine and law. Already in 1964 Raymond Aron had remarked that the increase in student numbers had not been an effect of democratization, but merely represented a rise in the middle-class intake[6] – a statement that to a less significant extent also refers to the situation in England.

Another study, by Dominique Bidou and his associates,[7] likewise highlights "the obscure mechanism for social selection which, outside and even within the school, contributes to eliminating or retarding children from less favoured social classes". Summarized, their findings show:

Twenty-three per cent of the sons of industrial workers and 24 per cent of the sons of agricultural workers have been in employment – often as primary school teachers – before entering higher education. This contrasts with 5 per cent of the sons of higher cadres and only 2 per cent of the sons of doctors and dentists.

Of those taking arts or science degrees, which traditionally lead to school teaching, 18 per cent of boys and 11 per cent of girls come from working-class families.

[6] Raymond Aron, "Combien d'étudiants?", *Le Figaro*, April 3, 1964.
[7] D. Bidou, P. Vrain and Geneviève Gontier, "Carrière universitaire et perspectives professionnelles", *Population,* Feb. 1970.

A corollary of this is that other courses, such as those in sociology and psychology, attract the more wealthy students. In law over half the students are from the very wealthiest classes. The same holds true for enrolments in the institutes of political science, which are the avenue to such institutions as the Ecole Nationale d'Administration, and thus to the top jobs.

The analysis therefore shows that rich and poor students study different subjects at university, subjects that, in the case of the rich, lead to the more rewarding occupations, both in terms of money and prestige.

The third and most recent study, that of Noelle Bisseret,[8] throws yet another light upon social inequalities in higher education. Her enquiry involved following through a whole generation of students of arts subjects at the Sorbonne since 1962. She refuses to accept genetic explanations to account for the lack of success of some students in their studies. Nor does she accept the thesis of Bourdieu and Passeron[9] that their failure may be ascribed to linguistic and cultural differences. She asserts that other social and economic factors are at work. She starts from the basic fact that in 1962 all students, regardless of social origins, had one chance in four of passing their first university examinations, taken after two years. Of those not working at the same time as they were studying, 54 per cent were successful (as, of course, against the overall success rate of 25 per cent). Whether or not a student was earning his living at the same time therefore made the significant difference. But only 17 per cent of students from the bourgeoisie were obliged to earn their living, whereas 52 per cent from working-class homes were obliged to do so. Employment was therefore one correlative of failure. Another significant factor was whether students had had to work for a year or two before beginning their studies, perhaps as primary teachers. Such students were notably less successful. A further interesting factor in success was whether the student had studied in a classical section for the baccalaureate examination. This section — the traditional bourgeois option — produced more successful university students. Thus the most favoured at university were those who had started their studies younger, had not been forced to work at the same time, and had had a classical background.

[8] Noelle Bisseret, *Les Inégaux ou la sélection universitaire,* Paris, 1974.

[9] P. Bourdieu and J. Passeron, *op. cit.,* pp. 92–93; cf. also P. Bourdieu and J. Passeron, "Les Etudiants et leurs études", *Cahiers du Centre de Sociologie Européenne,* The Hague, 1964.

According to Noelle Bisseret, social and economic factors even affect psychological traits such as ambition. Only 13 per cent of those who were classified as very ambitious, but who lacked the three advantages just mentioned, did in fact realize their intention of achieving a comparatively high position, as compared with 30 per cent, similarly inclined, but possessing these advantages, who did in fact achieve their ambition.

None of the different facets of social selection in higher education revealed in the studies is new. (One remedy would seem to be to increase the size of student grants so that students would not be dependent upon employment either before or during their studies. Although some improvements have been made, French students are not so well treated as are English students.) The Faure proposals did not deal directly with the demand for democratization of higher education. On the other hand, the matter was raised by the Communist Georges Cogniot (in a Senate debate on the Law of Orientation, October 24, 1968). He suggested that grants for the first two years of university should be made on *social* criteria. For studies thereafter, up to the master's degree, the criteria should be academic. As for students preparing for a "third phase" doctorate, these should be paid a salary, subject to satisfactory progress. But the problem of how to broaden the social spectrum of higher education was not solved after 1968.

The other catchwords of 1968, autonomy, participation and interdisciplinarity, were taken more seriously. In order to understand why reform that embodied these principles was necessary the past development of universities must be briefly summarized.

The universities did not emerge from their "long stagnation"[10] after the Revolution until about a century later. Even then, despite the intention of reformers such as Liard and Goblet, the law of July 10, 1896, which theoretically re-created fifteen universities — one for each "academy" — merely brought together loose groupings of faculties, largely independent of each other, into a corporate body rather than into an articulated institution of higher education. Between the five faculties of medicine, pharmacy, law, letters and science (theology had been abolished at the Revolution, save in Strasbourg), there remained comparatively little communication.

After 1945 the universities had been subjected to many partial reforms,

[10] A. Prost, *op. cit.*, p. 223.

particularly in the organization of studies. The propedeutic (or preparatory) year had been used as a means of eliminating unsuitable students, since the filter of the baccalaureate had palpably failed to do so. This was particularly true in the faculty of letters, which was enlarged to include the social sciences. The science faculty lacked almost any technological bias, but this situation was partly remedied in 1965 by the creation of the University Institutes of Technology. Other faculties suffered from similar gaps, some of which were progressively rectified. Thus in 1954 already the law course had been extended to four years; in 1959 the law faculty had been extended to include economics; by 1965 legal studies as whole had been reformed. In medicine a preparatory year had been reintroduced in 1963; closer links had previously been established between the faculty and the teaching hospitals. In 1966, to cope with the influx of students, seven new universities had been established. But the system was blatantly in need of further reforms.

Some of these had been carried out by Fouchet during his tenure as Minister of Education (1963–1966). The reforms then made largely concerned the faculties of letters and science, where studies had been reorganized into three phases [a two-year introductory course, with yearly examinations; a second phase leading after one year to the "licence" (bachelor's degree) or two to the "maîtrise" (master's degree), and a third phase to a junior doctorate]. Although Faure's Law of Orientation of Higher Education, passed in 1968, did not alter drastically this pattern of studies, it did change fundamentally the organization of the universities themselves.

The pre-1968 system had concentrated decision-making in higher education either within the Ministry of Education, for matters such as the award of qualifications, the establishment of syllabuses or the allocation of financial credits; or in the hands of "mandarin" professors, who determined their own teaching methods and regulated almost absolutely the careers of their subordinates; and within the Faculty Council, whose sole but important function was to recommend appointments to professorial chairs. Reorganization meant a reallocation of these powers. It was first accomplished by dissolving the old faculty system, breaking up most of the university institutes that existed, and even fragmenting subject disciplines. The basic grouping was to be the new "unit of teaching and research" ("unité d'enseignement et de recherche" – UER). Some 700

UERs have now been set up in sixty-five universities and para-university institutions.[11] These embody not only the principle of autonomy but, as will be seen, that of interdisciplinarity (or pluridisciplinarity, as it is now more commonly called). Thus, with certain specific exceptions, the UERs, no less than the universities in which they are grouped, may determine their own teaching and research activities, their teaching methods and their assessment procedures. The exceptions, however, are important. Any national diplomas which are "protected" — usually in France those such as in medicine, pharmacy, law and teaching which confer the right to practise a profession — are still regulated by the State. On the other hand, any university has the right to award other qualifications, for which it may or may not seek State approval. The UERs are of three kinds: those with a teaching function only; those with a research function, including the preparation of future researchers through the doctorate degree; those former university institutes, including the University Institutes of Technology ("instituts universitaires de technologie" — IUT) which already had some element of pluridisciplinarity in their work.

Title II Art. 6 of the Law of Orientation explained the intention behind pluridisciplinarity: ". . . universities . . . should associate as far as possible the arts and letters with science and technology. They may however have one predominant vocation." In some cases, moreover, UERs may correspond exactly to the former faculties; in others they need not be pluridisciplinary; in others they may represent a level of study (e.g. the first phase of university education). However, the majority of "teaching" UERs do represent a mixture of disciplines, as in the field of the environmental or social sciences. Further examples may show what is meant. The former English department in the old Faculty of Letters in Paris is now divided into a number of UERs, each attached to a different Paris university (there are now thirteen universities in the Paris area). One of these UERs combines the study of English language and literature with the history of ideas; another is concerned with producing future school teachers of English; another with producing translators and interpreters; another with giving English instruction useful in business and industry; yet another combines English studies with other subjects such as history,

[11] There were in 1975: 43 universities outside the Paris area; 13 universities within the Paris area; 5 "university centres"; 5 public independent institutions (the Institut d'Etudes Politiques in Paris and the engineering schools, which are now grouped together).

psychology or linguistics. (It has been alleged that this breaking up of a department which once numbered 8000 students has political overtones, since it was accompanied by an exodus of teaching staff to the UER corresponding most to their political persuasion!) Other types of UER have been innovatory: urban studies at Grenoble, rehabilitation techniques at Lille, or Mediterranean research at Aix-Marseille, to give only three examples.

Basically the view that different disciplines should not remain isolated from each other has much to commend it. Mathematics, for example, has many applications in the field of the humanities as well as the sciences, although literary scholars may well remain ignorant of its potentialities. In the past the bringing together of different disciplines has often engendered new knowledge. The sole condition should surely be that such unions should not be "shot gun" marriages. One commentator[12] quoted the case of a forced union between scientists and doctors, many of whom declared: "We have neither the same mentality, the same habits nor the same objectives. In fact, beforehand we had never exchanged a word with each other." Another problem (which is now not unknown in Britain) arises from the different academic education of teachers who may be teaching the same subject: one future French teacher may know nothing of linguistics, another nothing of literature, because the particular UERs in which they studied did not offer such courses. Such incidental consequences of the reform were not envisaged at the time.

The universities proper have derived much benefit from the new structures, particularly in respect of size. The thirteen universities of the Paris area, six of which are distributed round the periphery, represent a necessary rationalization of the single, elephantine institution that existed before. Those universities of the "inner area" are limited to no more than 20,000 students. Paris is "zoned" for students, so that the institutions located on the Left Bank, which once attracted a third of all the students of France, including 50,000 foreign students, are no longer so over-crowded and unwieldy. This is not to say that Paris, with its rich resources for learning, does not remain the Mecca, particularly for university teachers.

[12] F. Gaussen, "De l'Ancien Régime au nouveau", *Le Monde,* Dec. 8, 1970. Some critics have seen the creation of so many small units as a "Balkanization" of the university (cf. G. Bayet, "La loi d'orientation, est-elle applicable aux réalités? Des principes aux réalités", *Le Figaro,* April 11–12, 1970).

In his grand design for a France that should be neither authoritarian nor anarchic and free from ideologies of either the Right or the Left, de Gaulle had conceived of "participation", the third principle of reform, as having three facets: university participation, industrial co-management by employers and workers, and regionalization, so that participation should exert an influence upon the central decision-makers. When the workers rejected industrial participation and when the cause of regionalization, which was an issue in the referendum which eventually brought about his resignation, was also rejected, only university participation was left. This therefore was, and remains, an anomaly in modern French society. Nevertheless, the principle has been retained. On occasion, however, it seems a little cumbersome, as can be seen in Fig. 7 overleaf showing the network of university government. One example given[13] is that of the University of Rheims, which in 1973 comprised over 10,000 students. The University Council, which holds monthly meetings and decides the key question as to how resources are to be allocated, was made up of 71 members: the President (elected by his colleagues), his 2 deputies, 29 academics elected by their peers, 21 student representatives, also elected, 6 representatives of the administrative and technical staff, and 12 representatives of the town, local industry and the trade unions. Below the University Council is the Council of the UER, also elected. The University is represented on the Regional Council, presided over by the Rector of the academy, who is ex-officio Chancellor of the University. At Ministerial level the regional councils have a voice on the National Council for Higher Education ("Conseil national de l'enseignement supérieur"), whose function is to advise the Minister. Such an elaborate apparatus appears to be a heavy price to pay for participation.

(On the other hand, a new body, the Conference of University Presidents, which was set up independently of the Law of Orientation of 1968, has proved remarkably effective. It holds monthly meetings under the chairmanship of the Minister and, since university presidents are elected for a period of five years only and cannot be re-elected, is more efficient than the National Council, which is top-heavy, having 150 members.)

Has participation satisfied those that were most vociferous in demand-

[13] P. Scott, "France: four years after the Faure reforms", *Times Higher Education Supplement,* Jan. 12, 1973.

The Network of University Government

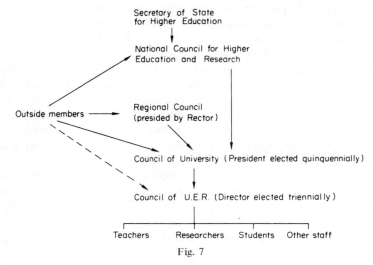

Fig. 7

ing it? Certainly the non-professorial academic staff have now a greater say: to this extent the considerable power once exercised by deans of faculties and professors has diminished. The key question is, however, how far the students are satisfied. Some — the "Gauchistes",[14] but not the Communists — have refused to take part in student elections to representative bodies because they say the representation accorded is insufficient. This it is, in the sense that student representatives cannot command a majority on any such bodies. In any case the number of students who use their right to vote is small: in 1969 the national figure of votes cast in university elections was 52 per cent; in 1972 this had declined

[14] The "Gauchistes" comprised the following groups: (1) The former "Gauche prolétarienne" (disbanded by the authorities; its leader, Alain Geismar, was imprisoned). (2) "Le mouvement du 27 mai" (the successor to the "Gauche prolétarienne"). (3) "Vive la Révolution" (a group of students at Nanterre). (4) "Humanité rouge" (orthodox Maoists, acknowledged by Peking). (5) "Ligne rouge" (Marxist-Leninist). (6) "Ligue communiste" (Trotskyist). (7) "Alliance des jeunes pour le socialisme" (Trotskyist). (8) "Lutte ouvrière" (Trotskyist). (9) "Alliance marxiste révolutionnaire" (Trotskyist). (10) "Parti communiste révolutionnaire" (Trotskyist). (11) "Anarchistes". (12) "Situationnistes" (opposed to any structured political organization).

to 27.4 per cent. Students whose courses are most directly related to their future profession are most zealous in voting; surprisingly, the percentage of voters among science students has been small. The attitude of those who deliberately abstain as a matter of principle remains revolutionary. Already in November 1968, after the troubles were over, Jacques Sauvageot, then vice-president of UNEF, the French national students' organization, declared: "We are preparing for the overthrow of the régime and do not conceal this."[15] In any case, the fields in which student participation was excluded were delimited very clearly in 1969 by Guichard,[16] who by then had succeeded Edgar Faure as Minister of Education: university teachers must be allowed the sole right to judge each other's worth, to choose who among them should be promoted, to decide what kind of research should be undertaken and to control examinations. These were all matters in which the students had wanted a say in 1968.

Student participation, therefore, does not seem to have come off. Perhaps the majority are not interested. By definition students are an unstable group: they cannot guarantee continuity as can virtually all the other elements in the system of co-management. Yet for them 1968 was not all loss. Amenities have been improved. They have been able to hold political meetings and to be free of police intervention. Disciplinary offences that they may commit are now judged within the university by bodies on which their peers sit as of right.

Autonomy, like pluridisciplinarity, has been only a partial success. It could in any case never be absolute. In a democracy the community is entitled to a voice in the aims and functions of the university. If, moreover, the university claims the right of acting as the "permanent critic" of society, this right must be mutual. In allowing each university to dispose of the funds allocated to it as it thinks fit the government conceded a great deal. However, in retaining the sole right to award national qualifications it preserved the whip hand in a vital domain.

Despite upheavals, the structure of studies in French universities has not as yet been drastically modified. In general the concept of three phases leading to an intermediate qualification, a first degree or a master's degree, and a junior doctorate has been preserved. Nevertheless a significant reform of the first phase was carried out in 1973. A new two-year

[15] Quoted by Minot, *op. cit.*, p. 59.
[16] Speaking before the Senate Commission for Cultural Affairs, Oct. 22, 1969.

diploma, the Diploma of General University Studies (Diplôme d'études universitaires générales"), was introduced for: law, economics, human sciences (with five sections: philosophy, psychology, sociology, history, geography), letters (with three sections: letters, letters and foreign civilizations, and applied foreign languages), and science (with two sections: sciences of structures and matter, and sciences of nature and life). To these traditional fields of study were added two other new fields: applied mathematics with social sciences, and economic and social administration. In each field the principle of pluridisciplinarity is implemented: there are main subjects, laid down nationally, which represent some 60 per cent of the course; there are also optional subjects, prescribed by the university, comprising about 20 per cent of the course, from which the student must choose; there are also "open-list" subjects from which the student has a completely free choice, comprising the remaining 20 per cent of the course. In all courses a modern foreign language must be studied for at least 5 per cent of the time, with the stress being upon the communication skills. Like the Diploma of Higher Education in Britain the new French Diplôme (the "DEUG") can be either a terminal qualification or lead on to a first degree.

The object of the DEUG was given as to enable students to gain an initiation into "methods of intellectual work", to give some acquaintance with a number of subjects and to broaden the general education of students so that they might become more aware of "the essential aspects of society and modern culture".[17] Students are evaluated partly by continuous assessment and partly by examinations, although those in full-time employment are exempt from attendance at the obligatory courses — 700—1100 hours depending upon the field of study chosen — and are assessed entirely upon formal examinations. The regulations stipulate a maximum time of four years for completing this first phase of higher education; this eliminates "perpetual students". The DEUG also closes the options open to the student for his degree course proper, since it must be taken in an appropriate field. On the other hand, it has been argued that the course is so diffuse that it will take longer for students to reach degree standard in their more limited field.

In one area, that of medical studies, there has been a great tightening up. A *numerus clausus* has been imposed since 1969 and the weeding-out

[17] Ministère de l'Education Nationale, *Informations rapides*, No. 10, Mar. 23, 1973.

of unsuitable students is strict. In 1972 a stiff second-year competitive examination was introduced which restricts the intake into the third year according to the number of places available in teaching hospitals. This severity is encouraged by the powerful Ordre des Médecins, which wishes to restrict the number of doctors qualifying to about 6000 a year. (France has at present 50,000 doctors and it is estimated that it requires double that number.)

The second phase of higher education leading either to the "licence" (bachelor's degree) or a master's degree is still in a state of flux. For letters and science the "licence" may be obtained one year after the DEUG; for law and economics the period is two years. In letters the master's degree may be taken after four years of higher education in all and a short dissertation is required. In science only course work is required.

The third phase was reorganized in 1974. It lasts two years and is intended to be a period of specialization. In medicine and pharmacy it marks the end of studies and is crowned by the award of a professional qualification. In other subjects it can lead to either a terminal diploma (sometimes only after a one-year course) for a specialist qualification or to the junior doctorate ("doctorat du troisième cycle"). (The complete structure of higher education studies in France is given in Fig. 8 overleaf.)

Following the appointment of a new minister independent of the Ministry of Education, a secretary of state for the universities, other changes have been proposed. The DEUG has failed to achieve any standing among employers as a marketable qualification. It is now proposed by the present Secretary of State, M. Soisson, to award a "licence" after only two years. This, it is argued, will give a viable qualification to students who do not wish to pursue their studies further, although it cannot be interpreted as anything other than devaluation of the first degree. A further reason advanced for the two-year degree is that it would give parity of esteem to general and technical education, since the main technical qualification, the diploma of technology, is awarded in an IUT after a two-year course. If the proposal for a shorter degree course were adopted, the next phase would be given over to a master's degree, prepared after a further two years.

Other proposals still under discussion relate to teaching staff. To the statutory 3 hours a week of lecturing that French professors are at present required to do would be added a weekly 1-hour seminar. Career structures

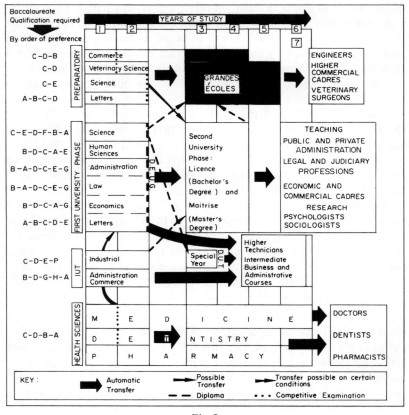

Fig. 8

would be unified into two grades: full professors and assistant professors ("maîtres assistants"). Internal promotion in the same university to full professorial rank would be forbidden, so that greater mobility would be encouraged. Provision would be made for sabbatical leave. These suggestions, outlined in a report specially compiled for the minister by M. Baecque, are likely to prove very controversial.

One outcome of the report of the "Commission des Dix-Huit", set up by Fouchet, the then Minister of Education, in 1963, was the creation, as has already been seen, of University Institutes of Technology (IUT). These institutions are now becoming separate "units for teaching and research" and integrated as such into universities, but still retain a certain autonomy. They were set up to provide two-year courses to train higher grade technicians for business and industry. Their purpose was therefore frankly vocational. They also fulfilled the object of taking the strain off the universities proper. The baccalaureate is not an absolutely essential qualification for entrance and in fact technician qualifications are accepted instead. The incorporation of such institutes into the university network is a significant departure, therefore, both because of the relaxation of entrance requirements and because for the first time the place of technology has been recognized in universities.

There was no doubt that the creation of the IUT was a necessary step. In the mid-1960s France was short of technical manpower. It had, in fact, some 12,000 trained engineers as against 5000 higher technicians, whereas these proportions should have been reversed. What was required was a training more concrete than that given to engineers, more general than that given to lower categories of technicians. In the secondary sector of employment the gaps to be filled were in mechanical construction, civil engineering, electronics, automation, chemical engineering and applied biology. In the tertiary sector also there was need for a different kind of higher technician in management, local government, documentation techniques, computing, etc.

How far have these institutions, which bear some resemblance to English polytechnics, fulfilled their role?[18] Numerically, their success has been limited. In 1972 their students comprised only 11.6 per cent of the total enrolment in higher education, and the majority were men. When the institutes were founded it was confidently expected that few who passed out from them would want to continue their studies further. Statistics, however, show otherwise: over one-third would like to continue their studies, and this proportion would be considerably increased if the third who have to go off to military service were taken into account as well. Indeed, those students who considered the course to be adequate without further study were, it seems, drawn from the lower socio-economic categories, a fact which confirms other studies. And in the event only 27 per cent of successful students from the IUT do enter employment immediately.

[18] For an evaluation of the IUT, cf. Janina Lagneau *et al*, *Les Etudiants des Instituts Universitaires de Technologie*, OECD, Paris, 1973.

Both industry and the universities view the institutes with suspicion. The industrialists say they ape the universities too much by stressing theory rather than practice. On the other hand, the universities take the opposing view, and argue that the two-year course is also too concentrated. Despite these criticisms, however, it would seem that these institutions have a key part to play in the differentiated model of higher education towards which the French, like other industrialized countries, are moving.

Another institution has also been integrated into higher education proper. The Ecoles Nationales Supérieures d'Ingénieurs (ENSI) have either been made part of universities or grouped together, as at Grenoble, Toulouse and Nancy, to form an Institut National Polytechnique in what have been described as the first French technological universities.

The Law of Orientation of higher education stipulated that universities should be involved in "éducation permanente" ("lifelong education"). The measures taken under the new laws relating to technological education for adults have already been mentioned. The Conservatoire National des Arts et Métiers, founded in 1819, has been very active in organizing "sabbatical leave" courses for industrial and salaried workers under these laws. But for general education the first requisite was plainly to relax university entrance requirements. Thus the university now known as Paris 8 (formerly the Centre Universitaire de Vincennes) was authorized to admit some students without the baccalaureate. Candidates had to pass tests, must be at least 24 (or only over 20 if they had already been working for two years), and were admitted after an interview. In 1973 some 30 per cent of students at Vincennes were admitted on this basis. Since many of the students were in full-time employment, many courses were given to overflowing audiences in the evening. As a "university of the second chance" Vincennes would seem to have proved its worth since it was started in 1968; nicknamed the "workers' university" — it has also a radical reputation — it now has 20,000 students. For a while it aroused suspicions as to its academic worth: using a unit-credit system of evaluation, there was in some disciplines 100 per cent success. This aroused protests against "cheapjack selling of diplomas"[19] and also brought down the wrath of the conservative Société des Agrégés. Nevertheless this novel experiment in France may well be generalized.

[19] Reported in *Le Figaro*, Nov. 13, 1969.

Lifelong education is, of course, more than allowing a person to acquire an initial qualification at any age; it must also mean the opportunity of updating one's knowledge, upgrading one's qualifications and retraining for different employment where necessary. Both the universities of Grenoble I and Grenoble II have been particularly active in this field, as has more recently the University of Paris VI, whose bias is mainly towards the sciences.

The theorists of "éducation permanente" such as Bertrand Schwartz[20] see it in a longitudinal perspective. Lifelong education would enable initial education to proceed at a more leisurely pace and perhaps be differently oriented. The legal stipulation that universities must concern themselves with it, even at levels lower than higher education, is one of the more interesting developments of 1968.

Another important facet of the Law of Orientation relates to assessment. In general, a credit-unit system has now been adopted. A series of "applicatory decrees" of the law lays down guidelines for assessment procedures by universities, particularly in respect of qualifications that have national validity. In accordance with the principle of autonomy, these decrees allow the Council of the university to prescribe its assessment procedures, after receiving the recommendations of the "unit for teaching and research" in the speciality concerned. The accredited teaching staff form the "college" to deal with all matters relating to assessment. It determines the "coefficient" ("weighting") to be assigned to each element in a course and sets the pass standard, which must not be lower than 50 per cent. The proportion of marks awarded either through continuous assessment or through a terminal examination must in neither case be less than 20 per cent nor more than 80 per cent (i.e. the ratio, continuous assessment: terminal examination, must lie between $80 \to 20$ per cent: $20 \to 80$ per cent). The actual proportions, between these extreme limits, may be determined by the university. Any intermediate examinations taken during the course of the year must be taken into consideration as part of the process of continuous assessment. Written papers and, where appropriate, oral, practical or clinical examinations, must constitute part of the evaluation. Thus, for example, the university now designated as Paris I, formerly the Paris law faculty (but to which other academic elements have been added), has decided that for a law

[20] B. Schwartz, *L'Education demain*, Paris, 1973.

degree 40 per cent of the marks will be awarded on continuous assessment and 60 per cent on terminal examinations. Continued assessment is carried out by qualified assistants, who run the "travaux dirigés" – the group work in classes and seminars. The professor considers the marks of his team of assistants at special coordination meetings and attempts to standardize them. One effect of this system is clearly to place more responsibility in the hands of subordinate teaching staff.[21] In order to obtain a degree, candidates have to accumulate thirty credit-units, at an optimal rate of ten per year. A credit unit normally represents 3 hours of teaching per week for one semester, either in lectures or in group work. The credit units give greater freedom of choice to the student, thus ensuring the flexibility in their courses which was one of the student demands in 1968, but are usually divided into obligatory and optional units, so that the particular bias ("la dominante") of a course is maintained.

The credit-unit system partially based on continuous assessment arouses mixed feelings among students. In some universities it works extremely well. In others, it is resented. At Vincennes, for example, students have complained of the strain of being continually "marked" and of, as they see it, the arbitrary character of the assessment, as compared with the anonymity of the traditional examination system, "which guarantees a fair, democratic selection". Such a comment, with hindsight, appears ironic. However, it looks now as if the system of "a degree by degrees" has come to stay, and not only in France.

Despite dissatisfactions, the results of the shake-up of higher education that followed 1968 have been positive. The French concept of the university as "functional" (rather than "idealist", as compared with the German or English) has remained unchanged, but has been modernized and refurbished.

---

[21] Information given to the writer by M. François Luchaire, President of Paris I, September 6, 1973 in an interview.

CHAPTER 16

The "Grandes écoles"

At the pinnacle of the French education system stand the "grandes écoles". These are specialized institutions giving high-powered courses of a professional kind. Access to them is severely limited by competitive examinations taken in a lycée one, two or three years after the baccalaureate. (This accounts for the presence sometimes of young men and women of 21 in a lycée.) What constitutes a grande école has never been officially defined. Although some pre-date the Revolution, the majority grew up during the nineteenth century. They stood outside the university faculties because their mission was to train higher cadres, particularly for the new scientific and technological occupations. They are not all institutions administered by the Ministry of Education, but are often controlled by the Ministry to which they are professionally most closely linked. Thus they train élites for the armed forces, the public service and private enterprise, and for the higher ranks of teaching and research. The "schools" — which in the English sense of the word they most definitely are not — may be grouped into four categories: commerce, veterinary medicine, sciences and the humanities.

Special post-baccalaureate classes are organized for preparation for the stiff competitive entrance examinations. These classes are particularly numerous in the large Paris lycées. Entrance to these classes is itself limited to those who have passed the baccalaureate with distinction ("mention"). For entrance to the "écoles vétérinaires" pupils follow a one- or two-year course in biology and mathematics. For the "écoles de commerce", of which the most famous is the Ecole des Hautes Etudes Commerciales, the course followed is more oriented to the humanities, and the social and economic sciences. But it is the courses in the humanities and the pure sciences that attract most applicants, because they prepare for the advanced teacher training institutions (the Ecoles Normales Supérieures) and the more prestigious scientific establishments, of which the best known is the Ecole Polytechnique.

221

A pupil wishing ultimately to enter an engineering grande école will have to choose one of the three scientific options that is centred on mathematics and physics. He will follow a strenuous timetable for 38 hours a week (mathematics 16 hours; physics 9; chemistry 3; French 3; first foreign language 3; second foreign language 1½; industrial drawing 3).[1] In addition, he will be expected to do some 20 hours a week private study. Perhaps only one in two who embark on this course will survive even as far as the competitive entrance examination. The examination then eliminates the overwhelming majority of candidates who sit it. Among the engineering grandes écoles, which are arranged below in a kind of hierarchical order which has deep historical and prestige reasons, Table 27 shows the success rate in the entrance examination.[2]

Table 27 (1973 figures)

Grande école	Number of candidates	Number successful	Per cent successful
Ecole Polytechnique	1600	300	19
Ecole des Mines,[3] Ecole des Ponts et Chaussées, etc. (Seven schools)	4100	355	9
Ecole Centrale and others (Four schools)	4200	710	17
Ecole de Physique et Chimie and Ecole de Chimie de Paris	2100	81	4

Two remarks must be made about the character of the potential intake to the grandes écoles. The first is that the age of entry to the preparatory classes in the lycée is very low (17.32 years), as compared with the average age of entry to the normal university fields of study, which also takes place after the baccalaureate (medicine, 19.42 years; science, 19.68; letters, 20.05; law, 20.97).[4] This suggests that the French system is

[1] *The Engineers' [sic] Training in France*, Service Scientifique, French Embassy, London, Mar. 1974 (revised).
[2] *Ibid.*, p. 8 (Table adapted).
[3] There are five Ecoles des Mines, of which the most famous is in Paris. Although originally specializing in mining engineering, they are now concerned with the whole field of industrial development.
[4] Etudes et Documents (Paris), p. 16, 1970.

admirably geared to the "production" of élites. The second feature is that girls are considerably under-represented in these institutions. In the grandes écoles as a whole only one in five students is a girl — a far smaller proportion than in the universities — and in the engineering grandes écoles girls form less than 4 per cent of the total.

The Ecole Polytechnique is undoubtedly the most well known of all the grandes écoles.[5] Founded in 1794 as a civilian school for the training of engineers, it was militarized by Napoleon. Although it now admits a dozen girl students a year it remains a military establishment whose director is a general and whose students are subject to military law. The purpose of the school has been defined as "to give pupils a general and scientific culture which will enable them, after specialized training, to assume highly qualified posts, or posts of a scientific, technical or economic nature demanding responsibility, in the civil or military branches of State service and in the various public services, and generally over the whole range of national activity".[6] It is therefore not surprising that it numbers among its former pupils many of the famous — and perhaps a few less reputable — names in French history. The school had already given to France two rather mediocre Presidents of the Republic, Sadi Carnot and Albert Lebrun, when a third ex-pupil, Giscard d'Estaing (who has also the very rare distinction of having also graduated from the Ecole Nationale d'Administration),[7] likewise was elected to the very highest office. It has numbered among its ranks at least one tragic figure, Captain Dreyfus, and one proponent of revolutionary violence, Georges Sorel. Among other contemporary graduates are to be found eminent economists such as Jacques Rueff and politicians such as Servan-Schreiber and Mendès-France. Indeed its graduates occupy many of the commanding heights of power within the civil service, the nationalized industries and key private undertakings.

Of the élitist character of "Polytechnique" there can be no question. In the written part of the entrance examination already half the candidates

[5] An interesting, although not always impartial, description of the Ecole Poly-technique and the influence it exerts in the 1970s is given in: J. Kosciusko-Morizet, *La "Mafia" Polytechnicienne*, Paris 1973. The author is a former "Polytechnicien".

[6] Senate debate on the reform of the Ecole Polytechnique, reported in *Le Monde*, June 24, 1970.

[7] Two graduates of the Ecole Polytechnique are admitted each year to the Ecole Nationale d'Administration, without having to sit the entrance examination.

are eliminated, after having completed stiff papers in mathematics and the sciences, summarized a difficult passage of French and undergone tests in languages, art and industrial design, as well as one in sport. The "happy few" that survive the oral examination may then enter the palatial new buildings at Palaiseau, in the suburbs to which the institution has recently removed from its traditional site in central Paris.

Five upper secondary schools alone provide all the successful candidates for "Polytechnique". The most well known of these is the Lycée Louis-le-Grand, to which would-be entrants come from all over France. Another highly successful school is the private Jesuit college of Sainte-Geneviève at Versailles.

Elitism not only distinguishes the intellectual quality but also the social origins of "Polytechniciens". In the early 1970s the social composition was as shown in Table 28.[8]

Table 28

	Occupation of fathers (per cent)
Farm owners	3
Independent businessmen and industrialists	15
Professional and higher cadres	56
Intermediate cadres	19
Other white-collar workers	2
Industrial workers	1
Others	4
	100

The predominance of the more wealthy is striking. No less striking is what might be termed the phenomenon of "élite succession". It has been calculated[9] that, given there are some 12,000 living ex-Polytechniciens – the "Anciens X", as they are known – the chances of a father having his son follow in his footsteps and enter Polytechnique are statistically two in a million. Yet in one recent "promotion" (year-group) the proportion of sons of "Anciens" was 10 per cent. Efforts have been made to diminish this social exclusiveness (which was condemned in the Lhermitte Report

---

[8] J. Kosciusko-Morizet, *op. cit.*, p. 157, quoting La Jaune et la Rouge (*sic*), the magazine of former "Polytechniciens", April 1972.
[9] *Ibid.*, p. 152.

of 1969) by allowing entry, through a separate entrance examination, to a small number coming from technical schools rather than general secondary schools, and whose social origins are likely to be more modest.

However, once entry is achieved the new "Polytechnicien" finds himself caught up in a web of tradition. Pressure is brought to bear upon him to conform to a Code of Honour designed to turn him into an "officer and a gentleman". The Code has also many amusing archaisms. The student may not, for example, have his hair cut on the Pont Neuf. (This, the oldest bridge in Paris despite its name, was once renowned for its open-air shops, hawkers and street singers.) Every student must master the special slang employed. Military discipline in the school is not too strict and many combinations of the various uniforms issued are permitted. So bewildering indeed is the choice of dress that, so the story goes, one cadet walked round in the pristine state of Adam, but was eventually put on a charge for not wearing braces!

Despite these light touches, the programme of work is very exacting. So often has the charge of encyclopedism been raised that the curricula have now been modified to include a common core of mathematics and science, with options in additional science, economics or computer science. There is also an element of liberal studies. In their studies, however, the "polytechniciens" are privileged. The teacher:student ratio is a generous 1:10. Teaching, given by some of the most eminent specialists in the field, takes place through lectures (known as "amphis" — from "amphitheatre"), seminars and work in small groups, with a strong emphasis on co-operative effort. Academic work is preceded by four months' initial military training, from which the student emerges with the rank of officer-cadet ("aspirant"). It is later interrupted for a short spell in an industrial undertaking. At the end of the two-year course the student passes out with the rank of second lieutenant and goes off to do a year's military service. The final qualification awarded is the Diplôme d'Ingénieur de l'Ecole Polytechnique. Failure is rare.

Although they have signed a ten-year engagement to serve the State in a civil or military capacity, about half the students resign their commissions at the end of their course in order to enter business and industry. There is a great demand for "Polytechniciens" in the private sector. They are then liable to repay the total cost of their board and tuition. Only very rarely does a student take up a permanent commission in the armed forces.

Those placed most highly in the pass list go on from Polytechnique to one of the "écoles d'application" (institutions of applied technology) which are run by the appropriate technical branch of the civil or military services. There are twenty such branches or "corps", as they are known. The école d'application most highly sought after is the Ecole des Mines; next in esteem is the Ecole des Ponts et Chaussées. Some also go into the Corps de l'Armement and other specialized institutions. In these institutions the "Polytechniciens" meet up again with those who were in the post-baccalaureate classes with them, but who, failing to pass into Poly-technique, entered directly an école d'application. These lesser mortals are destined never to achieve the highest technical posts in the public service, which are reserved almost exclusively for "Polytechniciens". In any case, for many the "corps" which they enter is often merely a stepping-stone to other sectors of the public service, both technical and non-technical, or eventually for top posts in the private sector. Thus in 1972, of the sixteen main public industrial undertakings such as Gaz de France, Air France or French Railways, all had at least one "Polytechnicien" at their head, either as chairman, vice-chairman or director-general. Furthermore, in the Private Office ("cabinet") of practically every minister is to be found at least one "Polytechnicien". In the private sector fifty of the largest industrial firms employ about 1000 of them, 150 in the very highest posts. They are in fact to be found in every walk of French life. Indeed about a hundred, in Stendhal's terms, have passed from the Red to the Black, becoming Catholic priests, usually in monastic orders and often Jesuits; in 1969 two were even bishops.

This quasi-monopoly of key posts in the national polity has given rise to accusations that an "old-boy network" operates. It is true that a very active association of former "Polytechniciens" exists, which publishes a year-book giving details of all living graduates of the institution and of their present employment. Within individual professions there exist organizations of ex-Polytechniciens. In the provinces similar groups of a sporting and social nature flourish. Furthermore, ex-Polytechniciens are noted for their accessibility to their fellows: the rawest recruit to Ecole Polytechnique has the right − even the duty − to address the most eminent of former "Polytechniciens" by the familiar "tu" form. Whether this amounts to more than what occurs in many similar situations in France or elsewhere is doubtful; it is certainly no stronger than the bonds of freemasonry, which is also very prevalent in certain high circles.

The Ecole Polytechnique has been accused of being over-selective, conservative, tradition-ridden and hidebound. It may or may not deserve this adverse side of its reputation. What is certain is that the institution has served France well. It gives a training geared to producing an intellectual aristocracy, in which the stress is on mental self-confidence — perhaps essential qualities in any power élites.

Only slightly less esteemed in the public eye is the Ecole Normale Supérieure, also founded during the Convention in 1794, reputedly by Lakanal. It was an all-male establishment, and the equivalent institution for girls was not founded till 1881 at Sèvres. Since 1843 the original "Ecole" (as it is always referred to by its graduates, confident as they are of the uniqueness of the institution through which they have passed) has been located on the slopes of the Montagne Sainte-Geneviève, not far from the Sorbonne. The original purpose was to train secondary schoolmasters — lycée teachers, "wise and philosophical young men" who would carry the torch of learning to every corner of the "hexagon". This still remains its nominal function, but many of its graduates today enter a university career or research. Some become distinguished later in fields other than the strictly academic. New entrants in fact join an illustrious band which in the past has included politicians such as Jaurès, Herriot, Pompidou and Léopold Senghor (also a poet), philosophers such as Bergson and Sartre, scientists such as Pasteur, and authors such as Péguy, Romain Rolland and Giraudoux. The institution remains élitist and its graduates ("les archicubes", in the peculiar jargon[10] of the school) form a closed corporation, characterized by "l'esprit normalien", characterized by those hostile to it as representing intellectual arrogance, scepticism and cynicism.

Students number only some 500 in all and are divided into "scientifiques" and "littéraires". They may become boarders if they so desire. In any case they enjoy great material advantages over the university student. In return for an engagement to serve the State in some capacity for ten years, they receive an adequate salary while studying, and food and accommodation are provided at cheap rates. Classes are small and, as in the

[10] For the jargon employed in the Ecole Normale Supérieure cf. of conversations of Jerphanion and Jallez, the two "Normaliens", in Jules Romains' *Les Hommes de Bonne Volonté*; cf. also the ten-page glossary of the jargon given at the end of the volume by: A. Peyrefitte, *Rue d'Ulm*, Paris, 1950.

case of the Ecole Polytechnique, students are taught by some of the most eminent professors in France. They sit the usual university examinations, taking the first degree in their stride, and eventually the "agrégation", the extremely difficult State teaching qualification. After a spell in school teaching many complete the State doctorate and move into university work. Incidentally, this movement from school to university has great benefit; to the school it gives an atmosphere of learning and scholarship; later, in the university, there is greater understanding of the problems that school teachers have to face.

Of recent years the Ecole Normale Supérieure has itself become a centre of political controversy. Within it the spectrum of opinion has always been broad, ranging from the extreme Left to the Right-wing Catholics, the so-called "Talas" (*"ils vont à la messe"*). This liberal tradition is in some danger of being weakened. The threat does not come from the Communists, who under the leadership of the leading Marxist philosopher Louis Althusser, a member of the teaching body, wish merely to see the privileges that the "Normaliens" enjoy extended to other students. The unrest arises in part from the fact that teaching in the lycée no longer carries with it the prestige that once it did, with the result that students in "Normale Sup.", as the institution is sometimes known, feel that their life style is under attack. The long strike of the students in 1971 caused many leading educationists to question its continued existence.[11] But for the time being it seems to have weathered the storm.

A third grande école that merits special attention is the Ecole Nationale d'Administration (ENA), which differs from the preceding two described inasmuch as all its entrants are graduates. ENA was founded in 1945 and has been a "nursery" for top civil servants. At the instigation of Michel Debré it was set up by de Gaulle for the express purpose of providing a uniform mode of recruitment to the top posts in the most coveted branches of the civil service, the "grand corps d'Etat": the Conseil d'Etat (a kind of supreme administrative court), the Cour des Comptes (the body which supervises public expenditure), the Inspection Générale des Finances (which is roughly equivalent to the Treasury). It also fills vacancies in the diplomatic, prefectoral and other careers in the public service of a non-scientific and a non-technical nature. It was also hoped to broaden the basis of recruitment to top posts. Certainly there is what has been termed an "énarchie" of graduates of ENA in French public life. By

[11] Cf. J. Capelle in *L'Aurore*, April 21, 1971.

1966, of the top 2947 civil servants in all branches, 21.2 per cent had been through the school. Just before the 1967 elections it was alleged that ninety-two graduates of ENA were serving in the Private Offices ("cabinets") of the ministers. These facts demonstrate the key role that this comparatively new institution has come to play in French public life. Political figures such as Couve de Murville and Chaban-Delmas graduated from it to become Inspecteurs des Finances before entering politics. The school has, however, not been very successful in democratizing its recruitment.

This is partly because of the procedures. Of the 500 students per year who apply for admission to ENA only 100 are admitted, and some 75 of these are graduates of the Paris Institut de Sciences Politiques. This institute has grown out of one that existed before the war. In those days intending entrants to administrative grades of the civil service (including, incidentally, would-be diplomats from Britain intending to enter the Foreign Office) enrolled at the Ecole Libre des Sciences Politiques, as it then was, a private institution in Paris charging high fees and familiarly known as "Sciences Po". This was nationalized after the war but remained, even after the Law of Orientation of 1968, unattached to any university. The present Paris Institut de Sciences Politiques, despite its 3500 students, has maintained its high standards: much work is done in small groups, known as "conférences", where students are taught how to present and argue cases convincingly and are taught administrative and management techniques. At the same time they prepare for a "licence" in law or economics or some other appropriate subject. Despite the fact that there are now eight other Instituts de Sciences Politiques – all, however, attached to universities – elsewhere in the country, the Paris Institute has supremacy.

The entrance examination to ENA is also open to Class B civil servants of five years' standing – a grade roughly corresponding to executive employment. Theoretically half the places in ENA should be awarded to these "in-service" candidates. In practice, however, the ratio is about seven "direct entry" students to only two civil servants already serving. It is not unknown for unsuccessful "direct entry" candidates to take a subordinate post in the civil service and then apply as "in-service" candidates again five years later. The vast majority of successful entrants to ENA come from the "bonne bourgeoisie", and mainly from the Paris area.

The ENA course lasts twenty-eight months. It comprises two options: general administration or economics (which has seventeen sub-options). The topics dealt with include administrative law, administration and management, public finance, social and economic studies. There are also a number of practical assignments. In 1970 there were only 370 students. Success in the course entitles the students only to an "attestation de scolarité" (certificate of attendance). What is important, however, is the rank order on the pass list, which determines the branch of the civil service to which successful candidates will be posted. Traditionally about a dozen posts are offered in the three "grands corps d'Etat" mentioned above, which offer better career prospects, higher salaries and more interesting work. Normally students have viewed with distaste the prospect of passing out so low on the list that they would be offered some bleak post in the Ministry of Cultural Affairs or banished to the obscurity of some sub-prefecture in a country town.

This system of training and allocation of posts was condemned as long ago as 1969 in a report compiled by the Bloch-Lainé Commission. The Commission advocated the creation of a unified corps of administrators, in which promotion would depend upon performance on the job. There have been signs also among ENA students themselves that they share the disappointment that the democratizing of the top civil service has not yet gone far enough. Certainly the students are not all pillars of the Establishment in their political views: a poll taken in 1972 showed that, whereas they comprised few Communists, there were only 29 per cent that supported the governmental parties.

Both the Ecole Polytechnique and the Ecole Nationale d'Administration have played a key role in the development of the Fifth Republic. Their role has given rise to the charge that France has been too much governed by technocrats and bureaucrats. In the early years de Gaulle preferred to appoint as ministers reliable civil servants, particularly for those areas of government which he had "reserved" for himself. In the elections of March 1967 twelve graduates of ENA were elected to the National Assembly. But the close link between the grandes écoles and the levers of power is best exemplified in the first government appointed by M. Giscard d'Estaing. In the spring of 1974 it comprised sixteen ministers in all. No less than seven were graduates of the most influential educational institutions: three had been at ENA, two at the Institut d'Etudes Politiques, and one each at the Ecole Polytechnique and the Ecole Centrale. (Of the rest, three were university graduates; the rest consisted of five industrialists and one journalist.)

In the past the whole system of the grandes écoles has rested upon competitive examinations. Other selection techniques have been hardly used. This spirit of emulation is indeed one of the characteristics of French education. But it has been argued that it also means that, through a once-and-for-all competition, access to the ruling élites is guaranteed for life. It has also been argued that the military character of the Ecole Polytechnique induces a certain conformism at an early age. With ENA, the system whereby allocation is made to a particular branch of the civil service has also been criticized. On the other hand, the English practice of moving young administrators from one ministry to another might be equally criticized. Above all, however, the question must be asked whether the system is *fair*. An Englishman may pose this question, but must also cast an uneasy glance over his shoulder to observe the persistent syndrome of the public-school/Oxbridge sequence as a mode of ascent to the power élites in his own country.

CHAPTER 17

Education and Politics since 1968

The elections of June 1968 had resulted in a resounding victory for the UDR as the "party of order". Edgar Faure, appointed on July 13 as Minister of Education, had, despite the covert opposition of Debré and Pompidou (replaced by Couve de Murville as Prime Minister), succeeded in drawing up his Law of Orientation of Higher Education, which had been passed in the National Assembly in November by 441 votes to nil. The new Minister was now able to turn his attention to secondary education.

The lycées, like the universities, had gone on strike during the "events of May". They had organized their own "lessons", replanned the curriculum, making it more relevant, as they considered, to modern life, and generally sought to move out from the "cultural ghetto" in which they considered themselves imprisoned. They wanted "participation", a say in how the schools were run; they wanted more human contact with their teachers and with society; they wanted freedom of political discussion in school. How many of these demands would find a responsive chord in the new Minister? That the secondary pupils could not just be ignored was self-evident. Politically they were well organized. The Vietnam war had sparked off the organization of anti-war committees. From these in May 1968 grew the Comités d'Action Lycéens (CAL — "secondary pupils' action committees").[1] Some of these committees were largely absorbed by the Communists into a new movement, UNCAL ("Union nationale des comités d'action lycéens"). Others became affiliated to the Parti Socialiste Unifié. After 1968 other "gauchiste" movements gained a foothold in the schools also. The CALs claim to be in the tradition of revolutionary syndicalism and are backed by those teachers who see the lycée as requiring the same kind of radical transformation as society. UNCAL, by contrast, is supported by Communist teachers who do not

---

[1] For an account of how a CAL was set up in a lycée, the Lycée de Kerichen at Brest, and the activities it undertook, cf. C. Jullien, *Les Lycéens, ces nouveaux hommes*, Paris, 1972, 319–323.

wish to see an *internal* revolution within the lycée. The broad mass of teachers and pupils, it must be said, held no such dogmatic views. But between the extremists and Faure there yawned a gulf.

Faure had made a number of piecemeal proposals regarding schools in his July speeches to the National Assembly.[2] He had wanted to "open up" the schools to higher education and to make the change between being a pupil and being a student a more gradual one. He held that this "décloisonnement" should also be effected within secondary education itself. The divisions between the literary and the scientific sections should be made less rigid, and science should be given greater importance. Too many pupils from the wealthier classes were able to climb the ladder to the university via the literary sections in the lycée, where their facility of expression and general cultural background gave them an undue advantage.

Faure was in favour of reshaping the curriculum. A "common core" of basic subjects should be learnt by all — the three "languages" of French, mathematics and a modern language — in order to train "au moins l'homme de trois paroles". The first two years of secondary education should be given over to the same curricular pattern for all pupils; this entailed the deferment of Latin until the age of 14. In the upper classes more "real-life" subjects should be taught, such as law, economics, accountancy and technology. The stress should be on "openness to the world", and to this extent the Minister praised the efforts of young people still in full-time education to meet with their counterparts in factories and elsewhere.

He was likewise in favour of "participation", not only in administrative matters, but in all facets of school life. This principle even applied to teaching methods, which had been over-passive. Henceforth there should be less reliance on memorization, on stuffing the brain with facts, and more emphasis on independent and group work, together with greater opportunity for discussion in class.

The principle of selection should be banished so far as possible. There should be progressive choices made in conjunction by pupils, parents and teachers. The principle of "orientation" should supplant that of selection throughout secondary education.

Such a declaration of intent showed that at least some of the criticisms of the school system that had emanated from the pupils themselves had been heeded.

[2] E. Faure, *op. cit.*, pp. 58 et seq.

On the right of political assembly within the school, which one commentator[3] has claimed to be the hinge upon which the success of school reforms turns, nothing was said — although several times since 1968 pupils have arrogated this right to themselves. Nevertheless Faure endeavoured to find an outlet for the political energies of the pupils by allowing them representation on the administrative councils and other representative bodies established within the school.[4] Unfortunately the pupils tend on occasions to politicize every issue that arises. (This attitude of "contestation" and "protestation" may well be fostered by the highly critical and individualistic views that the intellectualistic tradition encourages pupils to adopt in school.) In pupils' sentiments regarding the administration of their schools it may emerge also; indeed, it may well be a manifestation of "the antagonism between democracy and government" which, according to Pierre Avril, characterizes French life.[5]

Faure also made a determined effort to refurbish the curriculum and assessment procedures. In lower secondary education the pattern of "le tier-temps pédagogique" (a triptych of intellectual disciplines, "curiosity-awakening" subjects and physical and artistic education) was more widely adopted. A tentative reform of the marking system was advocated. It was recommended that a five-point letter grade system should be substituted for the traditional grading from 0 to 20 (at a time when in England precisely the opposite was being canvassed!) and there should be no rank orders of pupils.[6] But such novel assessment procedures caused such an outcry that they were quietly dropped for the time being.

Indeed Faure was not given time to develop further his ideas on school reform. The defeat of de Gaulle in the 1969 referendum meant the accession of Pompidou to the Presidency. To placate the more conservative supporters of the UDR Faure was dismissed. In June 1969 Guichard was appointed as Minister of Education in the Chaban-Delmas government, a post which he occupied till July 1972, the second longest holder of the portfolio since the founding of the Fifth Republic.

Guichard was more inclined to see education as a matter of successful management techniques. A graduate of "Sciences Po.", he himself had had

[3] R. Brechon, *op. cit.*, p. 86.
[4] Decree and "arrêté" of Nov. 8, 1968, supplemented by circulars of Mar. 7, 1969 and May 27, 1969.
[5] P. Avril, *op. cit.*, p. 14.
[6] Circular of Jan. 6, 1969.

a sound administrative career ever since he had entered the General's Private Office in 1947. He had embraced the new definition of a humanism which included technology. He believed that education must link this new humanism to economic and social problems. He accepted that the primary mission of the school was "collective advancement" through democratization. But he was aware that the real problems of education also related to teachers and the climate of the school. He realized that, in judging the success of an educational policy the public did not distinguish between the government, which determined policy, the administrators who carried out that policy, or the teachers. If these three elements in education were at loggerheads then society would exact retribution on all three.[7]

He faced and dealt with a number of practical problems. One of his first acts, which earned him a little fleeting popularity in the teaching profession, was to reduce the number of normal teaching hours of primary teachers from 30 to 27. He authorized experiments that would allow the "setting" of pupils by subjects and for the introduction of options into upper secondary education.[8] Reforms (as reported elsewhere) were introduced into French and mathematics teaching. In 1972 the so-called "classes pratiques" in lower secondary education, designed for those of lower ability, were replaced by terminal classes and measures were taken to increase the numbers leaving school with some form of vocational qualification − at the time some 200,000 did not possess one on leaving school. The reform of the "orientation" system was sketched out. No longer would the rather impersonal process of the "conseil d'orientation" take place in isolation. In its stead there would be engaged a "dialogue between teachers and parents" in which all interested parties would be brought into the discussion. If these could not agree as to the appropriate type of education for a pupil an appeal would be made to an independent tribunal or, ultimately, to a formal examination.

Several measures were taken in the interests of efficiency. The problem of grade-repeating and failure in school was intensively studied. In a report published in April 1970 the Education Commission of the Commissariat

[7] Press conference by Guichard on relinquishing office, reported in *Le Monde,* July 8, 1972.

[8] J. Quignard, "Recherches sur l'organisation des seconds cycles généraux et techniques en vue d'améliorer l'orientation: thèmes de réflexion", Paris, Institut Pédagogique National (roneographed), n.d. [1971?].

Général au Plan had again drawn particular attention to this "wastage" of resources, human and otherwise: one-third of all children were repeating the first grade in school; 47 per cent of children in the fifth grade were above the normal age; the failure rate in the baccalaureate was 38 per cent; the lack of qualification for employment was pinpointed. It was considered that these deficiencies were caused in part by a lack of information. Thus two information agencies were set up. The Office National d'Information sur les Enseignements et les Professions (ONISEP — National Information Office on Education and Employment) was started in 1970 to provide information and documentation for all "users" of the education system. The other, the Centre d'Etudes et de Recherche sur les Qualifications (CERQ — Study and Research Centre on Qualifications), was to assist ONISEP in its task by studying the types of occupation, the qualifications required for them. and future employment prospects. A decision was also made to reduce the size of secondary schools: 900 pupils for a college of secondary education and 1500 for a lycée were held to be the optimum.

In higher education the installation of the new universities was successfully accomplished. On the thorny question of teacher training no solution was found.

Guichard also undertook a long overdue reform of the central Ministry. After taking up his post he had declared, "There is no political or administrative post in France that is as monstrous as that of national education minister. The notion that a politician can supervise 811,000 civil servants and a budget of 27 milliard francs with the help of a skeletal headquarters staff is far-fetched."[9] Thus Guichard, using the principles of management by objectives, set up directors of objectives and directors of ways and means. For the posts concerned with objectives he would have preferred special ministers to have been appointed, but had to content himself with civil servants instead.

For Guichard the continuance of the arrangements for aid to private schools was a matter of urgency. The Debré Law of December 31, 1959 had been due for renewal after nine years, but could be prolonged for a further three. This renewal had taken place in 1969, after Peyrefitte had been unable to introduce a new law because of the uprising of 1968. The Minister was anxious not to revive the bitter quarrels that had

[9] J. Hayward, *op. cit.*, p. 199.

characterized the passing of the original law. In some ways his path had been smoothed. The Catholic authorities, although intent on safeguarding their schools financially, seemed not over-reluctant to shed some of their secular responsibilities. In particular, the lack of recruits coming forward for the teaching orders of the Church made their position difficult. The declaration of the French bishops meeting at Lourdes in November 1969, in which it was stated for the first time that the State school was worthy of the "esteem of Catholics and their pastors" had been seen as a gesture of appeasement. Contrasting, however, with the Catholic authorities, Catholic parents, grouped in the Union Nationale des Associations de Parents d'Elèves de l'Enseignement Libre (UNAPEL), still seemed rather militant.

In the spring of 1971 it was reckoned that one-sixth of all pupils were in private schools: 1,905,696 pupils in all, of which 1,730,953 were in Catholic schools. The distribution was as shown in Table 29.

Table 29. Percentage of pupils in private sector, 1971

Pre-primary	Primary	Lower secondary general	Upper secondary general	Technical and Professional
14.2	13.9	18.2	23.1	25.7

The comparatively larger figures for the secondary schools reflect the dissatisfaction that some of the bourgeoisie felt with State schools, particularly since 1968. Whether practising Catholics or not, some have preferred to pay fees to send their children to a Catholic collège rather than a State lycée.

It will be recalled that the Debré Law had envisaged two types of contract between private schools and the State. The *simple contract* was the one which surrendered the least the autonomy of the school. In return for payment of teachers' salaries the school had to see that its staff were fully qualified and fulfil three other lesser conditions. In 1971 private schools containing 62 per cent of all private pupils were governed by this type of contract. The *contract of association* imposed stricter conditions regarding programmes and timetables on the school, but in return the State paid not only teachers' salaries but all other running costs. A further condition imposed for this type of contract was that the school should fulfil "a recognized need" in the locality. Some 27 per cent of pupils were in schools which had signed this type of contract. The remaining pupils, some thirteen per cent, were in private schools that had preferred to remain completely independent of State aid.

In 1971 the government proposed that primary schools could opt for the simple contract for a further period of nine years. This was tantamount to establishing this arrangement permanently. Catholics welcomed this wholeheartedly. The other limb of the proposal, that by 1980, unless they wished to remain completely independent, the private secondary schools must sign a contract of association, was not so welcome. It was taken to mean that after 1980 the option of contracting-in would be removed from those schools that remained independent. It was feared by the Catholics that this was a first step towards the nationalization of all secondary education. There was also the question of what constituted a "recognized need", which was again left vague. However, the government was adamant. It held that what was at stake was the principle of the orientation and guidance system that had become one of the lynchpins of all reform. It was manifestly unfair that secondary pupils who had been in State schools but who at 15 had not been selected for the lycée could leave and go into a private school of their choice, subsidized by State funds. Indeed, the government went one farther and stipulated that the whole apparatus of orientation and guidance should also be introduced into the private schools. What was ultimately envisaged was the complete harmonization of public and private education.

Some of the secularist organizations raised the almost ritual outcry regarding these new arrangements, which would continue to subsidize private education, but finally the law was passed. There is no doubt, however, that it marks a further step towards more direct control of private education and was therefore acceptable to many of its nominal opponents. And the entire quarrel must now be viewed in the light of the decline in religious belief, which, although less marked than in England, is nonetheless apparent in France.

This is not to say that various interest groups are not still active. In the National Assembly there is still a strong Catholic lobby. In 1973 the Association Parlementaire pour la Liberté d'Enseignement numbered 152 deputies, mainly drawn from the UDR and including the then Minister of Education, M. Fontanet, and the future President of the Republic, M. Giscard d'Estaing. After the passing of the law Catholic education was undoubtedly strengthened: in 1971 State credits allocated to private schools amounted to 8.85 per cent of the education budget; by 1973 this had risen to 9.6 per cent. This increase was accounted for by the growth of the number of teachers employed, rising in the private sector by 2 per cent per year, and by the assistance that had been given in the training of private primary school teachers. The Minister, however, was at pains to state that the government would not allow the staff–pupil ratio in private schools to be better than that in the State system.[10] There was also a proposal made that the "free" Catholic faculties, grouped in Institutes, should be allowed to conduct examinations for degrees and qualifications which would be recognized by the State. This proposal would have broken the monopoly the State had enjoyed in the granting of degrees since 1879. It aroused such hostility that it was referred to the Conseil d'Etat, which promptly declared it illegal. When in 1975 the then Minister, M. Haby, dropped the adjective "national" from the title of his office and became plain Minister of Education this aroused resentment because it was feared that private education would benefit still further from State support. For some out-and-out secularists, such as Jean Cornec, until recently head of one of the largest parents' associations, eternal vigilance was seen to be necessary. He declared that the Church is always alert to take advantage of special circumstances to advance its educational claims. He cited 1914, when the closure of Catholic schools was halted by war; the Vichy interlude, when subsidies were given to Catholic schools; the Marie and Barangé Laws, which were voted during the Indo-China war; and the Debré Law, which was passed during the Algerian war. The fact that some 600 Catholic chaplaincies are still allowed to operate in State boarding lycées is also another source of irritation[11] – despite the fact that many chaplains are so dissatisfied with their ineffectiveness in these schools that they are leaving these posts.

It is doubtful, however, whether the mass of the French population, as distinct from special interest groups such as the teachers, or extremists at either end of the spectrum, whether "ultra-violet" or "ultra-red", feel passionately any longer about the "religious question".

On the other hand, some educational issues can still arouse the general public very easily. One such occasion occurred in 1970. Guichard, using

---

[10] Press conference given by Guichard, reported in *Le Monde,* Sept. 6, 1973.
[11] G. Cogniot, *Laicité et réforme démocratique de l'enseignement,* Paris, 1963.

only the instrument of a circular and not the more formal apparatus of decrees and regulations, changed the regulations concerning the teaching of modern languages. In an effort to lighten the load of the school curriculum he stipulated that the study of a second modern language in the third year of the lower secondary school, hitherto compulsory for the two top streams in that school, would become optional. Those who did not wish to learn a second language could instead have extra oral work in their first foreign language, which is usually English. This comparatively modest curricular reform, which denied nobody anything, struck up the most heated quarrel of the year. It had come like a bolt from the blue and had been announced without consultation with the interested parties. Immediately the measure was opposed by all the secondary teachers' organizations, some of the unions in higher education, one of the larger parents' associations, the Communist-oriented students' organization, UNEF-Renouveau, and the similarly oriented pupils' Comités d'Action Lycéens. Some teachers and would-be teachers of foreign languages other than English feared for their livelihood. Ambassadors of foreign powers — Italy was particularly mentioned — are alleged to have protested at the Quai d'Orsay on the grounds that the proposal would ensure the hegemony of English in French schools. This reasoning also aroused an anti-Anglo-Saxon lobby in the National Assembly. A tense situation, which led to teacher, student and pupil strikes, was only relieved when the Minister announced that, far from facilities for learning other languages being curtailed. they would be extended. The incident, although trivial, has a number of object lessons. The first is the undoubted political reaction that any educational innovations invoke in France — as contrasted with the apathy of the English when these occur. The second is the fact that the breakdown in communication was absolute: "legislation by circular" was universally condemned.[12] The third is the prickliness that exists in France over education, particularly when intellectual standards are considered to be under attack.

Other matters turned out to be more serious. Unrest continued to be latent in the lycées and in higher education throughout the period.

[12] Jean Papillon, the education correspondent of *Le Figaro,* commented in the newspaper on Feb. 18, 1970: "Let us recognize once again that a reform of the pattern of the secondary curriculum has had to be winkled out from a circular . . . [for which] no explanation has been given to the consumers, teachers, parents and pupils."

Occasionally, as in the spring of 1973, the tinder of revolt was almost kindled to flame again. Two matters aroused particular indignation. The first was the introduction of the new two-year university diploma, the DEUG, which could be either a terminal qualification or be a necessary step towards continuing for a full degree. Students and some teachers' unions argued that this was tantamount to selection, and that the new qualification would be no more than a "super-baccalaureate". Left-wing critics saw in the new arrangement a plot hatched up by the régime with employers to provide trained manpower with only a modicum of higher education, and one which was also aimed at cutting down the embarrassingly high number of university students. The government argued that all the signs were that some qualification lower than a degree was required, which would allow students to enter middle-grade management posts and the tertiary sector in general. It was here that jobs were available, rather than in the higher cadres.

The "affair of the DEUG", as it came to be known, was linked with another measure which affected students directly: the new proposals for the deferment of military service. A law sponsored by Debré when he was Minister of Defence had set a period of one year's obligatory military service, allowing those liable to choose the date of their call-up at any time between the ages of 17 years 9 months and 21 years 10 months. When the law had been passed in 1970 it had been considered by a special committee dealing with relations between the armed forces and youth, on which a number of representative bodies had sat. The measure had been approved by this committee with only one dissentient vote, although the Communist committee members had abstained. In 1973 it was proposed to apply the law to students born in 1951 and after, thus making students' conditions of deferment the same as those for other young men. (The sole exceptions were for medicine and dentistry, where students would still be allowed to defer military service until they had completed their course, but would then be required to serve for a slightly longer period.) The proposal to apply the law to students aroused a storm of protest. It was argued that it would mean an interruption of studies for most of them, with all the disadvantages that this entailed, and would bear particularly hard upon those who had no financial backing from their parents. The poorest students already reached the university at a later age and it was argued that it was likely that they would not even have completed their studies for the new two-year qualification, the DEUG, before they would be obliged to break them off and do military service. In that case there was a strong likelihood that they would never return to university afterwards. On the other hand, the government could legitimately argue that to grant postponements freely to students at university would disadvantage other young people who might also have good reasons for deferment, since in any case the quota of "le contingent" had to be equalized in numbers from year to year. Indeed, the system of deferment in the past had often worked to the disadvantage of students: they had been unable to take up employment immediately after completing their studies, since often jobs in France are advertised as being open only to applicants free of their "military obligations".

The situation was aggravated by the views of some high-ranking officers who argued, as had Lyautey and Pétain before them, that the school and the Army were the joint educators of the nation. They considered that since the family and religion were failing in their duty in fostering the moral and civic virtues, it was up to the Army to undertake this task! For this reason the break between school and military service should be as short as possible, so that new recruits would still be in their formative years.[13] The cry went up that this was an attempt to make youth toe the line — "une mise au pas" which was quite unacceptable. Indeed, the dispute quickly developed from one about the deferment of military service, which young men had usually, if reluctantly, accepted with good grace, but about the necessity for conscription at all, or indeed for any national defence force. The new slogan[14] was:

"Les sursis on s'enfout,
On n'veut plus d'armée du tout."
("We don't give a damn about deferment — we don't want any army at all.")

The quarrel brought tens of thousands of demonstrators on to the streets throughout France in the spring days of 1973. In early April the figure was put as high as 300,000. The students were out in force, as were the older school pupils, the principal federations of trade unions, the parents' federation (Association Cornec), the Communists and the Socialists. They carried banners with messages such as "Down with the army of capitalism", and "We want to study, not to kill".

[13] General Vanuxem, in: *Carrefour*, April 9, 1969.
[14] Quoted in *Le Monde*, April 4, 1973.

The "lycéens" took the opportunity to revive their old demands: they demonstrated, they organized sit-ins. Their slogans were the usual ones: "The syllabuses are boring", "We lack contact with our teachers", "The lycée is inhuman". Fontanet, the then Minister, was in favour of taking a firm line from the beginning, even to the extent of closing the schools if all else failed. He also hinted that boarders who "struck" might be sent home and that scholarships and family allowances might be cut.

On the question of military service an accommodation was eventually reached and a more liberal system of deferments for students was adopted. Debré, who had been the unwitting author of these disturbances, declared after the March 1973 elections that he would not accept the post of Minister of Defence in the Government of Pierre Messmer. This may be because he anticipated further trouble. Left-wing politicians and students did indeed begin a campaign to reduce the period of military service to six months and pressed for the granting of a "soldiers' charter" which would ensure "freedom of expression, association, thought and religious observance" in the armed forces. These demands are still current. Once again, however, as on so many occasions in recent French history, education had almost become the catalyst for a wider flare-up in society.

That 1968 had not entirely resolved the crisis in the schools was demonstrated by the report of the Joxe Commission.[15] Guichard, it will be recalled, had set up this committee of enquiry in December 1971 to look at "the teaching function in secondary education". The chairman of the Commission, Louis Joxe, had himself been a Minister of Education in the early days of the Fifth Republic. His remit from the present Minister had been to investigate:

(a)   What is the situation of the secondary teacher *vis-à-vis* his pupils, the administrators, society and his colleagues?

(b)   How may the function of the teacher be defined today?

(c)   What recommendations might be made for future policy?

The Commission reported in June 1972. It set out ten principles and made eighteen recommendations. The principles may be summarized as follows: (a) the school unit must be the basis of education; (b) real decentralization must take place; (c) school organization must be pupil-

---

[15] *La Fonction enseignante dans l'enseignement du second degré* (Joxe Report), Paris, 1972. This report is sometimes referred to as the report of the "Commission des Sages".

centred and open to the world outside the school; (d) teachers must work no longer in isolation, but in pluridisciplinary teams; (e) teachers' conditions of service must be modified; (f) teachers must be in touch with a network of ancillary services, from educational technology to research; (g) the teaching profession must be unified; (h) the general inspectorate must adopt a new role; (i) a social policy must be evolved for teachers; (j) the Ministry must cultivate a public relations policy to explain what happens. These principles, admirable in themselves, can only be described as vague. They were viewed by some teachers as a threat, by others as a promise of improvement.

Eighteen recommendations were nevertheless evolved in the light of these principles. They may be summarized as follows:

1. No school should contain more than 700–800 pupils.
2. Schools must have freedom to experiment in teaching methods.
3. Although the total time allocation should continue to be laid down centrally, how this should be distributed over the school year and whether it should form an element in a pluridisciplinary approach should be left to the school to decide.
4. Within a global budget the school should be able to spend its money how it wishes.
5. Every school should have a "documentation centre" (perhaps better translated as "resources centre"), adequate laboratories and workshops.
6. Teachers should be grouped in pluridisciplinary teams which should comprise coordinators, guidance counsellors, subject teachers, educational assistants and specialists such as doctors and social workers.
7. Each team should have wide powers.
8. Criteria must be laid down for appointments of school principals.
9. Schools should be purpose-built to be able to use the new methods.
10. Examinations should be reformed.
11. Experimental schools should be set up.
12. The initial and in-service training of teachers should be transformed and extended.
13. The various grades of teacher must be constituted in a unified profession.

14. Social measures must be taken to help teachers in matters that affect them.
15. Teachers' duties and obligations must be reformulated.
16. The procedures for the assessment of teachers must be modified.
17. The role of the general inspectorate must be modified.
18. The training of educational administrators must be changed.

Some of these proposals were deliberately vague; few were novel; all had far-reaching consequences and by no means received universal approbation. But they represented a distinct advance in the procedure for formulating new educational policy. For the first time a report of a semi-independent body, as in England free to speak its mind, constituted of teachers, inspectors, university professors, planners and others, had been given wide diffusion among the general public. The days when the Ministry had acted more secretively and autonomously were over. The formula of public debate, of "dialogue with the nation", was one that was henceforth to be increasingly employed.

In another area, which has been dealt with elsewhere, legislation had been successfully carried through. The laws on technological education had been passed in 1971 and had found approval practically everywhere.

Before, however, the content of the Joxe Report could be considered in detail not only did the outbursts of the spring of 1973 confirm the "malaise" that existed among teachers and the "boredom" of pupils, both of which had been mentioned in the Report, but a general election brought all reforms to a halt for the time being.

The British observer cannot but be impressed by the high priority that is accorded to discussion of education in French election programmes. This was particularly noticeable in the March 1973 parliamentary elections. Seven main political groupings put forward candidates, although there was an increasing tendency towards the bipolarization into Left and Right becoming more marked. On the Right the principal contenders were those who rallied round the Gaullists (the UDR itself, the Independent Republicans, and Modern Progress and Democracy – the three parties who loosely constituted what was termed the "Majority"). On the Left was the so-called "Union of the Left", consisting of the re-formed Socialist Party of 1969 and the Communists. Two lesser protagonists were the Reformers' Party – the former Radical Socialists and Social Democrats – and the Unified Socialist Party, small but influential. Each of these had much to say about the future of the education system.[16]

The "Majority" saw its future programme in terms of continuing the work in which it had been engaged as the ruling alliance for the previous fifteen years. It boasted that during the period the national budget for education had increased from 12 to 18 per cent of the total budget; lower secondary and technical education had been transformed; higher education had been reformed; and a start had been made upon developing lifelong education. It saw the goal as the continued "democratization" of education. The Prime Minister, M. Messmer, in an important speech at Provins, had announced that the small number of educational institutions still controlled by the municipalities would be brought under national control, school equipment and transport would be supplied free — at least until the end of compulsory education — and eventually all children would begin some form of nursery education¹ from the age of 2. Last but not least, he wished to see restored the authority of school principals, which had been considerably weakened after 1968. His Minister of Education, M. Fontanet, had his own "shopping list", the chief items of which were the adoption of the recommendations of the Joxe Report, a reform of the system of school guidance, the development of lifelong education, and an increase in aid to pupils and students.

Within the "Majority", the UDR attached priority to a fundamental reform of the content of education, particularly in secondary schools, where an initiation into economics and the stimulation of interest in technology were vital national concerns. In higher education the autonomy of the universities, and competition between them, had to be developed. Universities should also occupy themselves with regional matters and have local representation on their governing bodies.

The Independent Republicans — the party of the present President, Giscard d'Estaing — were in favour of a general law on secondary education which would mirror that on higher education passed in 1968. In particular, it would spell out precisely the degree of "participation" in schools. In higher education they sought to give help to the independent Catholic Institutes and to encourage — as did the UDR — greater autonomy and competition between universities. They advocated that the content of education should be made more "European". They wanted more strictly pedagogical training of teachers.

[16] Cf. Association des Journalistes universitaires, *Les Partis politiques devant l'école,* Paris, 1973.

The Modern Progress and Democracy grouping sought to divorce the administration of the teaching force from that of the civil service as a whole, to establish a common form of teacher training, to make upper secondary education less specialized and to increase university autonomy.

The Union of the Left, as the main Opposition grouping, envisaged a gargantuan programme of reforms, although this could not be carried out within the lifetime of one legislature. Their first priority was the achievement of social integration. One important step in this direction would be achieved by extending compulsory education from 16 to 18, a proposal that goes back to the Langevin-Wallon Plan of 1974. It is not clear whether this proposal implied full- or part-time education for all up to that age. A number of other measures would serve to iron out social inequalities: free books, equipment and transport; better provision for the handicapped; more crèches and nursery education; the abolition of "streaming" in lower secondary schools; the ending of the practice of "grade-repeating"; a better guidance service for those leaving school; the updating of the content of education. Likewise, lifelong education would be developed; in higher education science and technology would be encouraged; on the other hand, competition between universities would be discouraged; the present moves towards autonomy would be continued, but this must not lead to anarchy. Teacher training would be overhauled and unified — although the pro-Communist Syndicat National de l'Enseignement Secondaire remained lukewarm about this proposal. The most drastic suggestion concerned the unification of the education system itself, by absorbing all private education into the State apparatus. Catholic clergy would, however, enjoy the right (at present denied them) of teaching in the State system. Moreover, all schools would remain strictly "neutral" as regards religious beliefs. This is, of course, a colossal programme, which would cost, as the Minister of Education at the time pointed out, a phenomenal sum.

The Unified Socialist Party did not present a programme of educational policy as such, but merely used education as an example of how society must be transformed. A cultural, social and political revolution would bring about a profound metamorphosis in education. Social and education selection (for, the party asserted, the two are synonymous) must disappear; lifelong education must not be tacked on as an "extra" to schooling, but be the main theme in the training of the worker; there must be adequate sports facilities for all; there must be freedom to challenge the content of education and even the institution of the school itself; schools must in any case become community centres for the young. There is no doubt that the Unified Socialist Party was more extreme in its demands than the Communists.

The results of the elections gave the "Majority" a clear preponderance over the opposition parties. Fontanet, as Minister of Education, made clear his determination to take a firm line with "agitators" in schools and universities. After the tumultuous spring he issued a circular which baldly stated that in the summer term "the continuance of agitation will not be permitted", and threatened sanctions. This ukase did not endear him to everybody. Nevertheless he pressed on with plans for reform.

He commissioned M. Raymond Barré of Paris I University and M. Jean-Louis Boursin of the University of Orleans to undertake a study of education among the member states of the European Economic Community as a preparation for further reform of secondary education in France. A draft law was submitted to Parliament in the spring of 1974, but lapsed upon the death of M. Pompidou. The new President, Giscard d'Estaing, then appointed a different Minister of Education, M. Haby.

The principle of "consultation and concertation" as a means of achieving a consensus has been continued by M. Haby. It represents a radical departure from the somewhat autocratic way in which successive measures of reform have been imposed since 1959.

In order to free himself to concentrate upon the task of producing a new law on primary and secondary education, the Minister set up the special secretaryship of State for nursery education, with a woman, Mme Lesur, at its head. Furthermore, the separate autonomous Ministry for Higher Education, under M. Soisson, was also created.

After holding innumerable consultations with as many interested parties as possible, including the publication of a tentative plan, "Propositions pour la modernisation du système éducatif français", the Minister, M. Haby, presented a bill to Parliament in June 1975. Opponents of the bill — and they are numerous — say that the text is too vague; on the other hand, Article 34 of the Constitution stipulates that Parliament has merely to determine "the basic principles of education" and not to agree on every detail.

The law is a comparatively short one, comprising only twenty-two articles in all. The proposed organization of the educational system is simple: a nursery school open to all before the beginning of schooling proper; a common education for all pupils, in both primary and lower secondary schools — in the latter, supplementary courses will be available; and, for upper secondary education, a branching system, with schooling given in either general or technical lycées. Elected bodies that will include representatives of all members of the school community, where feasible, will assist in the running of the schools.

The text of the law[17] is given below:

ARTICLE 1

Every child has the right to schooling which, completing that given in the family, contributes to his education.

Such schooling is compulsory between the ages of six and sixteen.

It fosters the development of the child, allows him to acquire a culture, prepares him for working life and for the exercise of his responsibilities as a man and as a citizen. It constitutes the foundation for lifelong education. Families are associated with the accomplishment of these objectives.

To promote equality of opportunity appropriate arrangements make it possible for everyone, in accordance with his abilities, to have access to the different types or levels of schooling.

These arrangements include free education during the period of compulsory schooling.

The State is the guarantor of respect for the personality of the child and for the educative activities of the family.

TITLE ONE: TEACHING

ARTICLE 2

Infant or nursery classes are available in rural as well as urban areas to children who have not yet reached the age of compulsory schooling.

At the age of five, if the family so desires, every child is to be able to be admitted to these classes or, failing this, to an infants' section in an elementary school.

Early training in reading and writing in these classes is not compulsory. The education given in them is designed to stimulate the awakening of the personality. It seeks to forestall difficulties arising in schooling proper, to diagnose handicaps and to compensate for inequalities.

The State provides the necessary teaching staff for these educational activities.

ARTICLE 3

Primary education is given in elementary schools following a common programme spread over five consecutive levels; the initial period may be of variable length.

[17] The text of the new law is given in: *L'Education*, No. 252 of Sept. 18, 1975.

Primary education ensures the acquisition of the basic tools of knowledge: oral and written expression, reading and arithmetic; it stimulates the development of the intelligence, of artistic sensibility and manual, physical and sporting skills. It affords an initiation into the plastic and musical arts. In conjunction with the family it imparts moral education and civic education.

ARTICLE 4

All children undergo secondary education in colleges. This follows without interruption upon primary education and is aimed at giving pupils a culture in harmony with the society of their age. It rests upon a balance of disciplines that are intellectual, artistic, manual, physical and sporting, and which allows their abilities and aptitudes to be brought out. It constitutes the basis for later general or professional education, whether this follows immediately or is given in the framework of lifelong education.

The colleges follow a common programme, spread over four successive levels. The last two may also include additional courses, certain of which may prepare for occupational training; these may include practical courses controlled by the State and carried out under approved specialists. The schooling for these two levels, since it includes the compulsory common course, may be carried out in preparatory classes attached to an institution of vocational training.

ARTICLE 5

Secondary education may be continued in the "lycées" which, in all types of education, give both a general and a specialized training. It leads to *either:*
- the award of diplomas as vocational qualifications allowing access to a higher level of training
  or:
- the award of the diploma of bachelor of secondary education, which may itself attest also to a vocational qualification.

The examination for the baccalaureate of secondary education attests to the acquisition of a balanced education and includes:
- the guarantee of a level of culture acquired in the teaching given in the first two years of the "lycée";
- the verification of the specialized knowledge acquired by the pupil in the courses followed during the terminal year.

This verification is carried out independently for each one of these courses.

ARTICLE 6

The State undertakes or encourages measures to fit for an occupation those pupils who leave school without having followed a vocational training course.

ARTICLE 7

In the schools and colleges special arrangements and supportive measures are envisaged for those pupils who experience difficulties. Where these difficulties are serious and permanent, pupils receive remedial teaching.

Moreover, in the subjects comprising the common course offered in the colleges additional teaching is given to those pupils who may derive benefit from it.

ARTICLE 8
The organization and content of courses are defined respectively in decrees and regulations laid down by the Minister of Education. Decrees stipulate the principles for the autonomy in pedagogical matters allowed to schools, colleges and "lycées".

ARTICLE 9
Decisions regarding the guidance of the pupil are arrived at after systematic observation of him. Each one of the decisions is taken in conjunction with the wishes expressed by the pupil's family, or by him himself if he is of the age of majority. They take into account his personal abilities and the paths that are open to him.

The pupil and his family are informed of the data that are taken into consideration for decisions regarding the guidance of the pupil.

An appeals procedure is envisaged. This may comprise an examination, the results of which are judged by an external panel of examiners.

ARTICLE 10
During schooling the evaluation of ability and the acquisition of knowledge are carried out by a process of continuous assessment made by the teachers under the responsibility of the school principal or the head of the institution.

ARTICLE 11
The State validates by national diplomas the various secondary courses.

Subject to arrangements made under Article 146 of the code for technical education, panels of examiners are made up of members of the body of State teachers.

For the purposes of the award of diplomas there may be taken into account either the results of continuous assessment or the results of terminal examinations, or a combination of the two.

Diplomas may be obtained through a system of credit-units.

ARTICLE 12
Courses in regional languages and culture may be given throughout the period of schooling.

TITLE TWO: SCHOOL LIFE

ARTICLE 13
In every school, college or "lycée" the staff, the pupils' parents and the pupils form the school community. Each must contribute to its smooth running, having respect for persons and opinions.

For the purposes of the exchange of information contact is established between the teachers and each of the pupils' families, at least until the pupils have attained the age of majority. In particular their object is to allow the family, or the pupil himself, if he is of the age of majority, to be kept informed of reports on his progress.

ARTICLE 14

A principal is responsible for the smooth running of a nursery or an elementary school. He is responsible for the necessary coordination among the teachers. The pupils' parents elect their representatives to form a parents' committee, which is summoned to meet from time to time by the school principal. The representative of the local community attends by right these meetings.

ARTICLE 15

Colleges and "lycées" are run by a head teacher. He is assisted by a school council comprising, in particular, the elected representatives of the school community and of the various local interests.

ARTICLE 16

The life of the school community is governed by general arrangements embodied in regulations. In addition it is subject to special arrangements adapted to local conditions. Each member of the school community has the duty of observing the rules.

ARTICLE 17

The architecture of the school has an educative function. It is an indispensable element in the teaching function and fosters the growth of artistic sensibility.

TITLE THREE: SPECIAL TRANSITIONAL ARRANGEMENTS

ARTICLE 18

Dispensations from the provisions of the present law may be granted for the purposes of undertaking an educational experiment, but are limited to the duration of the experiment, under conditions stipulated by decree.

In such a case easy access to a school or educational institution not participating in the experiment must be guaranteed to those pupils whose families so desire.

ARTICLE 19

Decrees will lay down the procedures for applying the present law and will fix the conditions under which it will progressively enter into force.

Before the first of June of each year the government will present to Parliament a report on the application of the present law and any laws that supplement it. This report must include the observations made by the various educational councils regarding the applicatory decrees of which they are apprised.

ARTICLE 20

Subject to the jurisdiction attributed to assemblies or elected councils in overseas territories the provisions of the present law may be made applicable either wholly or in part in the overseas territories by means of decrees promulgated in the Conseil d'Etat, which will contain the adaptations made necessary by the particular organization of such territories.

ARTICLE 21

The provisions of the present law relating to education are applicable at the same time to State education and, with respect for the principles defined by the law No. 59–1557 of December 31, 1959 as modified by the law No. 71–400 of June 1, 1971, also to private education under contract.

ARTICLE 22

Decrees made in the Conseil d'Etat will fix in what conditions the provisions of the present law may, in whole or in part, be applied to French schools and educational institutions abroad, taking account of their special situation and of agreements concluded with foreign States.

The law, No. 75–620, was passed by the National Assembly, and signed by the President on July 11, 1975.

There is no doubt that it represents a watershed in French school education, just as did the Law of 1968 for higher education. Two other laws will be required to complete it. The first will deal with teachers and revise the many different categories now existing, their working conditions and number of teaching hours, as well as pre-service and in-service training. There is no doubt that official thinking is tending towards a more unified profession, which will inevitably arouse hostility. A second law will attempt to define with greater precision the conditions under which the schools must function, and in particular the degree of financial and pedagogical autonomy they will enjoy. Here much depends on whether the concept of the school as a community, specifically referred to in the law just passed, can be made a reality. Another important task will be the systematic revision of the content of education, with subjects grouped in interdisciplinary "fields" rather than taught as autonomous entities. The new law, as it stands, has been, as already mentioned, criticized severely for its lack of detail. It has been argued that the text contains many stock phrases that have been well used before; there is little indication that the objectives proposed will fit in with the kind of society that is envisaged for the year 2000. The use of the French word "formation" rather than "éducation" (a usage which cannot be always exactly rendered in the translation of the law given above) has also been criticized, because it would seem to imply the subordination of the cultural and individual purposes of schooling to those of society as a whole, insisting upon the "training" rather than the purely "educative" function of schooling. Another significant omission in the law concerns the problem of access to higher education, which remains unresolved.

The applicatory decrees ("décrets d'application") of the law will be hammered out with the interested parties in 1976, and the supplementary laws will also be presented to the National Assembly during the course of the year, if all goes smoothly. Thus the law may come into force progressively as from the autumn of 1977, a procedure which will cause the least disturbance to those pupils passing through the schools at the moment.

CHAPTER 18

Conclusions

A national education system reflects the culture of a people; indeed the totality of Man's inventions, whether material or in the realm of ideas form the subject-matter of education. The ideals that are uppermost in the minds of men at any one time, the practical achievements realized by a generation, condition the ways in which the older generation think the young should be "socialized". If this be so, what makes 1959 a decisive date in the history of French education?

The Gaullist era was the first occasion that had been vouchsafed any French government since 1945, indeed since 1918, to realize the ideals formulated in the aftermath of the First World War by the Compagnons de l'Université Nouvelle. Those ideals may be epitomized in the phrase "equality of opportunity", or as the French preferred eventually to say, "democratization". But this objective was conceived of in a specifically French way. It expressed a desire to open up the "high culture", that intellectual patrimony which is so eminently represented in France, to all young people. There was to be no dilution of this culture: all had the right of access to it; all efforts must be directed towards attaining it.

This was, of course, an impossible goal. It was unrealistic to assume that all children would wish to steep themselves in a bookish, literary culture which seemed to bear little relation to the world in which they found themselves. De Gaulle realized, none better, that the content of education needed updating. He had taken over the leadership of a nation which, through war and exploitation, lagged behind in industrialization. The new dimension that had to be imparted to French culture, and thus eventually to the education system, was scientific and technological. The secular idealism which had characterized the old classical learning and which for so long had informed French education had to be superseded by a new doctrine of instrumentalism, pragmatic and utilitarian. France had to enter the twentieth century; the schools and universities were an important agency in this process.

At the same time the schools must be what they had been under the Third Republic: a force for national unity. De Gaulle found a France uncertain of itself as a nation, lacking that confidence to take up its rightful place in the world. He aspired to a society which would be neither capitalist nor Communist. For him egalitarianism was best expressed in terms of participation. In this respect the educational institutions might become the mentors of the nation. All the measures taken, from the simple "orientation" procedures outlined in 1959, where for the first time all the partners in education were brought into consultation, to the elaborate Law of Orientation of Higher Education in 1968, can be interpreted as attempts to promote participatory ideals.

Democratization, egalitarianism, participation: this trilogy leads ineluctably to a meritocracy. This was undoubtedly the kind of society de Gaulle sought to promote. Yet a meritocracy is a form of élitism which, it can be argued, may be even more pernicious than one based upon wealth. In Western society, however unfair it may be, there is a residual, faint hope that even the poorest child may become a millionaire. In a perfected meritocracy that hope may no longer be entertained. That cruellest of yardsticks by which to judge a man, the accident of birth which determines how much brainpower he will possess, will in a meritocracy inexorably determine social position and life expectations, conferring a fixed status from which there is no possibility of escape.

In any case, the practical politicians that surrounded de Gaulle, who had not much flair for economic matters, held a slightly different view of education. In a world dedicated to the pursuit of affluence the schools had an important part to play. Education must be organized to meet the manpower needs of the economy, to supply the skilled workers and cadres that France needed. The refurbishing of the schools and universities must take this into account.

In any case, that refurbishing could not, for other reasons, have come at a more difficult time. The "social demand" for education came when population increase already was bearing down heavily upon the provision of facilities. Moreover, the turbulent 1960s were the period of the emancipation of the young, when the clash of the generations was a world-wide phenomenon. For the first time young people became aware of the political power that they could wield. The occasion for their discontent was the education system, then in the process of reconstruction.

Their attitudes provoked a counter-reaction. In 1968, as in 1830, as in 1848, the bourgeoisie set its face against radical reform, out of fear for what the future might have in store.

In any case, those without whom all educational reform will run like water into the sand, the teachers, remained profoundly hostile to the régime. The teachers, spurned, scorned and vilified by de Gaulle, suspecting a government which, despite its claim to be the mirror-image of the people of France, they considered to be profoundly rooted in the Right (whereas the majority of the teachers' organizations were at least part of the moderate Left), hostile even to the sensible arrangements that were made with the Catholic schools, could find few educational reforms acceptable. The slightest detail gave rise to "contestation", so hypersensitive had they become.

This attitude of "contestation" is perhaps the least understandable by the foreign observer. In 1963 a régime characterized as being of the Right introduced a form of comprehensive education which, in those days, would have won the unqualified support of the moderate Left everywhere in the world, as at least being a step in the right direction. This progressiveness in Gaullist educational policies, expressed also in a willingness to experiment, to decentralize power, to give educational institutions greater freedom (provided that it did not diminish equality), is something that cannot be denied.

To this, of course, the opponents of the régime would retort that changes did not go far enough, that everything remained fundamentally unchanged, that it was, as the Germans say, a "Scheinreform". Setting aside, however, the committed ideologists on both sides, how far are the mass of Frenchmen satisfied with the new edifice of education that has now been erected? What little evidence there is is conflicting. A poll by a French institute for public opinion taken in January 1971[1] revealed that 50 per cent of those asked thought that the school carried out its functions rather well, and 38 per cent thought the contrary. On the other hand, an anonymous survey[2] of "satisfaction ratings for different aspects of life" showed that among the EEC countries the "satisfaction rating" for education was low in France as compared with West Germany and Britain. The comparative percentages that declared themselves "satisfied" with the

[1] The results were published on the TV programme, "A armes égales", Jan. 18, 1971.
[2] Reported in *The Times,* Europa Supplement, Nov. 5, 1974, p. x.

education given in their own countries were: France 8 per cent; West Germany 20 per cent; Britain 31 per cent. But in none of the three countries is the proportion who declare themselves satisfied high.

What of the future? One of the educationists who supports the régime has remarked that there are growing convergences, at least on pedagogical questions, among those who hold differing views on education. Louis Cros[3] notes that, regarding the content of what is taught, there is more agreement that there must be a common core of subjects studied by everybody, and that this should be supplemented by options suited to the individual. In lower secondary education there is an increasing consensus that the "track" system should disappear and be replaced by "enrichment programmes" for slow learners. Teaching methods must become more individualized, and be based upon activity and creativity. The value of group work is recognized. Examinations are increasingly being called into question and may eventually be replaced by guidance and continuous assessment. The fact that there is such broad agreement is a hopeful sign for the future.

In the end, however, the nature of the education system must depend upon the nature of the society towards which men strive. On this there is as yet no agreement. The only firm conclusion that one may come to is that the concept of a stable, fixed education system is dead.

[3] L. Cros, "Convergences pédagogiques", *Education,* Sept. 19, 1974, pp. 27–30.

BIBLIOGRAPHY

The most comprehensive bibliography of French education published in English is: *Education in France. A Union List of stock in Institute and School of Education Libraries,* edited by Joan V. Marder (with a Foreword by W. D. Halls), Librarians of Institutes and Schools of Education, London, 1971. This lists 1157 titles.

There are numerous bibliographies of education in French. For articles, books, research reports and theses the best is the *Bulletin signalétique.* Sections 19–24. *Sciences humaines. Philosophie* (fascicule, "sciences de l'éducation"), published three times a year by the Centre National de la Recherche Scientifique. This is international in scope. It dates from 1946, but since 1969 the section on "sciences de l'éducation" has been sold separately. Another bibliography which is also international in scope is: E. Natalis, *Un Quart de siècle de littérature pédagogique. Essai bibliographique, 1945–1970,* Gembloux, 1971. This lists some 15,000 titles in twenty-four languages. Another recent bibliography is: P. Juif and F. Dovero, *Manuel bibliographique des sciences de l'éducation,* Paris, 1968. For the most recent works, apart from the general French bibliographies, there is the running list of acquisitions published at intervals throughout the year by the Service des Etudes et Recherches Pédagogiques, Institut National de la Recherche et de la Documentation Pédagogiques (INRDP) under the title: *Livraison Documentaire. Acquisitions: ouvrages intéressant la recherche en éducation. Liste annotée.* In 1971 the INRDP also issued a useful: *Bibliographie des articles français intéressant la recherche en éducation, 1968–1971.*

For general works in English relating to modern France the reader is referred to the lists which appear in general books mentioned below, such as those by Hayward, Ambler and Pickles.

The Selected Bibliography given below lists works and sources that relate to the present work. The Additional Bibliography which follows relates specifically to education and includes other relevant works (but not articles) published before 1971 and omitted from the Union List mentioned above, as well as works published since. It lays no claim to be exhaustive.

SELECTED BIBLIOGRAPHY

Official Publications

Journal Officiel
Bulletin Officiel de l'Education Nationale
Documents relating to syllabuses, programmes, examinations and teaching methods appearing in series sold by SEVPEN, Rue du Four, Paris. These are too extensive to list.
Occasional publications of the French Embassies in London and Washington.

Reviews and Periodicals

L'Education
Revue française de pédagogie
Cahiers pédagogiques
Le Figaro
Le Monde
L'Aurore
Times Higher Education Supplement
Times Educational Supplement

Articles and Monographs. etc.

Aron, R., "Combien d'étudiants?", *Le Figaro,* April 3, 1964.
Aron, R., "Quelques problèmes relatifs à l'enseignement", *Archives européennes de la sociologie,* 1962.
Assemblée Nationale, Document 136, Rapport Capelle (première session ordinaire de 1970/1971).
Bayet, G., "La loi d'orientation, est-elle applicable aux réalités?", *Le Figaro,* April 11–12, 1970.
Bidou, D. *et al.,* "Carrière universitaire et perspectives professionnelles", *Population,* Feb. 1970.
Bourdieu, P., "L'école conservatrice: les inégalités devant l'école et devant la culture", *Revue française de sociologie,* VII, 1966.
Bourdieu, R. and Passeron, J., "Les étudiants et leurs études", *Cahiers du Centre de Sociologie européenne,* The Hague, 1964.
Buriez, M., "Je ne peux plus être professeur", *Le Nouvel Observateur,* Feb. 17, 1967.
Capelle, J., "L'Université face aux problèmes de l'accès à la culture et aux emplois", *Le Monde,* Nov. 30, 1969.
Cesbron, G., "La plage et la grève", *Le Monde,* April 4, 1973.
Clark, P. P. and Clark, T. N., "Writers, literature and student movements in France", *Sociology of Education,* Fall 1969.

Clerc, P., "La famille et l'orientation scolaire au niveau de sixième", *Population,* Aug.–Sept. 1964.

"Déclaration des quatre-vingt-douze universitaires sur le bilinguisme en Alsace", *Le Monde,* Mar. 21, 1972.

Dejonghe, E., "Un mouvement séparatiste dans le Nord et le Pas de Calais sous l'Occupation (1940–1944): Le 'Vlaamsch Verbond van Frankrijk' ", *Revue d'histoire moderne et contemporaine,* XVII, Jan.–Mar. 1970.

Education et Gestion, Paris, numéro spécial, 1972.

(The) Engineers' (sic) Training in France, Service Scientifique, French Embassy, March 1974 (revised).

"Enseignement: retour à la vie", *L'Express,* Nov. 7, 1971.

Gaussen, F., "De l'Ancien Régime au nouveau", *Le Monde,* Dec. 8, 1970.

Gaussen, F., Europa Supplement, *The Times,* Dec. 8, 1974.

Gilly, M., "L'influence du milieu social et de l'âge sur la progression scolaire à l'école primaire", *Bulletin de psychologie,* No. 257, 1967.

Girard, A. *et al.,* "Enquête nationale sur l'entrée en sixième et la démocratisation de l'enseignement", *Population,* Jan.–Mar. 1963.

Girard, A. and Bastide, H.. "La stratification sociale et la démocratisation de l'enseignement", *Population,* July–Sept. 1963.

Halls, W. D., "Les effets de l'urbanisation sur l'éducation française", *International Review of Education,* 1966:4.

INRDP, *Le Mouvement éducatif en France, 1971–73,* Brochure No. 2032, Paris, 1973. (Under this title reports on changes in French education are reported biennially.)

Janina Lagneau *et al., Les Etudiants des Instituts Universitaires de Technologie,* OECD, Paris, 1973.

Marquet, P., "Quel français, demain?" *L'Education,* May 10, 1973.

Ministère de l'Education Nationale, Informations Rapides No. 10, Mar. 23, 1973.

Ministère de l'Education Nationale, Note d'Information No. 74–08, Feb. 26, 1974.

Nourry, P., "L'enseignement secondaire et l'égalité des chances. II. L'école moyenne, a-t-elle trouvé ses murs?", *Le Figaro,* Dec. 16, 1970.

Nourry, P. and Bois, P., "Français et égalité des chances: I. La maternelle", *Le Figaro,* Oct. 27, 1970.

Sauvy, A. and Girard, A., "Les diverses classes sociales devant l'enseignement: mise au point générale des résultats", *Population,* Mar.–Apr. 1965.

Scott, P., "France four years after the Faure reforms", *Times Higher Education Supplement,* Jan. 12, 1973.

Tournier, Michèle, "Women and access to university in France and Germany, 1861–1967", *Comparative Education* (Oxford), 9:3, October 1973.

Vial, J., "L'évolution des méthodes pédagogiques en France", *International Review of Education,* 1967:3.

Books

Allan, C., *Instituteurs et Professeurs,* Paris, 1964.

Alexandre, P., *Le Duel de Gaulle–Pompidou,* Paris, 1970.

Ambler, J., *The Government and Politics of France,* Boston, USA, 1971.

Amoureux, H., *La Vie des Français sous l'Occupation,* Vol. II, Paris, 1961.

Aron, R., *La Révolution introuvable,* Paris, 1968.

Association d'Etude pour l'expansion de la recherche scientifique. *Pour une école nouvelle: formation des maîtres et recherche en éducation. Actes du Colloque national d'Amiens, 1968.* Paris, 1969.

Association des Journalistes universitaires, *Les Partis politiques devant l'école,* Paris, 1973.

Avril, P., *Politics in France,* Harmondsworth, Middlesex, 1969.

Berger, Ida and Benjamin, R., *L'Univers des instituteurs: étude sociologique sur les instituteurs et institutrices du Département de la Seine,* Paris, 1964.

Besançon, J., *Les Murs ont la parole* (pub. by Claude Tchou), Paris, 1968.

Bisseret, Noelle, *Les Inégaux ou la sélection universitaire,* Paris, 1974.

Boirard, H., *Contribution à l'étude historique des congés et des vacances scolaires en France du moyen-âge à 1914,* Paris, 1971.

Bourdieu, P. and Passeron, J., *La Reproduction: éléments pour une théorie du système d'enseignement,* Paris, 1970.

Brechon, R., *La Fin des lycées,* Paris, 1970.

Capelle, J., *Tomorrow's Education: the French Experience* (tr. by W. D. Halls), London, 1967.

Capelle, J., *Contre le baccalauréat,* Paris, 1968. (In same volume, J. Cornec, "Pour le baccalauréat".)

Castel, R. and Passeron, J., (eds.), *Education, développement et démocratie,* Paris, 1967.

Chapsal, J., *La Vie politique en France depuis 1940,* 2nd edition, Paris, 1969.

Citron, Suzanne, *L'Ecole bloquée,* Paris, 1971.

Clark, J. M., *Teachers and Politics in France. A Pressure Group Study of the Fédération de l'Education Nationale,* Syracuse, New York, 1967.

Cogniot, G., *Laïcité et réforme démocratique de l'enseignement,* Paris, 1963.

Condorcet, *Sketch for a Historical Picture of the Progress of the Human Mind,* London, 1955.

Coombs, P. and Hallak, J., *Managing Educational Costs,* London, 1972.

Crémieux-Brilhac, J., *L'Education Nationale,* Paris, 1965.

Crozier, M., *The Bureaucratic Phenomenon,* Chicago, 1963. (Translation of: *Le Phénomène bureaucratique.*)

Dale, R., *From School to University,* London, 1954.

Daudet, Y., *Les nouveaux statuts des enseignants du second degré,* Paris, 1974.

Decaunes, L., *Réformes et projets de réforme de l'enseignement français de la Révolution à nos jours,* Paris, 1962.

De Gaulle, *Memoirs of Hope: Renewal, 1958–1962; Endeavour, 1962–* (translated by T. Kilmartin), London, 1971.

Delanoue, P., *Les Enseignants: la lutte syndicale du Front Populaire à la Libération,* Paris, 1973.

Durkheim, E., *L'Evolution pédagogique en France.* Vol. II. *De la Renaissance à nos jours,* Paris, 1938.

Emmanuel, P., *La Révolution parallèle,* Paris, 1975.

Faure, E., *L'Education Nationale et la participation,* Paris, 1968.

Fontaine-Garnier, Nicole, *Un Bilan: dix années d'application de la loi du 31 décembre 1959,* Paris, 1969.

Fournier, J., *Politique de l'éducation,* Paris, 1971.

Fraser, W. R., *Education and Society in Modern France,* London, 1973.

Gagnon, P., *France since 1789,* New York, 1964.

Grégoire, R., *Report on Vocational Education,* OECD, Paris, 1967.

Guérin, J., *La FEN. Un syndicat?,* Paris, 1973.

Guillemoteau, R. and Mayeur, P., *Traité de législation scolaire et universitaire.* Vol. 3. *Enseignements élémentaire et pré-élémentaire,* Paris, 1970.

Gusdorf, G., *L'Université en question,* Paris, 1964.

Hartley, A., *Gaullism. The Rise and Fall of a Political Movement,* London, 1972.

Hayward, J., *The One and Indivisible French Republic,* London, 1973.

Isambert-Jamati, Viviane, *Crise de la société, crise de l'enseignement,* Paris, 1970.

Jullien, C., *Les Lycéens, ces nouveaux hommes,* Paris, 1972.

Knaup, Gisela, *Die französische Beobachtungs- und Orientierungβtufe,* Hanover, 1974.

Kosciusko-Morizet, J., *La "Mafia" Polytechnicienne,* Paris, 1973.

Langevin-Wallon, *Le Plan Langevin-Wallon de réforme de l'enseignement.* Compte rendu du colloque organisé par le groupe français d'éducation nouvelle et la Société française de Pédagogie, Paris, 1964.

Legrand, L., *L'Organisation des premiers cycles secondaires et l'individualisation de l'enseignement.* Recherches pédagogiques No. 41, IPN, Paris, 1970.

Malraux, A., *Les Chênes qu'on abat,* Paris, 1971.

Michelet, J., *Le Peuple,* Paris, 1846.

Minot, J., *L'Entreprise Education Nationale,* Paris, 1970.

OECD: *Educational Policy and Planning: France,* Paris, 1972.

Papillon, J., *L'Ecole, pourquoi faire?,* Paris, 1965.

Paxton, R., *Vichy France. Old Guard and New Order, 1940–1944,* London, 1972.

Pickles, Dorothy, *The Government and Politics of France,* Vol. I, London, 1972.

Ponteil, F., *Histoire de l'Enseignement en France. Les grandes étapes, 1789–1944,* Paris, 1960.

Prost, A., *L'Enseignement en France, 1800–1967,* Paris, 1968.

Quignard, J., *Recherches sur l'organisation des seconds cycles généraux et techniques en vue d'améliorer l'orientation: thèmes de réflexion,* IPN, Paris, n.d. (1971?), roneographed.

Rapport d'Enquête du Ministère de la Jeunesse et des Sports, Paris, 1967. (Also known as the Missoffe Report.)

Rapport de la Commission des Etudes: La fonction enseignante dans le second degré, Paris, 1972, (Also known as the Joxe Report.)

Renan, E., *La Réforme intellectuelle et morale de la France,* Paris, 1871.

Ridley, F. and Blondel, J., *Public Administration in France,* 2nd edition, London, 1969.

Ruby, M., *La Vie et l'oeuvre de Jean Zay* (Thèse de doctorat de troisième cycle, Faculté des lettres et sciences humaines, Paris, 1967), Paris, 1969.

Sauvy, A., *La Montée des jeunes,* Paris, 1959.

Schwartz, B., *L'Education demain,* Paris, 1973.

Siegfried, A., *Tableau des partis politiques en France,* Paris, 1930.

(Le) Sixième Plan, La Documentation Française illustrée, Numéro spécial, Sept.–Oct. 1971.

(Le) Sixième Plan de développement économique et social, 1971–1975, Rapport général: Les objectifs généraux et les actions prioritaires du VIè Plan. Imprimerie officielle, Paris, n.d.

Soustelle, J., *Vingt-huit ans de gaullisme,* Nouvelle édition, Paris, 1971.

Talbott, J., *The Politics of Educational Reform in France, 1918–1940,* Princeton, N.J., 1969.

Thomson, D., *Democracy in France since 1870,* 4th edition, London, 1964.
Touraine, A., *Le Communisme utopique,* Paris, 1968.
Tournis, G. and Clarys, R., *Nouveau vade-mecum de la Direction de l'école,* 3rd edition, Paris, 1972.
Vial, F., *Trois siècles de l'enseignement secondaire,* Paris, 1936.
Villars, G., *Inadaptation scolaire et délinquance juvénile.* T. I. *Des écoliers perdus.* T. II. *L'organisation du désordre,* Paris, 1972–1973.
Vincent, G., *Les Professeurs du second degré,* Paris, 1967.
Wadier, H., *La Réforme de l'enseignement n'aura pas lieu,* Paris, 1970.
Wylie, L., *Village in the Vaucluse,* New York, 1957.

ADDITIONAL BIBLIOGRAPHY

Asselain, J., *Le Budget de l'Education Nationale (1952–1967),* Paris, 1969.
Avanzini, G., *L'Echec scolaire,* Paris, 1967.
Bachy, J. and Bachy, C., *Etudiants et la politique.* Documents présentés par . . ., Paris, 1973.
Baudelot, C. and Establet, R., *L'Ecole capitaliste en France,* Paris, 1971.
Béraud, J. and Millet, L., *Le Refus des jeunes,* Paris, 1971.
Boudon, R., *L'Inégalité des chances,* Paris, 1973.
Bourdieu, P. and Isambert-Jamati, Viviane, (eds.), *Sociologie de l'éducation. Revue française de sociologie,* numéro spécial, 1967–1968.
Brunold, C., *Demain ils seront des hommes,* Paris, 1963.
Cahiers des universités françaises. Cahier 1. *De l'Université aux universités, octobre 1968–janvier 1971,* Paris, n.d. (1972?).
Changer l'école. L'enseignement en procès. Expériences nouvelles. Professeurs et élèves parlent éducation et révolution sociale, Paris, 1970.
Chombart de Lauwe, P., *Pour l'université. Avant, pendant et après mai 1968,* Paris, 1968.
Comités d'action lycéens. *Les Lycéens gardent la parole,* Paris, 1968.
Daumard, P., *Le Prix de l'enseignement en France* (Préface d'Edgar Faure), Paris, 1969.
Delion, A., *L'Education en France. Problèmes et perspectives.*
Didier, P. *et al., Le Bouton du mandarin: l'école face à notre avenir,* Paris, 1966.
Duquesne, J., *Les 16–24 ans,* 2nd edition, Paris, 1963.
L'Ecole en question, par 11 auteurs, Paris, 1973.
Eliade, B., *L'Ecole ouverte. Témoignage et propositions pour aider à la mise en place d'une éducation permanente et populaire,* Paris, 1970.
Fourastié, J., *Faillite de l'université?* Paris, 1972.
Fraser, W. R., *Reform and Restraints in Modern French Education,* London, 1971.
Freyssinet-Dominjon, J., *Les Manuels d'histoire de l'école libre, 1882–1959,* Paris, 1969.
Giscard d'Estaing, Olivier, *Education et civilisation. Pour une révolution libérale de l'enseignement,* Paris, 1971.
Guichard, O., *L'Education nouvelle,* Paris, 1970.
Hassenforder, J., *L'Innovation dans l'enseignement,* Paris, 1972.
Jousselin, J., *Le Devenir de l'éducation,* Paris, 1969.

Kesler, J., "L'influence de l'Ecole Nationale d'Administration sur la la rénovation de l'éducation", *in: Société française de sociologie, Tendances et volontés de la société française,* Paris, 1966.

Lewandowski, O., *La barrière et le niveau: le baccalauréat,* Centre de sociologie européenne (roneographed), Paris, 1966.

Mangenot, M. *et al., Les Jeunes face à l'emploi,* Paris, 1972.

Michaud, G., *Révolution dans l'Université,* Paris, 1968.

Ministère de L'Education Nationale, Rapports d'orientation. *Pour une rénovation des formations supérieures. Groupe d'étude des formations supérieures,* Paris, 1971.

Mucchielli, R., *Comments ils deviennent délinquants,* Paris, 1965.

Niel, Mathilde, *La Crise de la jeunesse,* Paris, 1965.

OECD: *Reviews of National Policies for Education: France,* Paris, 1971.

Oury, F. and Pain, J., *Chronique de l'école-caserne,* Paris, 1972.

Palau, A., *Le Devoir à refaire,* Paris, 1971.

Commissariat Général du Plan: *Rapports des Commissions du VIè Plan, 1971–1975; Education,* Paris, 1971.

Revue internationale, La remise en question de l'université, mai-juin, 1969, Numéro spécial, July 1968.

Robert, F., *Un Mandarin prend la parole,* Paris, 1970.

Monique de Saint Martin, *Les Fonctions sociales de l'enseignement scientifique,* The Hague, 1971.

Snyders, G., *Pédagogie progressiste,* Paris, 1971.

Snyders, G., *Où vont les pédagogies non-directives?,* Paris, 1973.

Zamanksy, M., *Mort ou résurrection de l'université?,* Paris, 1969.

Index